THE OTHER PLATO

SUNY series in Contemporary Continental Philosophy

Dennis J. Schmidt, editor

SUNY series in Ancient Greek Philosophy

Anthony Preus, editor

THE OTHER PLATO

The Tübingen Interpretation of Plato's Inner-Academic Teachings

EDITED BY
DMITRI NIKULIN

STATE UNIVERSITY OF NEW YORK PRESS

Printed in the United States of America

For information, contact
State University of New York Press, Albany, NY
www.sunypress.edu

Production, Laurie D. Searl
Marketing, Anne M. Valentine

Library of Congress Cataloging-in-Publication Data

The other Plato : the Tübingen interpretation of Plato's inner-academic teachings / Dmitri Nikulin.
p. cm. — (SUNY series in contemporary Continental philosophy)
(SUNY series in ancient Greek philosophy)
Includes bibliographical references (p.) and index.
ISBN 978-1-4384-4409-3 (hardcover : alk. paper)
ISBN 978-1-4384-4410-9 (paperback : alk. paper)
1. Plato. I. Nikulin, D. V. (Dmitrii Vladimirovich)

B395.O75 2012
184—dc23 2011050354

10 9 8 7 6 5 4 3 2 1

CONTENTS

ACKNOWLEDGMENTS

The essays included in this collection have been previously published as:

H. J. Krämer. ΕΠΕΚΕΙΝΑ ΤΗΣ ΟΥΣΙΑΣ: Zu Platon, *Politeia* 509B. *Archiv für Geschichte der Philosophie* 51 (1969): 1–30.

H. J. Krämer. Platons ungeschriebene Lehre. In *Platon: Seine Dialoge in der Sicht der neueren Forschung*, ed. T. Kobusch and B. Mojsisch, 249–275. Darmstadt: Wissenschaftliche Buchgesellschaft, 1996.

K. Gaiser. Platons Zusammenschau der mathematischen Wissenschaften. *Antike und Abendland* 32 (1986): 89–124.

Th. A. Szlezák. Die Idee des Guten als *arche* in Platons Politeia. In *New Images of Plato: Dialogues on the Idea of the Good*, ed. G. Reale and S. Scolnicov, 49–68. Sankt Augustin: Academia, 2000.

J. Halfwassen. Monism and Dualism in Plato's Doctrine of Principles. *Graduate Faculty Philosophy Journal* 23 (2002): 125–144.

V. Hösle. Platons Grundlegung der Euklidizität der Geometrie. *Philologus* 126 (1982): 184–197; rpt. *Platon interpretieren*, 145–165. Paderborn: Ferdinand Schöningh, 2004.

I would like to thank the publishers, Academia Verlag, De Gruyter, Ferdinand Schöningh Verlag, Wissenschaftliche Buchgesellschaft, and the *Graduate Faculty Philosophy Journal* for permission to include translations of the essays in this volume.

I am also grateful to Mitchell Miller and Burt Hopkins for their very helpful comments on the manuscript, to Mario Wenning for exemplary translation of five articles included in this collection, and to Duane Lacey, Erick Raphael Jiménez, and Joseph Lemelin for their help and dedication with the editing of the manuscript. Without their persistence, as well as without the generous support of the Alexander von Humboldt Stiftung in the form of research grants at the universities of Tübingen and Heidelberg, this book could not have been published.

ONE

PLATO: *TESTIMONIA ET FRAGMENTA*

Dmitri Nikulin

Plato is a unique character among the *dramatis personae* in the history of philosophy. No other thinker arouses so much emotion and dissent among readers and interpreters. Passions are inevitably stirred when one tries to answer a simple question: What does Plato want to say, and what does he actually say? Plato wrote dialogues, which are fine pieces of literature and reasoning but which may always be read and interpreted differently, especially since the speakers often do not commit themselves to any particular philosophical position and the question discussed frequently remains unanswered and sometimes not even explicitly asked. Moreover, it is neither easy to discern Plato's own position at any given moment in the discussion, nor who is speaking behind his characters. When Socrates is engaged in a dialectical debate of a subject (such as wisdom, courage, love, friendship, temperance, etc.) does he *really* mean what he says, if one takes into account his undeniably ironic stance? And is it Plato who speaks through Socrates, Socrates himself, or an anonymous voice ascribed to Socrates, made to say what he has to within the logic of the conversation? Plato appears to always escape and defy any final and finalized conclusion, being an Apollo's bird, the swan that, as Socrates predicted, still remains not captured by generations of later readers and interpreters.

Because of the seeming uncertainty of what has actually been said, reading Plato is a fascinating yet risky enterprise, for we might need to reconsider not only our understanding of a text but also the very principles of philosophical reading and interpretation. It is perhaps not by chance that modern hermeneutics arises with Schleiermacher and flourishes in Gadamer as primarily an attempt to make sense of the Platonic dialogues, of their intention and proper sense. Yet, since the dialogues appear to be open to a variety of consistent but mutually conflicting interpretations, reading them leads to so much disagreement, misunderstanding, and even mutual mistrust in the guild of fellow Plato scholars.

THE TÜBINGEN SCHOOL

Among recent notable attempts to provide a different reading of Plato is the so-called Tübingen interpretation, both an original attempt at reading and understanding Plato, and at the same time one rooted in a philological and philosophical tradition that goes back to the end of the eighteenth century while echoing Platonic (Neoplatonic) interpretations of Plato. This interpretation of Plato originated in the works of two students of Wolfgang Schadewaldt, Hans Joachim Krämer and Konrad Gaiser, who were also joined by Heinz Happ, Thomas A. Szlezák, Jürgen Wippern, and later by Vittorio Hösle and Jens Halfwassen. In Italy, Giovanni Reale became the main proponent of the Tübingen interpretation, and in France, Marie-Dominique Richard. The two path-breaking works were Krämer's 1959 *Arete bei Platon und Aristoteles* and Gaiser's 1963 *Platons ungeschriebene Lehre*, which were followed by a number of other relevant publications.

The Tübingen reconstruction attempts to provide a systematic understanding of Plato based on the evidence preserved in the tradition of the transmission and interpretation of his texts. Dietrich Tiedemann and especially Wilhelm Gottlieb Tennemann, both of whom predate the Romantic reading of Plato and still continue the line of Neoplatonic interpretation, had already argued in favor of the existence of a systematic oral teaching in Plato. It is because of this tradition, which pays attention to the evidence preserved in earlier philosophical works and stresses the necessity of meticulous philological research oriented toward a philosophical understanding of the text, that we now have Diels and Kranz's *Fragmente der Vorsokratiker*. It is this tradition that made such a profound impact on ancient scholarship of the nineteenth century, including Jacob Burckhardt and Nietzsche, and the whole of twentieth-century Continental philosophy, including the Neo-Kantians, Heidegger, Hannah Arendt, and Hans Jonas.

In the late-nineteenth and early-twentieth centuries, the existence of a systematic teaching developed by Plato within the Academy was accepted and argued for by Eduard Zeller, Heinrich Gomperz, Léon Robin, and Julius Stenzel. Thus, in his book of 1908, *La théorie platonicienne des idées et des nombres d'après Aristote*, Robin attempts to show that, if one reads Aristotle carefully and takes seriously what he says about Plato, especially in *Meta-*

physics M and N, then one has to assume an account of first principles and ideal numbers in Plato.

The original publications of Krämer and Gaiser have provoked extensive debate, especially in the 1970s and early 1980s. Yet the majority of scholars in the Anglo-American world remained unconvinced that the Tübingen interpretation offered a glimpse into the historical Plato, maintaining rather that it provided a crafty interpretation of a number of texts considered secondary. However, recent work in the history of Platonism and new publications of fragments by Speusippus and Xenocrates (by M. Isnardi Parente and L. Tarán) shed new light on the connection between later ancient works and those of Plato and his disciples, which makes reconsidering the Tübingen position rather timely. Thus, John Dillon (Dillon 2003, 16–22) argues that one cannot properly understand what Xenocrates and Speusippus were doing without seriously taking into account the reports of Aristotle and other ancient writers about Plato's inner-school teachings and discussions.

HISTORICAL, CRITICAL, AND SYSTEMATIC INTERPRETATION

A distinguished feature of the Tübingen interpretation is its emphasis on the reconstruction of Plato's doctrine or, rather, of a set of related and mutually consistent doctrines in a *historical*, *critical*, and *systematic* way. Such a reconstruction presupposes, and allows for, the possibility of deducing different kinds of entities from simple principles and for reducing all things back to these principles. (Krämer pays particular attention to the reduction to the principles.) The critical philosophical and historical reconstruction of Plato's views is based on a careful reading and interpretation of his own texts *and* the preserved texts of other ancient thinkers, beginning with Plato's closest disciples. In this respect, the Tübingen School stands within the tradition of *Quellenkritik* insofar as it pays attention to the transmission of Plato's oral doctrines as they are reflected within the extant texts and the history of their interpretation.

This tradition of close textual reading and historical interpretation pays particular attention to *testimonies*, since *any* text or extant testimony might turn out to be important and its careful historical and philological consideration might lead to a new understanding and reconstruction of a philosophical position in its entirety. The Tübingen approach thus attempts to reconsider the understanding of Plato in a systematic way that uses any available means and sources, including all relevant evidence from later writers, which, however, is read not for its own sake, but with a view to a systematic interpretation of a reconstructed whole, within which a fragment might fit—in fact, within which a fragment will only make sense and obtain a *new* meaning.

The collections of ancient Greek texts that have been preserved only in part in contemporary and later writers—such as Diels and Kranz's *Fragmente der Vorsokratiker*, Jacoby's *Fragmente der griechishen Historiker*, or Bernabé's *Poetae et epici Graeci*—are commonly divided into two parts: the indirect *testimonia* and the direct *fragmenta*. We are fortunate to have had the whole *corpus Platonicum* passed down to us from antiquity, which realized the importance of Plato's works and built itself philosophically around reading and interpreting them. However, we also have a number of testimonies about and fragments of Plato's inner-Academic teachings that do not appear in the dialogues and are preserved in Aristotle's writings and those of Plato's other contemporaries, as well as in late ancient thinkers who might have known of the inner-Academic tradition and its transmission. An important source of testimonies is book X of Sextus Empiricus' *Adversus Mathematicos* (X.248–283), which Gaiser (1963, 32), together with Merlan (1953) and Wilpert (1949), considers a summary report of the inner-Academic teachings, independent of Aristotle's report in *Metaphysics* A.5–6. For the first time, the *Testimonia Platonica* (= *TP*) were collected and published by Gaiser as an appendix to his book on Plato (1963, 441–557). It is quite remarkable that no one undertook this attempt before Gaiser (in part, some of the texts appeared in the appendix to Findlay 1974) and that this important collection of testimonies remains still not fully appreciated and not fully translated into English.

If one takes the testimonies about Plato's inner-Academic teachings and discussions seriously, one is likely to find a picture of Plato quite different from the one Platonic scholarship has been presenting for the better part of the last two centuries. The simplistic two-world scheme—that of the ideal world of forms and the world of the becoming of bodily things—is simply not there. The ontological picture that arises from testimonies is more subtle, nuanced, sophisticated, and complex. However, such an interpretation neither contradicts nor ignores the existing texts of Plato but complements them and in fact clarifies certain points that remain either not fully spelled out, or only raised and slightly touched on, in the dialogues.

If one decides to take both dialogues and testimonies into account, one might further distinguish a "strong" and a "weak" reading of Plato. The strong reading would stress that the reconstructed theories genuinely represent Plato's teachings at the Academy. A weak reading, on the contrary, would suggest that we do not know whether Plato did indeed hold the views ascribed to him, and yet they are consistent with both the existing evidence and the dialogues. The Tübingen interpretation offers a strong reading of Plato, which Krämer, Gaiser, and Szlezák justify through meticulous and detailed philological and philosophical interpretation of the relevant texts.

Yet, even if one accepts the weak interpretation, the systematic reconstruction of the inner-Academic doctrines still remains valid, being consistent with both Plato's dialogues and the extant testimonies.

Krämer insists on the historical character of his interpretation and suggests a view of Plato's thought that originates in a critique of the Presocratics (primarily, of the Eleatic thinkers), continues in the Old Academy, is further transmitted and appropriated by Middle Platonism, and then is taken up by Neoplatonism (see Krämer 1959, 95; 1964, 45–49). Since, however, the Tübingen approach also insists on the importance of orality in the constitution and transmission of philosophy, it attempts to integrate both literary and indirect oral Platonic traditions. The existing testimony thus complements, and does not contradict, Plato's known texts. According to the Tübingen interpretation, a systematic doctrine, or a set of closely related doctrines, has distinct traces in many of Plato's dialogues but is never expressed in its entirety in any one of them. These teachings, referred to by Aristotle as the ἄγραφα δόγματα, or "unwritten doctrines" (*Phys.* Δ.2, 209b14–15: ἐν τοῖς λεγομένοις ἀγράφοις δόγμασιν), are mostly *oral* in character yet constitute a *systematic* philosophy (see Krämer 1990, 191–217). It might be better to refer to the ἄγραφα δόγματα in the plural, as Halfwassen suggests, as "the unwritten doctrines" or teachings. That these teachings come in the plural is further supported by the fact that (1) they were delivered at the Academy on a regular basis; (2) they were oral discussions with the students; and (3) they embrace a number of claims that are related closely and systematically, yet each one of them may be discussed independently on its own (e.g., the doctrine of opposites).

THE INDIRECT TRANSMISSION OF TESTIMONIES

The ways of transmitting the inner-Academic doctrines have been explored by Heinz Happ, Konrad Gaiser, Hans Joachim Krämer, Hellmuth Dempe, and Walter Burkert, who establish several parallel lines of passing on the testimonies (see Richard 1986, 79–82; for references, see *TP*). One has to approach the evidence of later ancient writers, such as Sextus Empiricus, Alexander, Iamblichus, and Proclus, with caution, in order to distinguish between properly Platonic elements and later Pythagorean doctrines, although the interaction between the Platonic and the Pythagorean components already began in the Old Academy—in Speusippus and Xenocrates (see Gaiser 1972, 475). And even if Plato's closest disciples, Speusippus and Xenocrates, substantially revised his theories of numbers and especially of ideas, and another disciple, Aristotle, wholly disagreed with and rejected them, their testimonies still need to be taken seriously.

(1) Much of what we know about Plato's inner-Academic teachings, which, from the point of view of the Tübingen School, were not explicitly present but often referred to in the dialogues, comes from the testimony of Aristotle, both in his extant and partially preserved works. Being a disciple of Plato for about twenty years, he certainly knew about the details of the inner-Academic debates and doctrines, which is why it seems very improbable to suppose, as Cherniss does, that Aristotle either misunderstood or deliberately misreported Plato's theories.

In Aristotle's now only fragmentary preserved texts (Aristotle, *Frag.* Ross; see Gaiser 1968, 209–214), the works that are relevant for the reconstruction of the ἄγραφα δόγματα are: (i) the dialogues *De philosophia* (Περὶ φιλοσοφίας) (paralleled in *De anima* A.2, 404b16–30, which contains a critique of Plato's theory of ideal numbers) and the *Protrepticus*. The *De philosophia* is partially preserved in Syrianus' and Pseudo-Alexander's commentaries on Aristotle's *Metaphysics* and the *Protrepticus* in Iamblichus' *Protrepticus*; (ii) Aristotle's philosophical works *De ideis* (Περὶ ἰδεῶν), *De bono* (Περὶ τἀγαθοῦ), and *De contrariis* (Περὶ ἐναντίων), which present an important doxographical account of Plato's inner-Academic teachings. These are partially preserved in Alexander of Aphrodisias (*In Met.* 59.28–60.2 = *TP* 22B), from whom they were passed on to Themistius, Porphyry (who originates the whole tradition of the Neoplatonic commentaries on Aristotle), Syrianus, Simplicius, Philoponus, and Asclepius. Here one should also mention Aristotle's *Diaireseis*, which are referred to by Alexander of Aphrodisias and Diogenes Laertius (III.80); and, finally, (iii) of paramount importance are testimonies in Aristotle's preserved works, mostly in *Metaphysics* A, M, and N (*Met.* A.6, A.9, M.6–9, and N.3–4 are particularly important) and *Physics* (especially *Phys.* Γ).

(2) The relevant text of one of Aristotle's disciples is Theophrastus' *Metaphysics*, which was commonly known throughout antiquity and is preserved in full, as well as in partial evidence from Eudemus, Aristoxenus, and Dicaearchus (a fragment from Dicaearchus has been discovered in the Herculaneum Papyrus 1021).

(3) The important testimonies come indirectly from other members of the Academy: Hermodorus' lost *Life of Plato* (the extant fragments are collected in Speusippus 1980), which through Dercyllides were transmitted to Porphyry and Simplicius (*In Phys.* 247.30–248.15).

(4) Fragments of Speusippus, in Proclus' commentary on the *Parmenides*, preserved only in the Latin translation of William of Moerbeke (*In Parm.* 40.1–41.10).

(5) Fragments of Xenocrates, passed on through the Middle Academy and probably preserved in Sextus Empiricus (*Adv. Math.* X.248–283), as well as in Simplicius' commentary on Aristotle's *Physics* (*In Phys.*).

INNER-ACADEMIC DOCTRINES: EARLY OR LATE?

Whether Plato's systematic reflection was a complete system or Plato kept working on some aspects of his philosophy till the end of his life is a matter of historical and philological reconstruction and dispute. And if Plato had indeed established a systematic doctrine, when did he begin using it? Krämer and Szlezák have argued that a definite system can be discerned in the dialogues relatively early on—in the *Euthydemus*, *Meno*, *Protagoras*, and in the first version of the *Republic*. Some, however—Ross, Paul Wilpert, Julius Stenzel, Cornford, Cornelia J. de Vogel, Enrico Berti, and John Dillon—have argued in favor of a later appearance of systematic theories in Plato in the course of the development of Plato's thought. Richard (1986, 240–241) argues in favor of a subtler genetic account of the ἄγραφα δόγματα, with reference to Gaiser (1968, 294–295), who argues that the mathematization of Plato's ontology begins first with the *Republic*. Two reports may be taken to support such an interpretation of Plato, in favor of the development of Plato's views concerning numbers as representing ontological patterns: *Met.* M.4, 1078b9–12, where Aristotle suggests that the theory of ideal numbers was developed after the theory of ideas, and Plato's own *Laws* (819D).

CRITIQUE OF THE TÜBINGEN APPROACH

Scholars who embrace positions similar to the Tübingen interpretation, although in some ways different from it, include W. K. C. Guthrie, J. N. Findlay (who has a monistic interpretation of Plato), Julia Annas, Gadamer, and John Dillon. Burnyeat (1987) argues that Platonic mathematics at least partly supports claims about the existence of systematic inner-Academic teachings.

Yet, since the publication of the first books of Krämer and Gaiser, the critique of their work, and of those who joined them, has been relentless. Harold Cherniss argued against the very existence of the ἄγραφα δόγματα even before Krämer's and Gaiser's publications. According to Cherniss (1945), Aristotle simply misunderstood Plato, and hence Aristotle's reports cannot be accepted; therefore, we have to ignore all later testimonies as untrustworthy and pay attention to the dialogues only. A number of prominent scholars have followed Cherniss in his criticism of the tradition and hence confined their efforts to the interpretation of dialogues alone and the logical arguments they contain. Among these are Gregory Vlastos, Luc Brisson, Holger Thesleff, and Margherita Isnardi Parente. Recently, continuing this line of argumentation and criticism, Mann (2006) has argued that one can explain the passages from the *Seventh Letter* and the *Phaedrus* without referring to the inner-Academic oral doctrines; moreover, there is no thorough agreement within the Tübingen School. The Tübingen followers do not provide a monolithic interpretation of Plato and sometimes disagree in details of their reconstructions, and yet they agree about the major theses of their interpretation. Some critics (Günther Patzig, Jürgen Mittelstraß, and Wolfgang Wieland) suggest that the reconstruction of the oral inner-Academic teaching, even if possible, is philosophically insignificant and trivial in comparison with the dialogues. Indeed, why trust a few dubious later fragments and then interpret several selected passages in Plato in accordance with them? Why divide Plato into *Plato minor* and *Plato maior* (as Tatiana Vasilieva [1985] has suggested)? Moreover, as the critics suggest, the number of testimonies about Plato's oral inner-Academic teachings is relatively insignificant compared to the amount of Plato's preserved works, and these testimonies appear often within a polemical context. Besides, much of the evidence concerning Plato's inner-Academic teachings is preserved in later authors, and hence appears dubious. Therefore, a systematic interpretation of Plato seems to be impossible and does not allow, and in fact obfuscates, a proper understanding of Plato based on, and read out of, his texts alone.

Recently, Charles Kahn (2005) argued that Plato has a systematic doctrine, but that it is not formulated in its entirety anywhere in his dialogues. Moreover, the same doctrine (the theory of ideas or the doctrine of recollection) is presented each time in a different form, according to the context of a particular question discussed in a dialogue.

Alternatively, one can opt for a careful reading of single dialogues without presupposing any overarching systematic interpretation behind and beyond them, and even without taking other dialogues into account. From this perspective, one can read a dialogue as a piece of literature and interpret it with a view to contemporary problems that Plato never faced, as well as to questions he never asked.

The Tübingen approach to Plato, however, takes seriously the oral tradition of the indirect, or doxographical, transmission of Plato. Stressing the reliability of the tradition of the transmission of texts, the Tübingen interpretation to a large extent suspends the fundamental principle of modern hermeneutical interpretation: the *sola scriptura*. This hermeneutic principle stresses the importance of going back to the "original" text as the *only* source of dependable interpretation, and hence implies the rejection of any oral tradition of transmission that is construed as only secondary and therefore untrustworthy. Yet, careful reading and interpretation of the extant texts can provide a picture of Plato that accords with both the later ancient tradition and the dialogues but is quite different from the usual two-world theory.

There is no reason why the ancient tradition of preservation and transmission of texts should not be taken as long-lasting and trustworthy. And if we agree that a fragment of Parmenides (DK B5) is and can be properly preserved in Proclus (*In Parm.* 708.16) or that of Anaximander (DK B1) in Simplicius (*In Phys.* 24.13), we might also agree that ancient writers could preserve the testimonies relevant to understanding Plato's inner-Academic teachings and debates.

SCHLEIERMACHER: INFINITE DIALECTIC

Sometimes, a systematic interpretation of Plato is rejected because it appears to be at odds with the open and aporetic character of the dialogues, where a dialectically discussed question often seems to be left undecided. According to Krämer and Szlezák, modern readings of Plato are dominated by the approach that Schleiermacher introduces in the famous *Einleitung* to his translations of Plato's works. According to Schleiermacher, the reader should be able to understand and interpret the meaning of what is said in a dialogue, even if it might appear incomplete (Schleiermacher 1804). Schleiermacher too pays attention primarily to Plato's dialogues (which in their entirety he takes as forming one living organism) as literary works in which there is an identity and coincidence of literary form and content.

The Tübingen interpreters of Plato argue against the 'infinite' reading of Plato, the origin of which Krämer finds in Fichte and further traces to Schleiermacher and Schlegel. Since, according to Schlegel, truth is infinite and thus unattainable, Plato can "approach it always and ever more through a restless, progressive striving, a steadily progressing philosophizing, an untiring inquiry and striving after truth and certainty, approaching a methodical formation and perfection of thinking and reflection" (Krämer 1999, 81). For Krämer, on the contrary, dialectic is to be considered not an infinite but a finite enterprise that leads from the specific to the general, and from the complex to the simple—a dialectic that can be established through a meticulous comparative analysis of the relevant texts of the dialogues and the indirect tradition.

EXOTERIC / ESOTERIC

Another objection commonly made to the Tübingen interpretation is that, if Plato's oral teachings are not contained, or only partially reflected and referred to, in the written texts, then such teachings should be esoteric and accessible only to the chosen or "initiated" few. Such an attitude toward readers was already perceived as arrogant and elitist in Kant (1977, esp. 388–389).

This objection, however, is beside the point, because it is based on a specifically modern understanding—or, rather, misunderstanding—of the relationship between writing and orality, the attitude to which was very different in antiquity. It needs to be stressed that the Tübingen interpretation of Plato has nothing to do with the "esoteric" interpretation of Plato by Leo Strauss and his followers. For Strauss, every philosopher at all times is in the situation of political persecution, and hence has to construct a specific way of writing, which on its surface is "exoteric," that is, meant for the general, unsophisticated reader, yet is "esoteric" in its hidden message, accessible only to few "thoughtful" and "careful" readers capable of understanding the true message of and behind a text by "reading between the lines" (Strauss 1988, 22–37). True philosophers, then, including Plato, "must conceal their opinions from all but philosophers, either by limiting themselves to oral instruction of a carefully selected group of pupils, or by writing about the most important subject by means of 'brief indication'" (Strauss 1988, 34–35). This account of Strauss is plainly contradicted by the fact that the Academy did not practice any secrecy, and that Plato himself delivered a public lecture on the good, where he presented his philosophy to the Athenian people in an accessible way (the lecture, however, did not go well, as we know from Aristoxenus' account, and many of those in attendance were disappointed, because they expected to learn about the acquisition of the goods of life).

To characterize Plato's inner-Academic teachings, the Tübingen School indeed uses the term "esoteric," in opposition to "exoteric," which, however, does not imply either secrecy or anybody's exclusion in any way, but is used as it was meant in Plato's times, when both terms, ἐξωτερικός and ἐσωτερικός, were routinely applied to describe different teaching and research procedures. "Exoteric" meant published works and speeches, i.e., those made public by being written and distributed to a wider circulation. "Esoteric" meant a set of doctrines established within a group of disciples or thinkers, who discussed and elaborated them in mutual conversations as part of an ongoing effort to refine and clarify them. In fact, the very term "exoteric speeches" (ἐξωτερικοὶ λόγοι) was coined by Aristotle in reference to those outside his own circle and school (see Aristotle, *NE* A.13, 1102a26; *Phys.* Δ.10, 217b30; Gaiser 1972; and Gaiser 1963, 336–337). In this respect, Aristotle's own doctrines would be considered "esoteric," as would any special modern theory, not because it is closed to the profane but because it uses specific terminology and refers to a particular set of texts and problems that need to be known to whoever wants to understand them.

In later antiquity, however, the use of "esoteric" and "exoteric" changes and becomes closer to what is ordinarily meant by "esoteric" today. Thus, speaking about ancient Pythagoreans, Iamblichus (*De vita Pythagorica* 40.15–52.19) distinguishes between the "esoteric" Pythagoreans, the so-called "acusmatics," and the "exoteric," or "mathematicians." The former instituted a conservative religious and political union and left a number of enigmatic prescriptions, ἀκούσματα (statements such as "do not speak without light" or brief responses to questions, such as "What is the wisest?" "Number" [τί τὸ σοφώτατον; ἀριθμός, Iamblichus, *De vita Pythagorica* 47.17]) that had to be interpreted as pointing to a hidden allegorical meaning. The "mathematicians," on the contrary, intended to discover mathematical theorems and properties of mathematical objects, transmit, and systematize this kind of knowledge. If one follows Iamblichus' distinction, then the Platonic mathematical studies in the Old Academy, which were very much in line with the mathematical activity of the Pythagoreans, were rather "exoteric."

"Esoteric" thus is meant to designate the research activity within a school, whereas "exoteric" reaches out to a broader audience, those who might not yet be familiar with the problematic and notions used within a particular scholarly tradition. In contemporary academic practice, "exoteric" would refer to all of one's published works, as well as public speeches, and "esoteric" to academic lectures and seminars one regularly holds for students, where, of course, nobody is excluded but everybody is welcome. In order to appreciate a theory and be in a position to develop it further, one needs to be introduced to, and study, a specific subject, learn certain things, be acquainted with a special literature and set of problems and categories. Every category is a condensed, wrapped narrative, and to be able to appropriate and use the category, one has to be aware of this underlying narrative. If one were to mention the amphiboly of the concepts of reflection to somebody who has never read Kant, it would sound rather "esoteric." Yet, there is nothing secret or exclusive about the amphiboly, and if one reads the *First Critique* or sits in on a seminar about it, one will be able to make sense of this notion.

Besides, clearly, we do not publish everything we think about, because some things we hold true are inevitably fragmentary, some not sufficiently elaborate, and for some we simply have no time to write them down in a way that would be acceptable for publication. From the very recent history of philosophy we see that such thinkers as Wittgenstein or Austin, despite their highly influential and profoundly original set of ideas, were almost reluctant to publish them, i.e., to make them "exoteric," remaining mostly "esoteric," i.e., in oral elaboration and discussion with students, friends, and colleagues.

ORAL AND WRITTEN: THE CRITIQUE OF WRITING IN PLATO

Plato's own critique of writing is well known from both *Phaedrus* 274B–278E and *Ep*. VII, 343A–344E. Here, he argues against writing—in writing, which appears ironic and performatively contradictory. Yet, one might say that Plato uses writing in order to suspend it and bring it to the limit of its very capacities. In a sense, writing dialogues is a minimal compromise one can reach in expressing and developing a thought without making it stagnant. From its inception, the critique is practiced and developed primarily as oral, although this does not mean that philosophy as a practice is incomplete and haphazard. The first systematic writer in philosophy in the modern sense was Aristotle. Yet other philosophers who developed their thought by means of arguments and thorough investigation of the terms they used—most notably, Plato—also tried to find some consistency in the presentation of their thought, for which purpose they investigated various forms of its presentation, including writing.

One should not think that publishing a philosophical theory in the times of Plato meant exactly the same thing as it does nowadays. Oral teaching was of extreme importance: Pythagoras and Socrates did not write at all, and yet the Pythagoreans authored a number of important philosophical insights, and Socrates attempted to formulate general definitions of moral virtues (Aristotle, *Met.* M.4, 1078b17–19), which is thoroughly testified to in Plato's written Socratic dialogues.

Any reconstruction that stresses the importance of the transmitted tradition, which apparently bears testimony to systematic yet oral teachings of Plato, appears to be an oxymoron to modernity, in which, if philosophy is systematic, it has to be written and, if it is oral, it has to remain unfinished or unsystematic. Our modern attitude toward writing in philosophy is strikingly different from the ancient one: only that which is written is worth consideration; the unwritten only represents a non-binding process of thinking, not (yet) verified and often gone astray, which thus is not worth writing down and publishing. And, vice versa, we write down and publish only those things that we consider important, and leave out those that are inconclusive and oral, those that are only a "work in progress" or testify to an ongoing debate that might be of some interest and yet remains inconclusive and hence does not need to be published. Besides, we write because writing is a pass to an immortality within cultural memory that might preserve the name of a writer better than oral speech, which tends to disappear with the dissipation of the living memory. Once again, as philosophers we feel justified *sola scriptura*, so that the oral can only serve as preparation for writing.

As Griswold suggests in his own reading of the *Phaedrus*, "the ideal of modern academic writing in philosophy is clarity of argument, unambiguity of meaning, and overt statement of the author's intentions" (1986, 221). Strangely enough, we do not seem to find any of these requirements explicitly met in Plato's writings. This means that we should try to approach the practice of writing, including philosophical writing, not from our contemporary perspective but from that of ancient writers, which perspective we have to reconstruct and read out of their writings carefully and without modern prejudices. In the last few decades, there has been a substantial and important discussion about the role of orality and writing in antiquity, which was originated by Milman Parry, and continued in the works of Albert Lord, Eric Havelock, Jack Goody, and Walter Ong.

If the oral philosophy that Plato tends to develop into a systematic enterprise within the Academy lies behind his critique of writing, and these efforts are reflected in the written dialogues, then there might be certain hints of the oral within the written texts. Krämer, Gaiser, and Szlezák have argued that the Platonic dialogues contain "self-testimonies" about the inner-Academic debates and teachings (Szlezák 1999, 19, 53, passim). As aforementioned, in ancient philosophy we find an attitude toward speaking and writing that in many ways is opposite the contemporary one: in Plato, it is the oral that is systematic, whereas the written is not. Hence, there are no systematic teachings in the dialogues—possibly only traces of them, alluded to and spoken indirectly, mentioned through deliberate withholdings, hints, and gaps. Thus, in the *Phaedrus* (278D8), Plato mentions "more valuable things (τιμιώτερα)" than those that one puts in writing in treatises, and in *Ep.* VII, 340B1–345C3 (esp. 344D4–5), he says that the greatest and more important things, or genera, τὰ μέγιστα and σπουδαιότερα, are unfit for the inflexible medium of writing and are the highest and first principles of all things, ἄκρα and πρῶτα (περὶ φύσεως ἄκρα καὶ πρῶτα).

When Socrates says in book IV of the *Republic*, "I am omitting much," what is he withholding? Krämer has argued that it is the thesis (apparent in *On the Good*) that the one (as the principle of all things) is the good (for all things). Besides, one can find a number of other significant omissions in Plato's dialogues (first discovered by Krämer; see Richard 1986, 59–64): in *Charmides* 169A, the problem is raised whether anything of the existent has a self-directed power; *Euthydemus* 290B–291A, esp. 291A4–5, hints at dialectic as practiced and discussed elsewhere; *Parmenides* 136D4–E3 can be read as making a reference to inner-Academic investigations; and in *Phaedrus* 246A Socrates mentions a human way of brief exposition, as opposed to a long and elaborate divine one. In *Timaeus* 48C–E Plato speaks about the difficulties in reasoning about the beginning of all things, which in the dialogue is referred to only by means of a plausible speech (a "myth"), and not within a systematic presentation. And *Timaeus* 53C–D mentions four elements that are reducible to geometrical entities, whereby the first principles are hinted at but not discussed in the dialogue, and yet they are said to be known to the philosopher or dialectician who is a "friend to god."

Why does Plato not entrust his philosophy to writing, and in fact argue that to fit philosophy into writing is impossible, so that a systematic theory does not have to presuppose a systematic written exposition? There might be several reasons for it, of which three seem to be important.

(1) In the *Phaedrus* (275D–E), Plato reproduces an argument made before him by Alcidamas (*On Those Who Write Their Speeches, or On Sophists*), that the written word is similar to painted lifelike statues that, however, are utterly lifeless and immobile and cannot talk back when addressed. Similarly, a written speech cannot defend or explain itself beyond what it does and has already said. Because of this, any text is insufficient for self-explanation and self-defense and requires further oral interpretation. The written, thus, may be easily misunderstood and misinterpreted. Moreover, the written originates in the oral, which always has *more* to say—and understands more—about a thing than is and can be presented in writing. Writing, therefore, cannot preserve one's thought in full: the thought that expresses itself in oral speech and argument, λόγος, can never fully fit the rigid Procrustean bed of a written text. Beautifully written and carefully crafted written dialogue is but an imitation of live oral speech and thinking, and thus can only hint at their fullness but never retain it. Writing makes oral thought "banal" and pinpointed to an immobile text, whereas thinking is a *living* activity.

(2) Against the modern attitude to publication as a preservation of thought, Plato tells us through Socrates, who himself puts it in terms of an Egyptian myth (*Phaedr.* 274C–275B; cf. *Ep.* VII 344D–E), that, quite on the contrary, writing does not provide for memory (μνήμη) but only for a reminder (ὑπόμνησις) in the form of notes. Memory stands for, and preserves, being, whereas reminder is meant primarily for oneself, in order not to forget certain things one deems important.

(3) And, finally, a reason why philosophy should remain unwritten is given by Plato in the *Laws* (968E), where, in playing with the form of words, he says that knowledge is inaccessible (ἀπόρρητα) without previous explanations (ἀπρόρρητα). Burnyeat (1987, 232) takes it that "sheer technical difficulty" was the main reason for Plato's not writing his doctrines in their entirety. In other words, the ability to properly and fully appreciate the content of philosophical teachings requires preparation and acquaintance with the discussed problematic and terminology. Otherwise, as Gaiser, Krämer, and Szlezák have consistently argued, the listeners or readers might be irritated and disappointed and leave philosophy without having begun practicing it.

So, why write, then? Why does Plato choose dialogue as the written form for philosophy? There might be several reasons for writing. Thus, other forms for presenting philosophical thinking that are familiar to us simply are not there yet, such as the systematic treatise, which begins with Aristotle. Another reason for choosing written dialogue is that it imitates real speech with all its twists and turns of argumentation. Moreover, dialogue falls within Greek theatrical agonistic urban culture, which is always present and reflected in the dramatic, political, or philosophical dialogue. Besides, as we learn from the critique of writing in the *Phaedrus*, dialogue can have a hypomnematic character, for example, as does the *Parmenides*, which claims to preserve a number of arguments that are central to understanding the one in the philosophy of Plato and remain such throughout in later Platonism.

Yet, the most important reason for writing dialogues seems to be that, if written dialogue does not, and cannot, fully contain and represent a systematic thought, but rather portrays it in its striving toward self-understanding and a reasoned account of the things that are, then dialogue can be an introduction to philosophy and philosophizing. In other words, Plato's ironic, aporetic, and elenchic written dialogue has a didactic and protreptic (i.e., exhortative or hortatory) character: it invites and introduces readers to philosophy and encourages them to keep practicing it (Aristotle, *Nerinthus*, fr. 1 Ross; see also Gaiser 1959; and Krämer 1964).

THE INNER-ACADEMIC TEACHINGS OF PLATO

In the reconstruction of the Tübingen School, the main points of Plato's inner-Academic teachings are the following (see Krämer 1964, 80–81; and Gaiser 1968, 221).

(1) There are two primary ontological principles that are the causes of all things. In establishing the principles, Plato follows the tradition of the Presocratic philosophers of thinking about the ἀρχή or ἀρχαί. Plato appears to be particularly influenced by the Pythagoreans (who also recognize two principles: the limit and the unlimited) and by the Eleatic philosophers. The Eleatic influence on Plato's ontology, however, is negative: for Parmenides and Zeno, the one (ἕν) is being (ὄν), and the many is non-being, whereas for Plato (in the second hypothesis of the *Parmenides*, 142B–157B) the one is opposed to being, on which account it is being that is the many, as the other of the one, and hence the one is beyond being, ἐπέκεινα τῆς οὐσίας (*Rep*. 509B; see Krämer 1981). Besides, Plato was equally influenced by Heraclitus, in that all physical things are in constant flux and change and thus cannot be known; even the very notion of "constant flux" is profoundly paradoxical. By choosing to write elenchic and aporetic dialogues, Plato follows and imitates Socrates in the very form and genre of Socratic dialogue. Yet, as has been mentioned, there is much affinity between the inner-Academic teachings of Plato and later Neoplatonic interpretations of Plato. Already in Plotinus, the one is the principle, and there are multiple layers of being. Many Neoplatonic philosophers make references to inner-Academic doctrines, and Proclus knew the teaching of Speusippus. Yet, an important difference is that the Neoplatonic interpretations of Plato are monistic, whereas Plato seems to have accepted two first principles.

(2) From these two principles comes a whole hierarchy of being: ideas and ideal numbers, intermediate entities that include mathematical entities and physical things (see Aristotle, *Met.* M.9, 1086a11–12). The ideal numbers are themselves limited in number (the first four numbers [τετρακτύς] play an important role in Plato, although Aristotle reports that they go up to the decad, *Met.* M.8, 1084a1–2; cf. N.3, 1090b24). The monad is the smallest but is not properly a number, so that the first number is two, of which the "elements" are the one (τὸ ἕν) and the great-and-small (τὸ μέγα καὶ τὸ μικρόν). The ideal numbers can also be called "idea-numbers," insofar as they *are* ideal forms, and all the ideas are structured in the same way as are numbers. The ideal numbers and ideas constitute a system of the highest categories of being. From these, one has to distinguish the (mathematical) numbers (μαθηματικοὶ ἀριθμοί), which are derived from, and are subordinate to, ideal numbers and ideas.

(3) From the ideal numbers come dimensional (geometrical) entities: line, plane, and solid (or length, breadth, and depth). Both mathematical numbers and geometrical objects represent the intermediate realm of mathematical objects, τὸ μεταξύ. The four ideal (one, two, three, four) numbers establish the sequence of geometrical entities and dimensions: for Speusippus, one corresponds to point, two to line, three to plane, and four to solid (Speusippus, fr. 4 Lang = Iamblichus, *Theol. arithm.* 84.10–11). In each case, the determining number is the number of points needed as limits to define the corresponding magnitude, or μέγεθος. However, according to Aristotle, Plato explicitly rejected the point, which he considered a geometrical "dogma," accepting instead the indivisible line, in which he was joined by Xenocrates (Aristotle, *Met.* A.9, 992a19–24; cf. [Aristotle], *De lin. insecab.* 968a1 ff.). For Plato and Xenocrates, then, what counts as geometrical counterparts of ideal numbers are dimensions, not points: one dimension for line, two for plane, and three for solid, whereas point has no dimensions. This explains the sequence in Plato which begins with an indivisible line, then two, then other numbers (Aristotle, *Met.* M.8, 1084a1). This position is shared by Xenocrates who takes it that a geometrical magnitude consists of matter and number: from two comes length, from three, plane, from four, solids (Aristotle, *Met.* N.3, 1090b21–24). In this sense, geometrical objects follow the numbers in the succession of number—line—plane—solid (Aristotle, *Met.* A.9, 992b13–15, τὰ μετὰ τοὺς ἀριθμοὺς μήκη τε καὶ ἐπίπεδα καὶ στερεά; cf. *Met.* M.6, 1080b23–24; M.9, 1085a7–9; Gaiser 1968, 510n; and Szlezák 1987, 46).

(4) After the intermediates come physical appearances, or sensual material bodies (see *TP* 68–72). There are thus three realms of being that are derivable from the first two principles: ideal entities (ideal numbers and

ideas); intermediate mathematical entities (mathematical numbers and geometrical objects); and physical things.

THE PRINCIPLES

In his inner-Academic teachings, Plato begins with an elaboration of the theory of principles or ἀρχαί, which are the one (ἕν) and the indefinite dyad (ἀόριστος δυάς) (see Aristotle, *Met.* A.6, 987b26). The two principles are not subordinated to one another but play a different role in the constitution of things. The one is the principle of *sameness*, whereas the indefinite dyad is the principle of *otherness*. However, since the principle is not that of which it is the principle, sameness and otherness are not themselves the principles but are their representations, in the forms, as the highest genera or μέγιστα γένη.

The first principle is the formal principle, whereas the second principle is a material principle that appears also as "great-and-small" (τὸ μέγα καὶ τὸ μικρόν), matter (ὕλη) (Aristotle, *Met.* A.6, 987b20–21, 988a13–15; *Phys.* A.4, 187a17–19; see also Simplicius, *In Phys.* 503.10–18). The great-and-small accounts for indefiniteness, disorder, and shapelessness (ἄπειρον, ἄτακτον, ἀμορφία) (Theophrastus, *Met.* 11b2–7; see also Sextus Empiricus, *Adv. Math.* X.261 and *TP* 49–55). As the other to the one, the second principle is also represented in the ἕτερον of Plato's *Sophist* (257B–259B). The indefinite dyad is not non-being per se (because non-being, properly speaking, *is not*), is not μὴ ὄν or χώρα (Plato, *Tim.* 52A–B), but an *ideal principle* of otherness (ἑτερότης) and inequality (ἀνισότης) that is further associated with motion (κίνησις, Aristotle, *Phys.* Γ.2, 201b20–21).

The two principles are thus the principles of *all* things, including ideal being(s). The one is responsible for the oneness and unity of each thing. The otherness or dyad introduces a difference and is *differently* present in different kinds of things. Within the ideas, the dyad is responsible for the plurality: there is a whole *multiplicity* of beings or ideas. Once again, being (ὄν) has to be considered and thought in its otherness to the one (ἕν). In numbers, the dyad is responsible for doubling a number and its division into halves. As Aristotle reports, Plato recognized *two* infinities: the great *and* the small (δύο τὰ ἄπειρα, τὸ μέγα καὶ τὸ μικρόν) (*Phys.* Γ.4, 203a15–16, Γ.6, 206a28). However, these are rather two different aspects of the same principle of the great-and-small that are present in increasing (e.g., in the addition in numbers) and decreasing (in the division of magnitudes). And, finally, the materiality of physical things is manifest in their changeability and constant change. Unity and multiplicity are thus present in things, and account for both identity and differentiation in all things, including the ideal forms and numbers. In other words, both unity and multiplicity in and of being come from the first principles.

TESTIMONIA ABOUT THE FIRST PRINCIPLES

Plato's *Parmenides* is the key dialogue for a systematic elaboration of the inner-Academic doctrine of the two principles of the one and many (cf. Plato, *Phil.* 16C–D; 26E–31B), which has been repeatedly emphasized by Stenzel, Krämer, Reale, Migliori, and Halfwassen. One might also count as Plato's "self-testimony" the passage in the *Phaedo* (107B4–10), where in a conversation with the Pythagorean Simmias, Socrates refers to ultimate "first presuppositions," at which the investigation should stop.

Besides, there exists consistent evidence from the closest disciples of Plato—from Aristotle, Speusippus, and Xenocrates. In *On the Good*, Aristotle explicitly mentions the one (μονάς) and the dyad as the first principles (Aristotle, *De bono*, fr. 2 Ross). And Speusippus' testimony (fr. 62 Lang = fr. 29 Isnardi Parente = Simplicius, *In Phys.* 151, 6f., in reference to Alexander) coincides with that of Xenocrates (fr. 27 Heinze = fr. 98 Isnardi Parente): "According to Plato, the principles of all things, as well as of the ideas themselves, are the one and the indefinite dyad, which is also called great-and-small," as Aristotle recalls in *On the Good* (κατὰ Πλάτωνα πάντων ἀρχαὶ καὶ αὐτῶν τῶν ἰδεῶν τό τε ἕν ἐστι καὶ ἡ ἀόριστος δυάς, ἣν μέγα καὶ μικρὸν ἔλεγεν, ὡς καὶ ἐν Περὶ τἀγαθοῦ Ἀριστοτέλες μνημονεύει). We also learn about the two principles of the ἕν and the ἀόριστος δυάς from Theophrastus (*Met.* 6a24–6b17; 11b2–7). Important testimonies about the two principles are found in Alexander of Aphrodisias (*In Met.* 85.15–86.23) and Philoponus (*In de gen. et corr.* 226.16–30) as well.

THE PRINCIPLES: SIMPLE AND INDIVISIBLE

If the principles are the principles of all things, what can one say about the ἀρχαί themselves? The principles have to be *simple* and *indivisible*, because they are the principles of everything else that is multiple and composite, as being constituted by the principles (cf. Plato, *Theaet.* 205D). This claim is also supported by the mentioned fragment of Alexander (*In Met.* 55.20–56.35). In its very notion (which, paradoxically, comes *before* the ideal notions in the proper sense, which themselves come from, and hence after, the principles), the principle is the first and incomposite (τὸ πρῶτον ἀρχὴ εἶναι καὶ τὸ ἀσύνθετον). In his account of the inner-Academic teachings, Sextus too (*Adv. Math.* X.250–251) takes the ἀρχαί to be simple and not evident, whereas the phenomena are—literally—evident: φαινόμενα). The principles of material things are not themselves material (not "visible"), because physical things are infinitely divisible, whereas the principles are not (*Adv. Math.* X.250).

Knowledge of the Principles. But, if the ἀρχαί are first and the source of all composition, how can they be known? For if the simple is ontologically and logically prior, then the cognition of it should be most difficult for us, who are composite and always begin with things that are complex. *Qua* simple and first, the principles can only be known *negatively*. The principle is unexplainable and unknowable from within itself: it is ἄλογον τε καὶ ἄγνωστον (Plato, *Theaet*. 205C9–10; cf. 201E). Since for Plato everything is and is known ultimately in reference to the first principles, for the principles *to be* and *to be known* is a negative determination: the ἀρχαί are different from those things that come from them. Hence, knowledge of the principles is negative, too: because they are simple, or incomposite, and are *before* the multiplicity of being as its (logical and ontological) beginning and cause.

Strictly speaking, from the perspective of the first principles alone there is no distinction between logic and ontology yet. This distinction becomes meaningful only with the multiplicity of beings, at which point one might say that the principles are first not only ontologically but also *logically*, insofar as they are represented in the first *genera*. In particular, in the *Sophist* (254B7–D3), Plato talks about the first genera of sameness and otherness as representations of the principles. In this, the principles can be said to be known *positively*, through logical (categorical) and ontological (mathematical or dimensional) reduction, as well as through the deduction of things from them, of which I will say more in what follows.

Principles as Causes. The two principles (ἀρχαί) are thus the first and ultimate causes (αἰτίαι, αἴτια) of other things, both ontologically and logically, but the principles themselves are not caused. Krämer considers a strict distinction and separation between ontology and logic to originate only with the Stoics; certainly, it is not there yet in Plato and the Old Academy, nor even is it explicit in Aristotle. (In this sense, one might say that Hegel returns to Plato.) Hence, both the being (the ontological aspect) and the knowledge (the logical aspect) of things depend on knowledge of their first principles and causes. In order *to be* and *to be known*, each thing has to be understood, that is, causally reduced to or deduced from these principles. As Aristotle argues, to know what a thing is (τί ἐστιν) is to know the cause of its being (τὸ αἴτιον τοῦ εἰ ἐστι) (*An. post*. B.8, 93a3–4; cf. *Phys*. A.1, 184a10–15). In this sense, Plato's philosophy is an *aitiology* in the sense of the Presocratics, i.e., an investigation of the first causes, principles, and elements of everything existent (Krämer 1981, 4–11).

Monism or Dualism of the Principles? If one accepts the requirement of assuming as few principles as possible (see Aristotle, *Phys*. A.4, 188a17–18), one might ask if it is possible to reduce the number of the principles in

Plato to one single principle. Most of the sources, beginning with Aristotle, mention *two* distinct and different first principles in Plato's ἄγραφα δόγματα: the one and the dyad. Other scholars, however, have supported a monistic interpretation of Plato. Thus, Hösle (1984, 459–490) argues for accepting one first principle as the unity of unity and multiplicity (*Einheit von Einheit und Vielheit*). And Halfwassen (2002) opts for combining a monism in the *reduction to* the one principle beyond being with a dualism in the derivation and *deduction of* being from the two ontic principles of the one and the many, even if the coming-forth of the principle of the many from the transcendent one cannot be explained rationally, i.e., by way of discursive thinking.

The former monistic interpretation of Plato is Hegelian, and the latter Plotinian. Halfwassen's interpretation is more in line with Speusippus, as well as with Proclus, who places the one beyond (any given) being, multiplicity, or otherness. On Speusippus' and Proclus' reading, the indefinite dyad, *interminabilis dualitas*, appears *after* the one (Speusippus ap. Proclus, *In Parm.* 38.25–41.10 [*TP* 50]), i.e., the two principles in this reading are not equal but rather hierarchically ordered. Discursive thinking, however, cannot discursively grasp either the identity of the unmediated opposites or the generation of the other, both of which are unthinkable. Hence, if there is either one first principle that embraces the same and the other, or if the one somehow engenders the other as multiplicity—in both cases the one single principle cannot be rationally conceived. On the contrary, Krämer and Gaiser are inclined to accept the dualism of Plato's "archeology," following the majority of ancient sources that speak about two ontologically equal yet functionally distinct first principles in Plato.

Principles as Opposites. The first principles appear as opposites to each other and in their representation and action within things. Even if the one (ἕν), *qua* principle, is one, unique, and simple, it is still opposed to the δυάς as its other. Both principles are present negatively in relation to each other, so that neither can be considered without the other. All other things can be deduced from the principles as their causes, but the principles themselves are not deducible either from each other or from other things. At the same time, the ἀρχαί are not absolutely symmetrical, because their roles are very different.

This conclusion finds support both in the texts of Plato and in the testimonies. Thus, in the *Sophist* (254E), Plato takes the same and other, the representations of the two principles in being, as paired opposites (along with motion and rest, although being [ὄν] does not have an opposite in the *Sophist* but is conceived in its relation to the opposites). In *On the Good*, Aristotle says all the contraries (τὰ ἐναντία) go back to the two principles of the one (τὸ ἕν) and multiplicity (τὸ πλῆθος); and the opposites are the elements (στοιχεῖα) of substance (οὐσία) (Aristotle, *De bono*, fr. 5 Ross = Alexander, *In Met*. 250.17–20 and Asclepius, *In Met*. 237.11–21). In Aristotle's *Metaphysics*, the one and many (ἓν καὶ πλῆθος) are taken also in opposition (ἀντίθεσις) to each other, as contraries (ἐναντία) (Aristotle, *Met*. Γ.2, 1004b28, cf. I.3, 1054a26; *Phys*. A.5, 188a19–20, 189a9–10). Theophrastus explicitly calls the principles of the ἕν and ἀόριστος δυάς opposites (τὰς ἀρχὰς ἐναντίας, *Met*. 11b7). And in Pseudo-Alexander (*In Met*. 615.14–17 [*TP* 41B]) the two principles are also considered opposites: the one as the same, like, equal (τὸ ἕν as τὸ ταὐτὸν καὶ ὅμοιον καὶ ἴσον); and multitude as different, unlike, unequal (τὸ πλῆθος is τὸ ἕτερον καὶ ἀνόμοιον καὶ ἄνισον).

Opposites (ἐναντία), however, can be considered either as allowing for a mediation (or middle, μέσον, μεταξύ), in which case they are contraries, or, if the opposites do not allow for mediation, they are in *contradiction* (see Aristotle, *Phys*. A.5, 188b21–23; and Pseudo-Aristotle, *Div. Arist*. 65–66 [*TP* 44A]). The opposition between the two principles of the one and the dyad (as not-one) is *contradictory*, because they do not allow for—and do not yet have—a mediation or anything to mediate between them. This is another reason why first principles in Plato cannot be considered as embedded in, or embraced by, one single principle. As Krämer has argued, even the logical principle of non-contradiction (Plato, *Soph*. 230B, 249B, 259B; cf. *Rep*. 436D) or of the excluded third implicitly presupposes a reference to the two principles (Krämer 1981).

The One as the Good. If the one and the indefinite dyad are two contradictory principles, then they are not hierarchically ordered, so that the one does not excel or transcend the dyad in its function. And yet, the one and the dyad are not altogether symmetrical or equal in their effect.

According to Krämer, the main thesis of Plato's inner-Academic teaching is the identification of the one with the good: ἕν is ἀγαθόν. In the *Republic* (506D2–507A2, 509C1–11), Plato *mentions* the good rather than giving it a proper definition, which is left out of the debate. A development of the thesis that the good is the one is found, however, in Plato's public lecture (ἀκρόασις) *On the Good* (Περὶ τἀγαθοῦ), which is different from a series of regular lectures delivered at the Academy of the same name (see Aristotle, *Met*. N.4, 1091b14–15; *EE* I.8, 1218a15–21; Alexander ap. Simplicius, *In Phys*. 454.17–455.14; *TP* 7–11).

Here, the one by itself is the good, yet in the relative constitution of things and numbers the one is responsible for ordering, unity, and equality, whereas inequality and differentiation is the "work" of the dyad (Gaiser 1988, 24–26).

Qua good, the one also constitutes the μέγιστον μάθημα ("greatest knowledge") (*Rep*. 504D2–3, 505A2), although, again, a detailed debate of what this knowledge is is postponed in the dialogue indefinitely and probably deferred to more specialized oral discussions in the Academy. As such, the one is, then, the ultimate element of all being. The one itself, however, is not being in the proper sense, but is "beyond being" (*Rep*. 509B). The good is the other of being which is represented in a multiplicity of beings, and yet the good is thinkable only in relation to the other of being. Because of this, Plato's inner-Academic "archeology" cannot be a strict monism. Hence, Plato's one is neither the Hegelian one, nor the Plotinian One of the first hypothesis of the *Parmenides*, but the one coupled with the many of the second hypothesis in the *Parmenides* (*Parm*. 137C–142B, 142B–157B).

If there are two principles in Plato, the one and the many, and the one is the good, then the other of the one—matter, ἀόριστος δυάς or τὸ μέγα καὶ τὸ μικρόν—has to be the cause of evil (κακόν), even if not necessarily evil *per se*. This conclusion is reflected in Aristotle's Pythagorean list of the ten opposites, in which the limit matches the one and the good but is opposed to the unlimited, multiple, and evil (Aristotle, *Met*. A.5, 986a 24–26). Speusippus already seemed to have been perplexed by this equating of the many with evil, which he tried to avoid by *not identifying* the one with the good (*Met*. N.4, 1091b32–35).

The One as Measure. As the principle of sameness, the one is also the measure (μέτρον) of all things (cf. Aristotle, *Met*. N.1, 1087b33; and Aristotle, *Politikos*, fr. 2 Ross: πάντων γὰρ ἀκριβέστατον μέτρον τἀγαθόν ἐστιν). The one, then, is the universal measure as the middle (μέσον) that balances the extremes of the excess and deficiency of the other principle (cf. Plato, *Polit*. 284A–285B).

In Krämer's reconstruction, the μεσότης doctrine plays a major role in *On the Good*, where it appears in conjunction with the theory of the principles and ontology (Krämer 1959, 287–289, 342ff.; also in Stenzel, Ross, and Wilpert). In particular, the one is defined as measure in the triple sense of scale, norm, and limit (Krämer 1980, 37).

As the universal measure and middle, the one emerges both in practical and in theoretical philosophy. In ethics, virtue (ἀρετή) is defined by Plato as measure (μέτρον) in relation to excess and deficiency. Thus, in the *Meno* (77A–B), Plato mentions moral excellence as measure defined by the good. As Dillon notes in support of Krämer, the notion of virtue as a middle is not distinctive to Aristotle but has a Pythagorean origin, which is evident in Plato (Dillon 2003, 18).

In theoretical philosophy, the one appears as the monad, which, however, is not a number properly but the principle and the beginning (ἀρχή) of number, insofar as the first measure is the beginning (τὸ γὰρ πρῶτον μέτρον ἀρχή) (Aristotle, *Met*. Δ.6, 1016b17–19). As the measure, the one balances the impact of the principle of otherness as excess and defect in numbers (Plato, *Prot*. 356D–357C), which results in the constitution of numbers. As

I will argue in what follows in more detail, the one accounts both for unity in ideal numbers, each one of which is one and unique, and for the units as elements in mathematical numbers, which are mutually commensurable.

Because various ontological realms are distinguished in Plato by their variously defined relations to the two principles, which are differently present in each ontological layer, the principle of the one is also present differently in different ontological spheres. This claim is clear and becomes elaborated especially in Speusippus (see Krämer 1964 [3], 89; Krämer 1966 [3], 429). As a *specific* one, in numbers the one is present as the unit (μονάς); in dimensional magnitudes as the indivisible line; in physical things as uniform circular motion; in music as the quarter tone, i.e., as the smallest interval in the scale (δίεσις); and in time, as the moment of "now" (see Sextus Empiricus, *Adv. Math.* X.276; Aristotle, *Met.* I.1, 1052b20–24 [ἕν], A.9, 992a20–22 [ἄτομος γραμμή], M.8, 1084b1, I.1, 1053a7–13 [circular motion; δίεσις; στοιχεῖον in speech]; N.1, 1087b35 [δίεσις], M.3, 1078a 12–13 [uniform motion]; *Phys.* Θ.9, 265b8–11 [circular motion as the measure and first motion]; Plato, *Polit.* 269E, *Legg.* 893C–D [περιφορά and κύκλος]; Aristotle, *Phys.* Γ.11, 219b10ff., Z.2, 233b33ff.; *DC* Γ.1, 300a14; [Aristotle], *De lin. insecab.* 971a17 [νῦν]; cf. Aristotle, *DA* A.2, 404b22 [νοῦς as τὸ ἕν]).

THE IMPORTANCE OF MATHEMATICS IN PLATO

Mathematics appears to be of utter importance for Plato. Gaiser did particularly much for a reconstruction of Plato's inner-Academic mathematical theories, both from his texts and from the evidence of the tradition. In Plato's times—and in Plato's school—enormous *progress* (ἐπίδοσις) was made both in *mathematics* (arithmetic and especially geometry) and *logic*. Aristotle tells us (*Met.* A.9, 992a32–b1) that Plato and his followers turned philosophy into mathematics, although they say that one has to do mathematics for the sake of other things, i.e., for the sake of philosophy proper. Indeed, in the *Republic* Plato argues that mathematics leads to dialectic, which further leads to a "synoptic" vision and understanding of being (*Rep.* 531C–534E, 537C). Dialectic is similar to mathematics and philosophy in that dialectic embraces a whole *plurality* of methods yet is based on only *a few* principles. Moreover, dialectic is a *logical* enterprise, some of whose methods are close to the analysis of *language* (λόγος). Thus, language and mathematics are the two spheres that are exemplary for the dialectician, because both enable establishing and justifying theories about the ideal (Gaiser 1988, 21). The connection of logic and ontology is further emphasized by the fact that, again, in Plato's times logic and ontology were not distinguished.

In particular, among the logical methods of dialectic Gaiser counts the following six (although the plurality of methods suggests that one can make other distinctions, e.g., by adding the method of definition [Alcinous, *Didask.* 6]). These are: (1) ἔλεγξις or ἔλεγχος; (2) συναγωγή and διαίρεσις, the collection of species under a superior genus and the division of a genus according to species (although the starting point for a dieresis is usually hypothetical, and each step in division is rather arbitrary, Plato, *Phaedr.* 265D–266C); (3) ἀνάλυσις and σύνθεσις (which identify elementary constituents [στοιχεῖα] within a complex whole): the model is that of speech as divisible into sentences, words, syllables, and *letters* (on the similarity of elements to syllables and letters in speech, see Plato, *Theaet.* 202E, 206B; *Tim.* 48C–E; *Soph.* 252B; *Polit.* 278A–D; cf. *Phil.* 16C–18D; and also Sextus Empiricus, *Adv. Math.* X.249–250; Diogenes Laertius, III.24; Iamblichus, *Protrepticus* 6, 38.14, 39.7–8; Proclus, *In Eucl.* 212.18–20); letters are simple yet multiple (which shows the work and presence of the dyad), whereas the whole is complex yet one (which shows the work and presence of the one); (4) μεσότης; (5) ὑπόθεσις; and (6) μίμησις (Gaiser 2004, 177–203).

A Herculaneum papyrus suggests that Plato was considered an "architect" who directed the mathematical research at the Academy (ἀρχιτεκτονοῦντος . . . καὶ προβλήματα διδόντος) (Dicaearchus ap. Philodemus, *Index Academicorum*, col. Y 2–7). Many outstanding mathematicians, such as Eudoxus, Archytas, Theaetetus, Menaechmus, and Theudius, were active in the Academy or were closely associated with Plato (cf. Proclus' "catalogue of geometers" [*In Eucl.* 64.2ff.]; Nails 2002, 275–278) and defined the development of mathematics up to the present day. They made a deep impact on Euclid's *Elements*, which thus may be considered an Academic work. Apparently, a number of mathematical problems were discussed and solved at the Academy. Such, for instance, is the Delian problem of doubling the volume of a cube, which was addressed already by Hippocrates of Chios, discussed within the Academy, and solved by means of the construction by Archytas and Menaechmus, even if Plato himself objected to the use of mechanical methods in the study of mathematics (see Proclus, *In Eucl.* 66–68, 77–78; Plutarch, *Quaest. Conviv.* VIII, 2.1, and *Vita Marcelli* 14.5–6). However, Plato was more interested not in the solution of mathematical problems as such but in the pedagogical and philosophical meaning of mathematics and its role in knowledge of being and the good (*TP* 15–21).

In Plato, there is a close connection between mathematics and ontology, which is apparent in his Περὶ τἀγαθοῦ, where he explains the thesis of the identity of the one and the good through mathematics by showing the deduction of ideas and ideal numbers, as well as mathematical numbers and geometrical magnitudes, from the two principles. Insofar as mathematics leads to the simplest yet most universal hypotheses (axioms and definitions) and notions—such as unity, measure, middle, and multiplicity—mathematics became a model for the understanding of the structure of being and the cognition of the first principles. Since Plato uses mathematics to describe and structure *being*, ontology itself becomes mathematical (see Aristoxenus, *Elem. Harm.* 2.30–31 = Aristotle, fr. 111 Ross). The famous μηδεὶς ἀγεωμέτρητος εἰσίτω, "Nobody unversed in geometry should enter," reportedly written above the entrance to the Academy, is probably a later rhetorical invention (as Plutarch says, Πλάτων ἔλεγε τὸν θεὸν ἀεὶ γεωμετρεῖν [*Quaest. Conviv.* VIII, 2.4, 719F), yet it captures the spirit of the Academic attitude toward philosophy.

Ideal and Mathematical Numbers. A crucial point for understanding Plato's philosophy of mathematics is the *intermediateness*, or middle position, of mathematical objects (Aristotle, *Met.* A.6, 987b14–16; see Gaiser 1963, 89–99; Gaiser 1988, 21; Merlan 1969, 112). In order to properly locate and understand this claim, one has to stress a crucial distinction in Plato's account of ontology and mathematics between the so-called "ideal" and "mathematical" numbers. Although ἀριθμός plays an important role in Platonic ontology and dialectic (cf. *Soph.* 254E), Plato does not speak explicitly about ideal numbers in his dialogues. However, a clear distinction between ideal numbers (εἰδητικοὶ ἀριθμοί) and mathematical numbers (μαθηματικοὶ ἀριθμοί) in Plato is testified by Aristotle (*Met.* N.2, 1088b34–35; N.3, 1090b32–33; *De philosophia*, fr. 11 Ross, ap. Syrianus, *In Met.* 159.33–35).

The objects of mathematics are intermediate (i.e., occupy a middle ontological position, μεταξύ) between the ideal and the physical (cf. Proclus, *In Eucl.* 3.1–7). Mathematical entities thus bridge the gap between the spheres of being and becoming by *both* separating and uniting them within the ontological sequence of the principles; ideal entities (ideas and ideal numbers); intermediate mathematical entities (mathematical numbers and geometrical objects); and physical things. As intermediate, mathematical entities are similar to the ideal ones in that both are immutable in their properties; and mathematicals are similar to physical things in being many (there are, for example, many number fives).

The intermediate character of mathematical objects establishes an ontological structure of things that is complemented and paralleled by the epistemological structure of cognitive faculties (see Plato, *Rep.* 511D–E, 522C–526C). Thus, the ideal entities—ideal numbers and ideas—are subjects of non-discursive thinking (νόησις). The mathematicals (which include mathematical numbers [studied by arithmetic], lines and planes [geometry], solids [stereometry], and regular motions [astronomy]) are thought by discursive thinking (διάνοια). Notably, the soul, which, in a sense, *is* διάνοια, because it thinks discursively through arguments, is itself intermediate within the structure of cognitive faculties, and is the "place" of ideas (see

TP 66–67, esp. Philoponus, *In de anima* 524.6–16). The soul thinks mathematical numbers and figures discursively. And finally, the appearances, or physical bodies, are conceived by sense-perception (αἴσθησις).

But what are ideal numbers? Aristotle is unambiguous in the *De anima* when he tells us that the ideal numbers (or "idea-numbers") are *ideas* (οἱ . . . ἀριθμοὶ τὰ εἴδη αὐτά, *DA* 404b24). In the Tübingen interpretation, ideal numbers are the ideal paradigms for mathematical numbers, which are intermediate between the ideal and the physical. Of course, as paradigms ideal numbers do not have the same properties as mathematical numbers or things. Rather, ideal numbers establish the structure of mathematical numbers and things and the pattern of their cognition (cf. *Tim.* 31C–32A, 35A–36B).

The mathematical Pythagorean approach of Plato is also reflected in the very terms he uses for the principles—the *one* (ἕν or μονάς) and the *dyad* (δυάς). The principles are the principles of numbers, although neither of them is properly a number. Since everything that is comes from the two principles, the ideal numbers, a synthetic unity of the same and the other, are deduced from them, too (cf. Gaiser 1988, 22).

But if ideal numbers are ideas, are ideas also numbers, i.e., are *all* ideas numbers, or are there ideas that are not ideal numbers? There is no clear indication in the *testimonia* of how Plato would address this problem, which is why Gaiser has speculated that, if ideas are numbers, this does not yet mean that *all* ideas are numbers. According to Gaiser, ideal numbers are the universal genera of being, and for this reason ideas are numbers. But at the same time ideas are also subsumed under numbers, as species under genera. Krämer, however, has a different solution of the problem: ideal numbers are not the ideas of numbers, although there are ideas of numbers, too; rather, *all* ideas are structured in the same way *as* numbers.

A notable distinction between the two kinds of numbers consists in that in ideal numbers, as Aristotle tells us, the monads are mutually *incommensurable* (ἀσύμβλητοι), as are ideal numbers themselves, whereas in mathematical numbers the monads are commensurable (συμβλητοί), as are mathematical numbers (Aristotle, *Met.* M.6, 1080a23, M.7, 1081a17, M.8, 1083a32–35). Thus, the dyad and triad, or the ideal numbers two and three, are ideal forms that establish a structure of mathematical number and patterns of things in the cosmos. Yet, they do not have a common measure, which would be a monad, because each monad that can be discerned in an ideal number is not commensurable with any other one.

Another important difference between the ideal and mathematical numbers can be further seen in that the limit has a stronger presence in the ideal numbers: the ideal numbers are *finite* in number, whereas the mathematical numbers are not limited in their number. In particular, the ideal numbers go up to ten only (Aristotle, *Met.* Λ.8, 1073a20–21, M.8, 1084a15 [μέχρι τῆς δεκάδος]; *Phys.* Γ.6, 206b32–33; Speusippus, fr. 4 Lang = Iamblichus, *Theol. arithm.* 83.6ff.).

Ideal numbers are the ideal paradigms for the natural numbers of the decimal system. However, the four "primal numbers" (1, 2, 3, 4) seem to have a privileged position within the ideal numbers, of which we have a hint in the very first sentence of Plato's *Timaeus* (17A), which is formulated as a question by Socrates: "One, two, three, and where is the fourth?" This opening sentence might be taken as a brief formulation of the whole program of Plato's mathematical ontology. The four first ideal numbers in sum form the decad, which is a "completion" of numbers and, as it will be argued later, are also the patterns for four-dimensional geometrical objects (point, line, plane, solid) as their limits (cf. Dillon 2003, 19).

But how do these four numbers relate to the ten ideal numbers? In Gaiser's interpretation, the four numbers of the decad (1, 2, 3, 4) precede the ideal numbers (Gaiser 1963, 115ff., esp. 137). This, however, seems to be an unnecessary distinction, because it leads to a genera-species logical hierarchy of being, which would be: the two first principles; the four primal numbers; the ten ideal numbers; and the infinity of mathematical numbers. Yet there is no indication in the testimonies that such a numerical hierarchy was conceived of by Plato. Krämer's suggestion that ideal numbers (without making a distinction between primal and ideal numbers) are the universal paradigms as structural patterns for all entities in their sameness and otherness, including ideas, mathematical entities, and bodies, appears more plausible.

A further problem with the interpretation of the role numbers play in Plato is that, whereas Aristotle in *Metaphysics* M and N clearly says that ideal numbers *are* ideas or forms, the distinction between the ideal and mathematical numbers is not clearly established later in Alexander, who is an important source of our understanding of the functioning and structure of numbers in Plato. Commenting on Aristotle, Alexander simply identifies εἴδη with ἀριθμοί (Alexander, *In Met.* 55.20–56.35). Moreover, both Theophrastus (*Met.* 6b11–15) and Sextus Empiricus (*Adv. Math.* X.258) report that the ideal numbers *precede* ideas and that the ideas are reducible to numbers.

The confusion might be explained by the fact that Speusippus and Xenocrates began a revision of Plato's doctrine of ideal numbers. Speusippus denies the very existence of ideal numbers and ideas, and asserts the existence of mathematical numbers only (Aristotle, *Met.* M.6, 1080b11–16; cf. Gaiser 1968, 224), whereas Xenocrates identifies ideal and mathematical numbers (Aristotle, *Met.* M.6, 1080b22–23). From all these accounts, it is clear, however, that number played an extremely important role in Plato's inner-Academic theories and that these doctrines have been much debated, revised, and to an extent rejected even by Plato's immediate disciples.

Deduction of Numbers. Alexander of Aphrodisias, in his commentary on Aristotle's *Metaphysics*, which preserves a substantial fragment from Aristotle's doxographic evidence of Plato's public lecture *On the Good* (Aristotle, *De bono*, fr. 2 Ross = Alexander, *In Met.* 55.20f.), explains the deduction or generation of numbers in the following way. Plato and the Pythagorean philosophers established numbers as the principles of all things. By its very notion, the first principle is the cause of a thing's being and of its being knowable as what it is with all its properties. The principles, however, have to be simple and indivisible. According to Alexander, the primary (τὸ πρῶτον) and incomposite (τὸ ἀσύνθετον) is the principle (ἀρχή). The units in numbers (αἱ μονάδες) are simple and incomposite, and, since units are numbers, numbers are therefore first and prior to everything existent. Since ideas are the forms of things and precede them, and since things only have their existence in relation to ideas, ideas are identical with numbers. This means that the first principles of numbers are also the first principles of ideas, and thereby of all things.

Since Plato took the opposites, which do not allow for mediation, to be the principles of all things, they are thereby also the principles of numbers: the one (μονάς) is the principle and cause of unity and equality, and the dyad (δυάς) is the principle of many and inequality in numbers. But because the many as the dyad is the other to the one, the dyad is also the source of duality as many *and* few, or great *and* small, in numbers and also of the double ("great" or "excess") *and* the half ("small" or "defect") in things.

At this point, we still only have two opposites as the beginning, source, and principles of everything existing, but we still have to deduce the primary being—or beings, since, as numbers, being always comes in the plural—from these two principles. Hence, the numbers come from the two principles of the one and the dyad (cf. ἐκ τοῦ ἑνὸς καὶ τῆς δυάδος τῆς ἀορίστου) (Aristotle, *Met.* M.7, 1081a14 and Xenocrates, fr. 3 Heinze = Ps.-Alexander, *In Met.* 819.37–820.7 Hayduck [*TP* 68B]). Yet, the principles of numbers themselves are not numbers: the one is not a number but the beginning and the measure of number (ἀρχὴ καὶ τὸ μέτρον) (Aristotle, *Met.* N.1, 1088a6–8).

As Alexander reports, and his account coincides with the testimony of Aristotle (*Met.* M.9, 1085b9; *De bono*, fr. 2 Ross), the first number is number two (for it is "one in its form"), which is different from the dyad as the principle of number and being. The first number is a product of the limitation of the other of the limiting principle (see Plato, *Phaedo* 96E–97C, 101B–C; Aristotle, *Met.* M.7, 1081a21f., 1081b10f., 1082a13–14, Δ.15, 1020b33–34; and Sextus Empiricus, *Adv. Math.* X.276–277). That is to say, when the principle of the limit limits the principle of the unlimited, there comes the very first being, which is the number two and is the result of interaction between the first two principles. Since, however, two is also an image of the great-and-small, it bears in itself the potency of being doubled or divided into halves and thus has the possibility of generating monads.

Now, we also need the unit of number as the simplest elementary number. Rather than dividing the number two into two halves, Alexander explains the production of the numerical unit by an act of further application of the principle of the one to the dyad ("great-and-small"). When the one applies itself to its only other (τὸ παρὰ τὸ ἕν), i.e., "limits" the dyad as a whole, there is the number two. But when the one applies to the potencies of the dyad (which "do not allow a thing to remain what it was"), i.e., to the "great" and the "small" as capacities for producing the double and the half, there come two distinct units. In this way, the numerical unit comes only after the two as the first number.

Thus, we now have the number two, which also comes with a potency of doubling everything to which it applies, and a numerical unit that can be added to any number. From here, we can deduce the numbers within the decad. However, rather than obtaining the next number by adding a unit or as the successor of the already deduced number, as does Peano, Plato on Aristotle's and Alexander's accounts derives even and odd numbers differently and separately from each other. We do not have a further explanation for this, yet the reason for a separate derivation of the odd and even numbers might be that odd numbers represent more the principle of the one, whereas the even numbers have more to do with the principle of the dyad, although, of course, the one and the dyad are present and act in every number, as also in every being and thing.

The even numbers are derived first by the application of the number two to itself, which means its doubling by itself: 2 x 2 = 4, and so on (cf. Aristotle, *Met.* M.7, 1081b21–22). The odd numbers, however, are derived by adding a numerical unit to the first number: 2 + 1 = 3. The first four ideal numbers are thus derived in succession: first number two, then number one as a unit, then number four (as the doubling of two), and then number three (as one added to two). Yet the four ideal numbers in their entirety constitute all the even and odd numbers within the decad (cf. Aristotle, *Met.* M.8, 1084a33–34). Thus, 3 x 2 = 6, 4 x 2 = 8, and 4 + 1 = 5, 6 + 1 = 7, 8 + 1 = 9, and 5 x 2 = 10. In this way, all the numbers within the decad are derived.

As has been mentioned, Alexander does not make an explicit distinction between ideal and mathematical numbers. However, the very way his deduction goes suggests that he is speaking about the derivation of ideal numbers as incommensurable wholes, which are paradigms for mathematical numbers and all things, rather than about numerical numbers that are constituted by a definite number of mutually commensurable units.

TWO REDUCTIONS AND A DEDUCTION

Once Plato establishes the first principles of all things, on the one hand, and a hierarchically ordered structure of being, on the other, he has to find a way to describe a relation of ontologically different entities to their causes. We may always begin with what is more evident to us and go back to the ἀρχαί, or we may also begin with the ἀρχαί and then deduce the existent from them. Both ways of reduction and deduction should be mutually convertible, even if the two methods themselves might be mutually independent.

There is thus a *double motion* of reasoning or argumentation *from* the principles (οἱ ἀπὸ τῶν ἀρχῶν λόγοι)—and *to* the principles (οἱ ἐπὶ τὰς ἀρχάς) (Aristotle, *NE* A.4, 1095a30–b3). The double motion from and to the principles parallels, and indeed implies, the synthesis and analysis methods that justify a claim by moving from or toward the accepted principle(s) of an argument, such as definitions, axioms, or postulates. We know that Plato practiced the method of analysis, which traces a proposition back to an acknowledged principle, and taught it to Leodamas (Proclus, *In Eucl.* 211.17–23; cf. Diogenes Laertius, *Lives* III.24). In the two kinds of examination, *of* the principles and *from* the principles, mentioned by Theophrastus (τῶν ἀρχῶν/ ἀπὸ τῶν ἀρχῶν ἡ ζήτησις) (Theophrastus, *Met.* 6b21–22), the study *of* the simple and non-evident principles (and there is nothing more difficult than to look into really simple things) implies a possibility of reducing all things *to* the principles (εἰς τὰς ἀρχάς) (Theophrastus, *Met.* 6b14).

Moreover, it is possible to distinguish further two different ways of reduction to the principles (Aristotle, *De bono*, fr. 2 Ross; cf. Gaiser 1968, 240–241; Gaiser 1963, 107–110; and Richard 1986, 180–190): a dimensional and a categorical reduction. The dimensional reduction is a mathematical ("Pythagorean") method, whereas the categorical reduction is a logical ("Socratic") method, which, once again, suggests a close connection between mathematics and logic in Plato's constitution of ontology.

Dimensional (Mathematical) Reduction. The dimensional reduction to the principles begins with the body and moves back (or "up") to the principles. Sextus mentions a distinction between sensual and noetic bodies in Plato (αἰσθητὰ σώματα / νοητὰ σώματα) (Sextus Empiricus, *Adv. Math.* X.253), which are physical bodies and geometrical figures, correspondingly. In order to proceed with the reduction to the principles, one has to move from the physical to the intelligible by way of the geometrical, which is intermediate between the two realms. A similarity between physical bodies and geometrical solids consists in that both are three-dimensional, yet the former are in flux, whereas the latter do not change over time. Further distinction and relation between the physical and the geometrical are not very clearly spelled out in Plato's dialogues and have to be reconstructed on the basis of the existing evidence. Thus, when in the *Timaeus* (54Dff.) Plato speaks about the primary triangles that constitute the four regular bodies of the four elements, he does not provide any explanation as to how and why geometrical bodies obtain physical properties (such as weight).

The dimensional reduction, then, follows the sequence: solid–plane–line–number, which leads to the principles of number, the one and the dyad, which are also the universal principles of all things. There are a number of texts within the tradition that testify to such a consecutive reduction (Aristotle, *Met.* A.9, 992b13–15; Δ.6, 1016b24–31; Z.2, 1028b16–18; M.9, 1085a7–14, N.3, 1090b5–7; *De philosophia*, fr. 11 Ross = Alexander, *In Met.* 117.23–118.1; Theophrastus, *Met.* 6a25–26; Sextus Empiricus, *Adv. Math.* X.257–262; Iamblichus, *Protrepticus* 6, 38.11–14; cf. *TP* 33–38). The dimensional reduction is not explicitly discussed in Plato's extant texts, although hints at it may be seen in the *Timaeus*, where Plato speaks about the constitution of the three dimensions of bodies in the cosmos according to a numerical proportion that connects four terms (*Tim.* 32A–B).

The reduction thus begins with the physical, then moves to the geometrical, where at each step the dimension of the figure is reduced by one, up to the one-dimensional object (line), then to the arithmetical (numbers), and then to the first principles.

That the cosmos in Plato is inherently geometrical and is structured according to a numerical pattern is supported by an interpretation of a passage from Plato's *Timaeus* (36C–D), which supports the conclusion that the Platonic cosmos, although spherical and unique, in its entirety preserves Euclidean, and not elliptic, geometry, insofar as the cosmos can be taken as topologically equivalent to a torus (see Nikulin 2000, 113–118).

Notably, point is absent in the geometrical sequence of solid–plane–line: because of its simplicity and partlessness, point always presents a difficulty for thinking for Plato and Xenocrates. In Speusippus' account of mathematical ontology, however, there is a clear parallelism between four ideal numbers and geometrical figures of different dimensions: 1–2–3–4 : : point–line–plane–solid. Numbers thus establish a pattern for the structure and consideration of geometrical entities, in which point stands for a unit (μονάς) that, as has been said, is not the first number but rather an indivisible basis of number and a representative of the one, of the principle of sameness. Similarly to unit in numbers, point is the indivisible *limit* of divisible geometrical figures. A difference between the numerical unit and point consists in that the unit has no position, whereas point has a position, i.e., is located in geometrical space (ἡ μὲν ἄθετος μονάς, ἡ δὲ θετὸς στιγμή] [Aristotle, *Met.* Δ.6, 1016b30–31]; τὰ δὲ σημεῖα εἶναι μονάδας θέσιν ἔχουσας [Aristotle, *De bono*, fr. 2 Ross]).

The second principle of otherness and multiplicity, the "great-and-small" or ἀόριστος δυάς, to which the dimensional reduction leads as well, is differently represented at different stages or levels of the reduction. In numbers, it is "many-and-few," whereas in dimensional (geometrical) entities it appears as "long-and-short" in lines, "wide-and-narrow" in planes, and "deep-and-shallow" in solids (Aristotle, *Met.* A.9, 992a10–17; M.9, 1085a9–12; N.2, 1089b11–19).

Now, if point is the indivisible limit and non-extended beginning of extended geometrical entities and, furthermore, is representative of the one as principle, then a problem arises of how to handle and interpret the indivisible within the geometrical, where all objects are extended and divisible. Plato opts for *excluding* point from the sequence of the dimensional reduction—denying point the status of a geometrical object—takes it to be the *limit* of geometrical figures, and consequently develops the doctrine of the extended yet indivisible lines as the elementary constituents of any extended line (see Aristotle, *Met.* A.9, 992a20–22).

There is, however, another way of considering the relation of the unextended, partless, and indivisible point to extended geometrical figures, which have parts and are infinitely divisible. As Sextus explains it, some "Pythagoreans" considered line as a product of the "flux" of point, which thus traces line in and by its movement. Respectively, the motion of line produces plane, and the motion of plane, solid. This position is different from that of their predecessors, Plato and his immediate disciples, who accept the deduction of numbers and, further, geometrical objects from the two first principles (Sextus Empiricus, *Adv. Math.* X.281–282). Indeed, the production of the continuous (line) by the motion of the discrete (point) is found in later Neoplatonic considerations of geometry, particularly in Proclus' commentary on Euclid. But such a production needs a specific geometrical or intelligible matter distinct from the matter of physical things, as an "ubi" where the motion of point and the tracing of line can take place (see Nikulin 2002, 245–254). Aristotle reports that in Plato motion and change are associated with otherness and inequality, and thus with the second principle (Aristotle, *Phys.* Γ.1, 201b16–26). Yet, this motion has to be associated with physical things, because in Plato there is neither a clear indication of a distinction between the two kinds of matter, physical and intelligible, or geometrical (cf. *Tim.* 48E–53A), nor construction of geometrical figures by motion.

The four ideal numbers are thus patterns for the dimensional sequence of unit–line–plane–solid, where each entity is defined by the corresponding number of points as its defining limits: two points define line, three plane, and four solid. In turn, each geometrical object is the limit of the object of a higher dimension: line is the limit of plane, and plane of solid. Here, however, one has to stop, because the tetraktys completes the sequence of ideal numbers, and three dimensions are defined either by four points or by the elementary solid, tetrahedron consisting of three triangles. On Aristotle's account (which itself is an explanation that presupposes dimensional reduction), the Pythagoreans do not proceed beyond three dimensions because three constitutes a completion of the beginning, middle, and end (*De caelo* A.1, 268a7–14).

In Plato, the elimination of the ontologically prior leads to the elimination of the ontologically posterior, but not vice versa (see Aristotle, *Met.* Δ.11, 1019a 1–3). Thus, the elimination of point leads to the elimination of line, and the elimination of line to the elimination of plane and, correspondingly, of solid (see Alexander ap. Simplicius, *In Phys.* 454.22 f. = Aristotle, *De bono*, fr. 2 Ross), yet line does not consist of points, which are its limits, and plane does not consist of lines, and solid of planes. The posterior does not consist of the prior but exists by and through the participation in the prior. The operation of elimination or abstraction (ἀφαίρεσις) used throughout the dimensional reduction is opposed to that of addition (πρόσθεσις) used in the deduction. Again, reduction and deduction correspond to the methods of analysis and synthesis.

Since ontology in Plato always is paralleled in epistemology, the sequence of the ideal numbers, 1–2–3–4, establishes not only the ontological structure of principles–numbers–mathematicals–physical things but also the structure of cognition and cognitive faculties: νοῦς is one, knowledge (ἐπιστήμη) is two (linear number), opinion (δόξα) is a plane number (three), and sense perception (αἴσθησις) is a solid number (four) (Aristotle, *DA* I.2, 404b19–27; cf. *TP* 67A). I have already mentioned that the soul *qua* discursive thinking or διάνοια is responsible for thinking mathematical entities and is itself intermediate between non-discursive νοῦς and sense perception, αἴσθησις. On Plato's account, the soul conceives mathematical entities as intermediate and embraces both knowledge (ἐπιστήμη) and (right) opinion (δόξα), whereas the whole motion of dimensional reduction goes epistemologically from sense perception (αἴσθησις) to thinking (νόησις) of the first two principles.

Categorical (Logical) Reduction. Categorical reduction in Plato moves from the species of being through the opposites to the highest genera of being. The opposites (ἀντικείμενα), such as equal and unequal (ἴσον and ἄνισον), are further reducible to the original opposition of the one and the indefinite dyad. As Alexander explains, the ἴσον is attributed to the one, μονάς, the ἄνισον to the excess and defect, ὑπεροχὴ καὶ ἔλλειψις (Alexander, *In Met.* 56.13f.; cf. Aristotle, *Met.* Γ.2, 1003b33–1004a2; Γ.2, 1004b27–1005a2; *Phys.* A.4, 187a12–21, *TP* 39–48; and Gaiser 1963, 86, 476).

An important source for the understanding of the categorical reduction is book X of Sextus Empiricus' *Adversus Mathematicos*, which explains that the division of all being for Plato falls into those entities that (1) exist by themselves (καθ' ἑαυτὰ ὄντα), which are separable and independent (κατὰ διαφοράν); (2) are opposite (κατ' ἐναντίωσιν); and (3) are relative (πρός τι) (*Adv. Math.* X.262–276). (In Alexander, the division is into καθ' αὑτά and opposites [ἀντικείμενα], and in the pseudo-Aristotelian *Divisiones Aristotelae*, 39–40, τὰ ὄντα are divided into τὰ καθ' ἑαυτά and τὰ πρός τι). That which exists by itself is that which can be thought and considered by itself (such are a human, horse, plant); opposite are those things in which the emergence of one yields the disappearance of the other (such are good and evil, just and unjust, useful and useless). And relative are those things in which the emergence of the one yields the emergence of the other, and disappearance of the one means disappearance of the other at the same time (such are left and right, up and down, double and half). Moreover, opposites do not allow for a middle or mediation, whereas the relatives do allow for such a mediation, which makes opposites contradictories, whereas relatives are contraries.

The categorical reduction in Sextus mostly agrees with the one reported by Hermodorus (ap. Simplicius, *In Phys.* 247. 30 sqq. Diels = fr. 7 Isnardi Parente; the fragment has been transmitted via Dercyllides and Porphyry; cf. Dillon 2003, 201), where all beings are divided into those that are "absolute," or exist by themselves (καθ' αὑτά), and those that are "alio-relative," or exist in relation to other things (πρὸς ἕτερα). The πρὸς ἕτερα are further divided into those that are relative to the contraries (πρὸς ἐναντία) and those that are relative to something (πρός τι), and the latter are further divided into those relative to something determinate (ὡρισμένα) and those relative to something indeterminate (ἀόριστα).

But how does one get to the principles by way of reduction? As Sextus explains, the two original principles are present within the three logical categories: that which exists by itself (one single thing), opposites (contradictories), and relatives (contraries). First, one has to establish the highest genus, or genera, in each category. In that which exists by itself, it is the one (τὸ ἕν), because each thing that is, is one, whereas the opposites are subsumed under the equal and the unequal (τὸ ἴσον καὶ τὸ ἄνισον), and the relatives under the excess and the defect (ἡ ὑπερβολὴ καὶ ἔλλειψις). Now, in the category of the opposites the equal can be reduced to the one in the category of independently existing things, whereas the unequal is reducible to the excess and defect in the category of the relatives. If, furthermore, as we know from other testimonies, the excess and defect represent the indefinite dyad (ἀόριστος δυάς), then we have reduced all categories to only two that are the principles of all things: the one and the indefinite dyad.

A question with the interpretation of the categorical reduction is: what does the category of πρός τι refer to? According to Krämer, because the proper distinction between the logical and ontological is not yet univocally established in Plato, the category of the πρός τι must refer to physical things only, and καθ' αὑτά to the ideas (see Krämer 1964, 158–161; and Krämer 1959, 439–440). Yet Happ (1971, 465–466), Gaiser (1963, 73–77, 353), and Richard (1986, 148–149, 189), on the contrary, argue that the category of πρός τι is applicable not only to physical bodies but also to the logical distinction within the ideas, insofar as they relate to each other (cf. Plato, *Soph.* 254C–D).

Deduction. The way to the principles can be reversed and complemented by the way from the principles, as analysis is complemented by synthesis. Thus, a mathematical proposition in Euclid is considered fully established and proven once it can be deduced synthetically from the accepted first principles, and then analytically reduced back to them. Hence, either of the two analytic reductions can be reversed to the deduction, which is a synthetic way of deriving the existent: the intelligible, the intermediate mathematical, and the physical. In a sense, deduction is a response to the question of how to explain the whole variety and multiplicity of things from as few principles as possible, the question which every philosopher in antiquity, beginning with the so-called Presocratics (or "physiologists"), had in mind.

That Plato was concerned with the deduction of the existent is confirmed both in his texts and in the doxographic tradition. Thus, in the *Laws* (894A1–5) we find a clear distinction between the ontological levels of being, established in a movement from the beginning, through an intermediate stage, to sensible things. And in Sextus there is a condensed description of the deduction from the principles (*Adv. Math.* X.276–280; cf. *TP* 49–72).

As has been already mentioned, in the reconstruction of the inner-Academic teachings the deduction begins with the two principles of the one and indefinite dyad, moves on to the ideal numbers that are the forms, then goes to the intermediate mathematical entities (mathematical numbers and geometrical objects of increasing dimensions: line–plane–solid), and finally brings about the cosmos and physical bodies. In a sense, the motion of the deduction is similar to the motion of discursive reasoning (διάνοια) in establishing an argument. Within and along the motion of deduction the effect of the dyad, seen in otherness and multiplicity, constantly increases, whereas the effect of the one diminishes. However, both principles are present at each stage of the deduction and in every sphere of the existent.

The details of the deduction require a good deal of reconstruction, especially since the deduction in its entirety embraces the whole of Plato's inner-Academic theories. (For a more detailed discussion, see Richard [1986, 190–205], mostly in reference to Gaiser's speculative reconstructions.)

Clearly, Plato is more interested in a mathematical—geometrical—description of being, which he also extends to the description of the cosmos and its structure (*Tim.* 53Cf.). Yet, how exactly the geometrical is translated into the physical, mathematical, thinkable solids, νοητὰ σώματα, into physical bodies, αἰσθητὰ σώματα, remains ultimately not explained mathematically but rather within a plausible "mythological" account.

This, finally, brings us to several problems that remain open in the interpretation of Plato posed by Gaiser (Gaiser 1968, 221; Gaiser 1988, 25). Thus, ideal numbers are ideas, but are all the ideas numbers? To which of the three ontological spheres belong spatial (geometrical) magnitudes, μεγέθη, which are reflected in the ideal numbers yet are also present in the physical? How significant is the notion of the indivisible line, accepted by Plato and Xenocrates but rejected by Speusippus? Do mathematical numbers come from the same two principles as the ideal numbers? Why is there a physical world at all (for the two primary principles are necessary but not sufficient conditions of its existence)? Why are there so many levels in the *Dimensionsfolge* (sequence of dimensions) of number–line–plane–solid–physical motion? Why are there exactly two principles? In Plato, the one and the dyad are equal in their status—as opposites and constituents of everything there is—and yet in their meaning and being they are not equal, for the one is established as the positive principle, while its other, the indefinite dyad, as negative in its effects. How does he explain it? These problems do not seem to find an immediate and straightforward solution in the preserved texts but require a thorough reading of the relevant texts within the historical and philosophical contexts.

With the reconstruction of Plato's inner-Academic theories we can go as far as the extant body of dialogues and testimonies allow us; the rest is a matter of consistent interpretations, which, hopefully, will go on in the scholarly debate.

OVERVIEW OF THE ESSAYS INCLUDED IN THE COLLECTION

In his seminal paper "*Epekeina tēs ousias*: On Plato, *Republic* 509B," Hans Joachim Krämer discusses the notion of the good in Plato's *Republic*, where the good is said to be "beyond being" yet remains not defined any further. Through a detailed analysis of Plato's texts, Krämer shows that Plato's understanding of the good as the principle of being and knowledge comes out of a critical exchange with the Eleatic thinkers, Parmenides and Zeno. Where Zeno sees an opposition between the one (ἕν), which is being, and the many (πολλά), which is non-being, Plato (in his *Parmenides*) sees a disjunction of the one and being. Such an interpretation of Plato fits thoroughly with the inner-Academic doctrine of the two principles: if the one is opposite to being, and not just its predicate, then being is associated with the many. Hence, one should speak about a whole *plurality*, of many *beings* (ὄντα) that constitute the realm of the intelligible or ideas. On such an interpretation, the one *is* the good, and as such is opposite to being as many, which explains Plato's thesis that the one is "beyond being."

In his other essay in this volume, "Plato's Unwritten Doctrine," Krämer first provides an overview of the role of writing in antiquity and then argues that there was a substantial philosophical debate in the Old Academy that was not put in writing. Krämer complements an exposition and a reconstruction of the "unwritten doctrines" with numerous examples from and references to Plato's dialogues that can be then reinterpreted and understood in a new way. There is also a discussion of the most significant publications on the ἄγραφα δόγματα and a short history of their transmission and reception. Due to the constraints on the length of this volume, the third part of the original essay, which polemically deals with the contemporary reception of Plato through the paradigm established by Schleiermacher and Schelling, had to be omitted. However, the main points of this critical exchange are reproduced in Krämer 1996 and Krämer 1999.

In his discussion of the synopsis of the mathematical sciences in Plato, Konrad Gaiser provides an overview of mathematics in Plato's dialogues, in reference to and concordance with the testimonies in the Academy and later authors. Gaiser argues that Plato adopts a mathematical model of ontology, where being is understood according to the pattern of number as constituted by sameness (the unit, "one") and otherness (the "indefinite dyad"). The importance of mathematical sciences and their methods for Plato consists in their allowing for a dialectical knowledge of the good. Due to the limitations of space, this essay, too, is published without its last section ("6. Plato's Evaluation of Mathematics from a Contemporary Point of View").

Thomas Szlezák discusses the notion of the good as the principle of knowability and of the being of both ideal and physical things in the *Republic* and comes up with an explanation of how Socrates' account of one single, highest, generic ontological and epistemological principle fits within a reconstruction of Plato's teachings that accepts two opposite principles. Szlezák argues that a close analysis and reading of the text, rather than establishing two different diverging theories, suggests that Socrates' discussion of the good presents an abridged version of the systematic theory of principles.

Jens Halfwassen carefully explores various logical and ontological possibilities of monistic and dualistic interpretations of Plato. A skillful interpretation of Plato's texts (primarily, of the *Republic* and *Parmenides*) and later testimonies (mostly, of Speusippus and Eudorus) allows him to claim that Plato's doctrine of the two first principles can be taken as a combination of a reductive monism of one principle with a deductive dualism of the two principles.

Finally, following Imre Tóth's suggestion that non-Euclidean (or, rather, anti-Euclidean) passages in Aristotle show that the Greeks already understood that the parallel postulate cannot be demonstrated by mathematical tools, Vittorio Hösle argues that Plato, who showed that intuition has no place in geometry, provided an ontological foundation for geometry that was in line with the inner-Academic teachings, which favored Euclidean geometry.

TWO

EPEKEINA TĒS OUSIAS

On Plato, *Republic* 509B

Hans Joachim Krämer

1.

It is well known that the allegory of the sun in Plato's *Republic* includes the difficult proposition: just as the sun is the cause (αἰτία) of becoming, without itself being becoming (οὐ γένεσιν αὐτὸν ὄντα), so the good is the cause of being, without itself being a being, i.e., is superior to being in its dignity and power: "the good gives being [εἶναι] and substance [οὐσία] to what is known, while the good itself is no substance [οὐσία], but is rather beyond being [οὐσία], exceeding it in rank and power."[1] This mysterious "throwing beyond" or "beyondness" (ὑπερβολή [509C2]; μειζόνως τιμητέον [509A4]; ὑπὲρ ταῦτα [509A7]) has been of repeated concern to modern interpreters,[2] and a convincing explanation has not been reached. The solutions that have been proposed so far can be summarized in four groups: (1) the good relates as an αἰτία to being, just as a principle relates to that of which it is the principle [*Prinzipiierten*]. Thus, the good cannot itself be a being.[3] (2) According to its essence, the good entails the end, highest perfection, or normative direction for everything that exists, and thus should necessarily be located beyond being.[4] (3) "Beyondness" marks the firstness, singularity, indivisibility, or absoluteness of the good, in contrast to every particular and dependent being.[5] (4) The good is the "transcendental"—and, even for Plato, concealed—condition of the possibility of being, knowledge, and truth, insofar as it is pre- or beyond being.[6]

Of these positions, the fourth is a transcendentally modernized variation of the first, which dismisses from the outset an adequate *historical* understanding of Plato's statement. But the third position also emphasizes only certain characteristics of the concept of a principle, and is thus subordinate to the first solution. The two remaining positions differ in that one—to put it in Aristotelian terms—presupposes the concept of a *causa efficiens* (and probably *formalis* as well), while the other is committed to a *causa finalis*. However, it is doubtful whether or not these are sufficient, and to what extent, if any, they can be proven. The relationship between a principle and that which is grounded by the principle also holds, *mutatis mutandis*, for the Presocratic question of ἀρχή as well. With respect to the Presocratics, however, it is not possible to find evidence of a differentiation that is similar to the Platonic one. The philosophical reason for Plato's having introduced this differentiation still remains unknown. The justification through a final principle, however, which immediately starts with the good, does not fully do justice to the more comprehensive function of the good as the principle of knowledge that is contained in the allegory of the sun.[7] In the case of the relationship between the good and οὐσία, it is highly questionable as to whether or not we are primarily dealing with a relationship of being [*Seinsverhältnis*]. This suspicion is supported by the fact that in book VI of the *Republic* Plato explicitly refrains from uncovering the real essence of the good (509D–E; cf. 509C).[8]

In light of this situation, it is not surprising that recent philosophical commentators on the *Republic* resign and dismiss any form of further "speculation."[9] Indeed, all attempts at explanation that have been proposed so far are stipulated conjectures, which often isolated the passage 509B from its historical background and often projected later philosophical positions onto it. In particular, it has not been sufficiently recognized that Plato's philosophical predecessors and contemporaries provide important clues for a historically grounded interpretation of the passage. Furthermore, the fact that Plato refrains from providing the essence of the good (τί ποτ' ἐστὶ τἀγαθόν) (509D8f.) in the *Republic* has been ignored, which necessarily takes the statements concerning the allegory of the sun out of context, because the *functions* of the good discussed there, must emerge from its concealed *essence*, and can thus only be adequately known based on the knowledge of this essence.

2.

To begin with, the surrounding Platonic Academy allows us to narrow down the meaning and importance [*Bedeutung*] of the beyondness of being [*Seinsüberwurf*] in Plato. Three different testimonies provide proof of the same conviction on the part of Plato's nephew and successor Speusippus concerning the original principle [*Urprinzip*] of the one (ἕν). The one of Speusippus, according to Aristotle, is "not even a being (ὥστε μηδὲ ὄν τι εἶναι τὸ ἓν αὐτό)" (*Met.* N.5, 1092a14f.), while the excerpt from chapter IV of Iamblichus' *De communi mathematica scientia*, which most likely refers to Speusippus,[10] also provides justification ("the one, which should not even be called being because it is simple and constitutes the principle of existent things, and the principle does not have the properties of the things of which it is the principle").[11] Here, the relationship between a principle and that which it brings about is explicitly expressed and applied to the beyond-beingness of the one, without, however, making explicit its systematic function and its historical position, for example, with regard to the Presocratics. A third testimony is the Speusippus fragment that is included in Proclus' commentary on the *Parmenides* (Proclus, *In Parm.* 1–5),[12] which was published in 1953 and has been preserved in Latin translation. In this fragment, Speusippus describes the beyond-beingness of the one (le unum enim *melius ente* putantes *et a quo le ens*) as the doctrine of "the ancients" (*placentia antiquis, antiquorum opinio*), and thus it contributed to many projections of the Academic doctrine onto the Pythagoreans.[13] That we are not dealing with a mere doxographic witholding of Speusippus' own doctrine becomes obvious throughout the course of the account, according to which "the ancients" have posited an opposing principle to the one in the form of the *interminabilis dualitas*. Clearly, this is the indefinite dyad (ἀόριστος δυάς) of the large-small (μέγα-μικρόν), which is neither Pythagorean (cf. the differentiation in Aristotle, *Met.* A.6, 987b25ff.) nor really Speusippean. Speusippus generally calls his opposing principle πλῆθος,[14] which is a rather characteristic feature of the Platonic doctrine. Hence, one may legitimately infer that here Speusippus is providing an account of Platonic doctrine.[15] Accordingly, the beyond-beingness of the one was not just held by Speusippus, but also by Plato.

The principles of the ἕν and the ἀόριστος δυάς belong to Plato's "unwritten doctrines" (ἄγραφα δόγματα). The doxography of the Speusippus fragment suggests that Plato discussed the beyond-beingness of the principle of being, not only in the *Republic*, but also in the ἄγραφα δόγματα. When interpreting why this may be the case, one should keep in mind that the one is also at the same time the good in the *Republic* where Plato mentions the good, whereas the ἄγραφα δόγματα deal with the one as the principle of being. Hence, the title Περὶ τοῦ ἀγαθοῦ, and conversely the good, concerns that which is explicitly not fully revealed, and which remains concealed in its essence.[16] We learn something more specific from the accounts of the ἄγραφα δόγματα in Aristotle and Aristoxenus, especially *Metaphysics* A.6, according to which for Plato the one was primarily (in Aristotle's terminology) the formal and efficient cause, i.e., the principle of being, that it was foremost for the ideas (Plato assigned "the one to forms" as "the cause of their essence"),[17] and was intended to fulfill the function of "balancing," "limiting," and "determining" (ἰσάζειν, περατοῦν, ὁρίζειν) in relation to the material principle.[18] The aspect of the final cause was introduced only secondarily (Plato "assigned the cause of the good and the beautiful to the elements, one to each of the two").[19]

Considering the presentation in the *Republic*, it follows that the relationship between the good that surpasses being (naturally, the value aspect of this principle is emphasized more strongly in this political work, as is the case with καλόν in the *Symposium*, and also with πρῶτον φίλον in the *Lysis*) and οὐσία should primarily be understood ontologically as a *relation of being* [*Seinsverhältnis*]. It also follows that the alternative teleological interpretation, which is based on the nexus of finality, can be dismissed.

3.

Now that a first approach toward an interpretation of the passage in question has been achieved, we need to address the prehistory of Platonic ontology. We will see that this solution, which already appears plausible, will also prove necessary.

Although, as we have shown, there is no direct connection between Plato's conception of being and Presocratic conceptions of the relationship between the principle and that which it grounds or 'principiates,' still the terminology of the passage (εἶναι, οὐσία) alludes to the horizon of the Eleatic question of being, which is the case for Plato's entire ontology. The doctrine of ideas, which is developed in book V of the *Republic* and is similarly presented already in the *Phaedo*, operates to the point of being expressed (in ὄν/μὴ ὄν, "being/non-being," ἕν/πολλά, "one/many," ἀλήθεια/δόξα, "truth/opinion," κατὰ ταὐτὰ ὡσαύτως, "in the same way," etc.)[20] within the framework of the Eleatic paradigm. Similarly, the distinction between τόπος νοητός and ὁρατός (the "intelligible" and the "visible" "places") cannot be conceived without taking into consideration the Eleatic school. Thus, because the presentation of the idea of the good in *Republic* VI logically builds on the doctrine of ideas of book V,[21] we must therefore raise the question as to whether or not, and to what extent, a differentiation was possible *within* the Eleatic approach to the problem [*Problemstellung*] that in turn led to the Platonic beyond-beingness (ἐπέκεινα τῆς οὐσίας).[22]

It is extremely important to keep in mind at this point that the Eleatic tradition, which Plato continues, is not a direct continuation of the Parmenidean didactic poem [*Lehrgedicht*]. Rather, Plato takes into account the Eleatic "school" in its diversity while dealing primarily with the advanced form of the Eleatic school; Plato is particularly concerned with Zeno. While the position of the Parmenidean teaching was primarily determined through the opposition of ὄν and μὴ ὄν, Zeno in his apology [*Apologese*], and also Melissus, placed the antithesis of the ἕν and πολλά at the center of their discussions:[23] the unity and singularity of the Parmenidean conception of being obviously provided the decisive impulse for the Eleatic school, which needed to be defended against the adherents of the multiplicity of being. W. Kullmann demonstrated that it is likely that the position of Zeno for the most part already occurred in the background of Parmenides' poem.[24] This makes the starting point of the Platonic discussion historically more authentic. What is important in this respect is that Plato presupposed a version of Eleaticism as the basis upon which the antithesis between ἕν and πολλά was decisive: apart from *Republic* V,[25] this is primarily shown in the *Parmenides*, where Plato directly refers to Zeno's work and apparently interprets Parmenides in Zeno's sense.[26]

At the same time, however, the *Parmenides* and the *Sophist* also make explicit why Plato dissolved the Eleatic doctrine of the ἓν ὄν and replaced it with the multiplicity of beings [*Vielheit von Seiendem*]. This first happens in the *Parmenides*—which only unfolds what has already been presupposed in the *Phaedo* and the *Republic*[27]—through the introduction of the doctrine of ideas into Zeno's schema of the ἕν and πολλά: although, as Zeno believed, it is true that individual objects are contradictory, still the εἴδη in which they participate are free from contradiction and unchangeable. While Zeno's refutations do not apply to them, individual objects can also exist at least insofar as they participate in the εἴδη (128Ef.). This proves that the multiplicity of being is possible. The second part of the *Parmenides* describes the dialectical relationship between the many and the one in an adumbrative manner. The *Sophist* continues this discussion in a more precise way through a logical analysis of the concept of ἓν ὄν (244B–245E). It assigns the concept of ὄν to multiplicity,[28] and limits that of the ἕν to pure undivided unity,[29] in this way integrating the Eleatic μὴ ὄν as an exponent of multiplicity into the ὄν by an indirect regress to Parmenides. This results in establishing the dialectical structure of being (237Af.; 241Df.; 258Cf.).

Based on the Eleatic question of being, the doctrine of ideas renews the Presocratic problem of the one and the many. The ideas receive all the qualities of the Eleatic ὄν: they are ὄντως ὄντα, unities (ἕν, ἑνάδες, μονάδες)[30] in opposition to the multiplicity of perceivable objects; they are self-identical, immortal, and are an embodiment of the ἀλήθεια accessible to νοῦς. What is important, however, is that it is not just the case that a plurality of beings is simply substituted for the Eleatic ἓν ὄν, but also that the pure, now dialectically conceived unity, ἕν, is preserved as the opposing concept to multiplicity, as is implied by the second part of the *Parmenides* and the *Sophist*, and supported by the unwritten doctrine: not only an individual εἶδος, but also the order of being as a whole, partakes in the one itself.[31]

The Eleatic / Zenoistic "dualism" of the ἕν and πολλά is also preserved by Plato, although there has been an important internal change in the disjunction: for Zeno, being is one, while the multiplicity of things is non-being. For Plato, on the contrary, the multiplicity of things and being are no longer one, but many. While for Zeno the ὄν was placed alongside the ἕν, with Plato it is placed on the side of the πολλά, which thus becomes ὄντα:

Table 2.1.

ἕν	πολλά	ἕν	πολλά
ὄν	οὐκ ὄντα		ὄντα
Zeno		Plato	

However, for Plato the opposition between the ἕν and πολλά remains. But since the πολλά have now become ὄντα, the ἕν therefore necessarily appears in opposition to the ὄντα. The ἕν is thus no longer an ὄν, but rather a non-being. But because the πολλά = ὄντα partake in the ἕν and can only exist because of that participation, the ἕν therefore appears not only as non-being, but also as beyond being. By ontologically raising the value of the many, or to put it differently, by placing being on the level of the many, *the opposition between the many and the one necessarily becomes that between non-being and beyond-being, and consequently moves into the position of* "ἐπέκεινα τοῦ ὄντος," *or* "ἐπέκεινα τῆς οὐσίας."

The beyond-beingness in Platonism thus does not proceed from an abstract analysis of the relationship between the principle of being and the world it brings about or 'principiates,' but has been forced upon Platonic philosophy through its engagement with the inherited Eleatic question. It is only the restructuring of the Eleatic disjunction, calling it into question, and the pointed reformulation of the concept of being within this discussion, that leads to the transcendence of being of the first principle. Today the reconstruction of the Eleatic position is necessary in order to make "beyond-beingness" fully understandable, especially since an adequate understanding of early Greek philosophy depends on it.

4.

The historical constellation responsible for the Platonic beyond-beingness also left its traces in the doxography of the Academy that appropriately support the position for which I am arguing. Apart from the already mentioned doxographical account of Speusippus, which now needs to be cited in its entirety,[32] there is a related passage in Aristotle whose importance was recently emphasized by Philip Merlan:[33]

Speusippus, Procl. *In Plat. Parm. Interpr.* G. de Moerbeka p. 40, 1ff. Klibansky-Labowsky:
Le *unum* enim *melius ente* putantes *et a quo le ens*, et ab ea que secundum principium habitudine ipsum liberaverunt. Existimantes autem quod, si quis le unum ipsum seorsum et solum meditatum, sine aliis, secundum se ipsum ponat,[34] nullum *alterum elementum* ipsi apponens, *nichil utique fiet aliorum, interminabilem dualitatem entium principium* induxerunt.[35]

Aristotle, *Met.* N.2, 1089a2f.:
ἔδοξε γὰρ αὐτοῖς πάντ' ἔσεσθαι ἓν τὰ ὄντα, αὐτὸ τὸ ὄν, εἰ μή τις λύσει καὶ ὁμόσε βαδιεῖται τῷ Παρμενίδου λόγῳ "οὐ γὰρ μήποτε τοῦτο δαμῇ, εἶναι μὴ ἐόντα," ἀλλ' ἀνάγκη εἶναι τὸ μὴ ὂν δεῖξαι ὅτι ἔστιν· οὕτω γάρ, ἐκ τοῦ ὄντος καὶ ἄλλου τινός, τὰ ὄντα ἔσεσθαι, εἰ πολλά ἐστιν.[36]

In the context of the passage in the *Metaphysics*, Aristotle deals with the Academy's dualistic doctrine of principles (στοιχεῖα, αἴτια); as the context shows, ἄλλο τι primarily means the ἀόριστος δυάς. The first principle is referred to as the ὄν in analogy to the original position of the Eleatic philosophers, but here the textual context (1088b29) also shows that we are dealing with the one (ἕν) of the system of elements.[37] The same doctrine of principles (*principium* = ἀρχή; *elementum* = στοιχεῖον; *a quo* = αἴτιον) is also present in the doxography of Speusippus (*unum–interminabilis dualitas*; ἕν–ἀόριστος δυάς), although here the functions of both principles are contrasted to mark out their differences.[38] The dualism of the principles is justified in both cases by stating that such dualism is necessary for the constitution of the multiplicity (πολλά, *alia*) of beings (ὄντα, *entia*).[39] If this is interpreted as a correction of the Eleatic position, we can assume without a doubt that the statements in Plato's *Sophist* have exerted their influence.[40] Yet it seems that the thought of expanding an original monism to a dualism in Speusippus also corresponds with the presentation in the *Sophist*, to which, as Klibansky has noted, Speusippus makes reference through certain expressions.[41] Thus, we can assume that Speusippus also had the Eleatic starting point of Plato's philosophy of principles in mind.

It is possible that, in both instances, we are dealing with a historical interpretation[42] of Plato's ἄγραφα δόγματα inspired by Plato's *Sophist*.[43] Such interpretations were common among Plato's students. However, since the position of the testimonies is much more general than that of the dialogues, it is quite possible that they originate in Plato's own oral remarks and self-interpretations,[44] which may be in line with, but are considerably more far-reaching, than the account in the *Sophist*.

First, Academic doxography confirms that Plato made positive use of the Eleatic disjunction by assuming the multiplicity of being. Secondly, this led to the continuation and elaboration of the Eleatic ontological approach to a theory of principles, which picked up and continued the Presocratic theme of the ἀρχή. On the one hand, the one (Aristotle calls it ὄν in Eleatic fashion) fulfilled the function of the principle of being with respect to the multiplicity of existing things; on the other hand, the multiplicity of beings itself required a material principle as a substrate (the Eleatic μὴ ὄν). In collaboration with the one, the latter constituted everything existing. If this interpretation is correct—and there is no reason to call it into question—then Plato's ἄγραφα δόγματα, with the dualistic doctrine of the principles of the ἕν and the μέγα-μικρόν (ἀόριστος δυάς)[45] at its center, resulted primarily from the dialogue with Eleatic philosophy.[46]

The account that goes back to Speusippus provides an additionally valuable corroboration of the pre-eminent role of the one: *unum melius ente et a quo le ens* (Klibansky renders this back into Greek as τὸ ἕν . . . βέλτιον τοῦ ὄντος . . . καὶ ἀφ' οὗ τὸ ὄν: "the one . . . is greater than being . . . and the source of being"). Although the introduction of the multiplicity of being and the introduction of an opposing principle was only developed later (*existimantes autem*), there can be no doubt that both lines of thought are close to one another, and that the superiority of the one already presupposes the pluralistic structure of being and its material principle. This becomes evident in the second part of the description of the one, according to which it is *a quo le ens*, i.e., still the principle of being. The internal connection of this thought, however, must be as follows: the introduction of a multiplicity of being apart from the one necessitates the assumption of a material principle (the *interminabilis dualitas*), *and at the same time raises the one as the principle of being above the constitution of beings*. Hence, the Academic doxography implicitly reaches the derivation of the Platonic beyond-beingness based on the restructuring of the Eleatic disjunction. Once the one is not conceived of independently and by itself (*seorsum et solum meditatum*, *sine aliis*, *secundum se ipsum*), but is conceived in contrast to a material principle and enters into the multiplicity of being derived from it (*alia*, *entia*),[47] then it cannot be a being but can only be a principle of being beyond being, i.e., it necessarily receives the status of a *melius ente* (βέλτιον τοῦ ὄντος, ἐπέκεινα τῆς οὐσίας).

5.

Plato's definition of the "good" in *Rep*. 509B as ἐπέκεινα τῆς οὐσίας ὑπερέχον, "residing beyond being," can be fully situated within the course of the Greek history of being [*Seinsgeschichte*] and properly historically understood. The definition does not originate in an arbitrary act of positing, but rather—when considered either from the point of view of the dialogues or the Academy—is a philosophical consequence of the Eleatic problem and its transformation in Plato. The point of departure is the opposition of ἕν and πολλά; the driving impulse is that of shifting the concept of being from unity to multiplicity. Unity thus also turns into the opposite of being, and becomes non- and beyond-being. However, since unity at the same time grounds and makes possible the multiplicity of being, a dialectical relationship is established between the ground of being [*Seinsgrund*] and the existent [*Seiende*], which corresponds to the relation and the essential difference between the principle and that which it brings about. This is the case because that which grounds being [*Seinsbegründende*] is different in kind from being [*Sein*], and hence is itself not existent [*Seiende*]. However, it would be misguided to interpret Plato's beyond-beingness as a result of two different historical constituents: that of the Eleatic doctrine of being, and that of the ἀρχή as a theme in other Presocratics. Rather, it can be shown that the beyond-beingness grew out of the proper movement of the Eleatic theory, and that it leads back to that theory in all of its determinations: the disjunction of ἕν and πολλά is implied from the beginning by the "ontological" approach of the Eleatics and cannot be separated from it. However, in this approach we already find the capacity for the difference between the principle and that which it grounds, and even for a dualism of principles. The Platonic reinterpretation of the concept of being was necessary for unfolding these possibilities. The idea of principles has thus been developed by Plato within the Eleatic position and its presuppositions, and has not been applied externally to the Eleatic doctrine of being. The idea of the beyond-beingness, then, is primarily also of Eleatic origin, and is not derived from the application of some other theory of principles to the question of being.

From these circumstances one can draw remarkable conclusions with regard to book VI of Plato's *Republic*. The presentation of ἀγαθὸν αὐτό there remains rather superficial insofar as Plato explicitly leaves out the *essence* (τί ἐστι) of the good, and only explains its *functions* by means of the allegory of the sun. Yet it is obvious that the functions and properties of the good, one of them being its beyond-beingness, have to be derived from and can only be adequately understood in reference to its essence. The analysis of beyond-beingness in Plato has just shown that, historically, it needs to be situated within the Eleatic disjunction of the ἕν and πολλά. This means that the supreme or beyond-being—wherever it comes on the basis of the Eleatic conception of being—according to its essence, can only be the one (ἕν). This doctrine of the *one* beyond-being is indeed confirmed not only by later Platonism, but also already by Plato's ἄγραφα δόγματα, and in differentiation from an Eleatic original position. For the presentation of *Republic* VI, this means that the "good" itself, which is characterized as ἐπέκεινα τῆς οὐσίας ὑπερέχον, "residing beyond being," has to be the one (ἕν) according to its proper essence, because beyond-beingness can only be explained historically from the ἕν. This, however, means that the authority of Plato's so-called ἄγραφα δόγματα has again been validated for the period of the *Republic*.[48]

Although this is primarily true for the first principle, the one,[49] this is also the case for the more elusive material principle: Academic doxography connects, as we have seen, the beyond-beingness of the one, and already the plurality of beings, with the assumption of an opposing principle. And the analogy of the allegory of the cave suggests that the "good" keeps the ideas within being just as the sun keeps perceivable objects in being; however, in both cases one needs a material substrate[50] (objects in nature are not just the outflow of the sun!). Presumably, Plato intentionally avoided uncovering and openly disclosing the material principle, which especially concerned the world of ideas, in a political work such as the *Republic*. The same is true for his early protreptric work in general.

6.

The attempt to situate Plato's unwritten doctrine of principles late in his work has thus been refuted by *Republic* 509B.[51] This yields further consequences for the most recent controversies about the central passages from books VI and VII of the *Republic*, especially those surrounding the other functions of the "good" that are introduced in the allegory of the sun.

To begin with, we need to keep in mind that the concept of the one in Plato not only changes its ontological position, but also its content. This is not the case for the Eleatic school. The one is no longer one being, but rather the one itself, i.e., the new dialectical method no longer regards it as a determination of something else (beings), but rather, and for the first time, as that which is pure "in itself," i.e., as the one "itself."[52] This dialectically purified concept of the one lacks determinate content, which also allows it to be "multivalent [*mehrwertig*]," especially since it itself lacks content and is not determinate, but rather "abstract" and general; at the same time, it can precede and ground different domains of objects. The movement of Platonic dialectic thus aims not only at the synoptic creation of the most general in the form of the one, but conversely also at the functional evaluation of the logically ambivalent and thus multivalent one in the form of dialectical derivations and justifications.[53]

For Plato, the one, according to its basic function, is the limiting, forming, and determining principle of its opposite, multiplicity. As limiting and determining, however, it unfolds different aspects. This is the case because that which is limited by the one is ontologically a determinate being, and epistemologically it is perfect, is knowable, and is axiologically valuable in the form of a "measure" (μέτρον, μέτριον), "limit" (πέρας), "middle" (μέσον), and "order" (κόσμος, τάξις). Hence, the one as a principle of limitation can at the same time be a principle of being, value, and knowledge [*Seins-, Wert-, und Erkenntnisprinzip*].

It is clear that this functional multivalence of the dialectical concept ἕν, which is sufficiently documented by the indirect transmission of the ἄγραφα δόγματα,[54] is closely connected to the functional multivalence of the supreme "good" whose essence remains concealed, at the end of *Republic* VI, as the principle of being, value, and knowledge. The repeated and sufficiently justified thesis[55] that the one of the ἄγραφα δόγματα, while intended here, is introduced in this political treatise under the aspect of value [*Wertaspekt*], i.e., as ἀγαθόν (in the *Symposium* as καλόν, in the *Lysis* as πρῶτον φίλον), has been strongly criticized by various critics. In what follows, their arguments will be examined meta-critically [*epikritisch*] from the standpoint we have achieved thus far.

In a noteworthy contribution,[56] H. M. Baumgartner has shown that the function of the "good" as the principle of being and knowledge is in no way as strange as it might seem to a fresh reader of the *Republic*, insofar as one tries to understand it in light of the transcendental is-ought distinction. Additionally, he tried to show that the formal dualism of the principles of unity and the dyad as it is present in the unwritten doctrine also requires an ultimate and materially mediated ground of meaning [*Sinngrundes*]—that of the good—that justifies and coordinates the principles, from which they can be constructed by means of Fichtean analytic tools. Baumgartner is concerned "primarily" with the "refutation of a substantive philosophical claim, namely the thesis that the ἀγαθόν is unable to ground beingness, knowability, and knowledge [*Seiendheit, Erkennbarkeit, und Erkenntnis*]."[57] Stated in such general terms, Baumgarten's remarks are correct. However, as soon as he claims that "presumably, the introduction of ἀγαθόν as the ultimate principle in Plato's *Republic* is already based on the idea that was only explicitly reflected on in Fichte's *Wissenschaftslehre*,"[58] that Plato's "reflections tend in this direction (of transcendental philosophy),"[59] and that "in terms of the doctrine of the good in the *Republic* . . . we need to remember that it once again surpasses the formal doctrine of principles,"[60] then we begin to have legitimate doubts about whether or not this really does justice to the historical Plato of the fourth century BCE. The ἄγραφα δόγματα subordinate the good to the universal one,[61] which has been affirmed by later Platonists. The good cannot mediate between the principles, because this is reserved only for the one. The known function of the good is accordingly not transmitted. What has been transmitted, rather, is the value-directed efficacy [*werthafte*

Wirksamkeit] of the one (as "limiting" and providing "measure"), which at the same time is the principle of both being and knowledge. Furthermore, one can hardly imagine how it should have been possible that an absolute normative 'ought' could have existed, given classical Greek thinking concerning values [*Wertdenken*] and its corresponding objectivism, according to which the good always adheres to what is essential (and not vice versa!). If one adds that the καλόν (*Symposium*) and the πρῶτον φίλον (*Lysis*) equally compete with the ἀγαθόν in Plato's writings, and that the essence of the good itself clearly is concealed in the *Republic*—a claim to which Baumgartner obviously does not do justice—then it is sufficiently evident that Baumgartner's interpretation of *Republic* VI not only over-interprets the thought of the historical Plato, but that he simply skips it. Baumgartner basically only renews the transcendental and final[62] explanation, which has been shown to be refutable.[63]

The polemical article by W. Bröcker,[64] directed against the more recent interpretations of the unwritten doctrine, works at a more modest level. Among other issues, it addresses the many functions of the one as the principle of being, value, and knowledge, which, according to Bröcker's opponents, is at the basis of the presentation in *Republic* VI. If Bröcker finds categorically "no philosophy at all, but rather empty talk" there, then it not only remains unclear how the critic takes the corresponding transmission[65]—which includes the combined justification of all three functions within the *limiting* action of the one[66]—or the lasting effect [*Fortwirkung*] of the later doctrine of transcendentals on the principle of convertibility [*Konvertibilitätsprinzip*], but also, the question remains open as to what extent the presentation in *Republic* VI, according to which the "good" is also supposed to be the principle of both being and knowledge, can, philosophically speaking, be more legitimate according to Bröcker's premises than it is according to the conception provided by the unwritten doctrine. Furthermore, Bröcker seems to doubt the proximity and contact that the Platonic doctrine of the principle has with Eleatic philosophy in general. This, however, is sufficiently contradicted by Plato's *Parmenides* and the doxography of the Academy (see above).

Apart from the two philosophers mentioned above, the philologist and historian K. von Fritz took a critical stand with his novel interpretation of *Republic* VI.[67] On the one hand, it is true that von Fritz is a self-confessed opponent of the conception that Plato purposefully left his ἄγραφα δόγματα unwritten.[68] The distinguished scholar too quickly passed over Plato's relevant self-portrayals (such as his references to writing in the *Seventh Letter* and the *Phaedrus*)[69] and instead listed general objections that either contribute rather little to the issues involved, or are based on misunderstandings.[70] On the other hand, however, von Fritz has lately been increasingly open to the evaluation of the indirect transmission and affirms its comparative reading [*Verknüpfung*] with the dialogues.[71] After all, he seems to value[72] an interpretation[73] that aims to show that the remarks of the allegory of the sun in *Republic* VI can be well understood in and of themselves and thus deserve further and closer attention.

Von Fritz does not address the controversial situation of the older textual interpretation, which is expressed in the resignation of certain commentators.[74] Without considering that Plato explicitly omits a definition of the essence of "the good," from which all of its effects originate,[75] von Fritz proposes an interpretation that leads to the view that the good could be the principle of knowledge, because "without constant preference of a 'good' or 'better' to the lesser good or worse there could be no knowledge of any sort."[76] The transition to the function of the good as the principle of what can be known and the principle of being cannot be executed by von Fritz without the concept of "shape [*Gestalt*]," because every preference "raises something shaped . . . out of the unformed and chaotic,"[77] which, admittedly, is "necessary also as a kind of unity."[78] Concerning this second step it has to be noted that K. Marc-Wogau already attempted earlier to combine the determinacy of the idea as a basis of its being and knowability with the good.[79] A.-J. Festugière logically inferred from the same characteristics in which the good is present (*unifiant*, déterminant) that the "good" is the *one*-good [*Un*-Bien] in the sense of the *Philebus* and the unwritten doctrine.[80] As soon as one tries to understand the "good" as the principle of being and truth, one cannot do without ideas such as that of "shape," "unity,"[81] "limitation," "determinacy," "unshaped," "chaos," etc., which almost naturally lead to the basic conception of the ἄγραφα δόγματα (πέρας + ἄπειρον, ἕν + πλῆθος → ὡρισμένον, πεπερασμένον, ἡρμοσμένον, τεταγμένον, μέτριον, ἴσον, etc.) and particularly to the principle of the "one." This leads us to a dimension in the investigation of the principles that always already *precedes*, and is thus capable of originally justifying, individual aspects of what exists. At the same time, it remains uncertain as to how these general characters, such as "shape," "unity," "determinacy," etc., enter into an "essential and necessary relationship,"[82] particularly with the good as such. The issue of subject-oriented "preference" or "selection" among possible objects of cognition, which von Fritz adopted from modern philosophy of science,[83] seems to be foreign to this conception, and cancels its internal unity. Such "preference" has been reported neither in Plato nor in later Platonism.[84] However, it has been reported for the Academy, and most probably with regard to Plato himself, that not only are the one and the simple everywhere the basis of what can be known,[85] but also that νοῦς, which represents the knower in *Republic* VI, is a form of being [*Seinsweise*] of the one,[86] similarly to how, in *Republic* VI, νοῦς, γνῶσις and ἐπιστήμη are said to be "agathoid" (ἀγαθοειδῆ, 509A).

Von Fritz's attempt to derive an epistemological function immediately from the good as such is not convincing, because it applies historically unfounded assumptions to the text, while also surpassing the tradition that we have and disrupting the possible unity of the Platonic conception. With his conception of the good as the principle of being and knowledge, von Fritz is pushed toward the direction of the ἄγραφα δόγματα. While this interpretation remains quite hypothetical and unfounded based on the mere wording of the allegory of the sun, it is nevertheless historically corroborated, and substantively justified by the ἄγραφα δόγματα. In any case, it is evident that Plato did not make his line of thought as explicit as he might have (as the history of research shows), which he could have done in order to avoid opacity and misunderstanding. Von Fritz regards Plato's comportment as "absolutely incomprehensible," insofar as he should have "mentioned such a central thought as the one at issue in a written work, but purposefully concealed its true meaning from the readers of the written work" and raises the question "for what purpose and for whom . . . did he state it in written form?"[87] Here, too, the necessity of circumspection provides the answer. It can be verified that Plato, in other passages of his work, used similar suppressions, for example, the "great number" in *Republic* VIII,[88] not immediately accessible to the reader, or the allusion to the order of dimensions in *Laws* X.[89] In these and other instances,[90] we are apparently dealing with the ὑπόμνημα theory of the written word introduced in *Phaedrus*.[91] "Hypomnematic" allusions are made for the sake of the hearers at the Academy in order to remind them of certain teachings and their deeper substantive presuppositions.[92] Thus, the allusions made in Plato's written presentation of the allegory of the sun are not without purpose, because they were properly understood by the students of the lectures at the Academy. But even for those readers who do not have knowledge of the essence of the ἀγαθόν, according to the lectures Περὶ τοῦ ἀγαθοῦ, the incomplete presentation of the allegory of the sun is not meaningless. They still acquire a concrete idea of the paramount position of the μέγιστον μάθημα, which facilitates further understanding of the *Republic*, namely, the subsequent discussions of the allegory of the line and the cave, and the following steps [*Stufenfolge*] in scientific παιδεία as it is introduced at the end of book VII.[93] The beginning of the allegory of the sun, where we find the "good" beyond being, has a well-considered psychagogic function within the economy of the whole work, even if it first appears to the reader—as it does to the interlocutor Glaucon—only "strange,"[94] because it presents the prominent position of that which is "greatest" in a suggestive and intuitive way, which at the same time is distinguished from alternative determinations[95] (φρόνησις, ἡδονή).[96]

While the alternative solutions of certain critics require questionable speculative artificial twists, and remain often implicitly unhistorical and founded in the project of modernity, the explanation of the ἄγραφα δόγματα starting from *Republic* VI has the advantage of making *all* of the functions of the "good" fully intelligible. Moreover, it *uniformly* understands these functions based upon a single ground of explanation and provides *historical* justification. Among its functions, the function of the "good" as the principle of order and unity in the state and soul is particularly important. It refers to the uniting, limiting, and balancing activity of the one.[97] Being, aptness, and making clear and knowable are only different aspects of the basic character of the good, which, according to Plato's ἄγραφα δόγματα, in every being originates in the one, and includes fixation, limitation, determination, identity, persistence, discreteness, balance, and order.

Additionally, in a different context it was shown[98] that the dialectical ascent from the uppermost ideas to the "good," as well as the definition of the essence (λόγος τῆς οὐσίας) of the good that is required in book VII, had to be established within the domain of the ἄγραφα δόγματα. The preceding investigation has shown that the beyond-beingness of the "good" is substantively and historically grounded through the unwritten doctrine of the principles. All of the essential properties of the ἀγαθὸν αὐτό in the *Republic* converge in, and have been traced back to, the ἄγραφα δόγματα of the λόγοι περὶ τοῦ ἀγαθοῦ.

Thus, we have provided a coherent argument based on mutually corroborating indications against previous speculative-experimental interpretation. The future interpreter of Plato's late dialogues, as well as of the *Republic*, has to take into account the indirect transmission of Plato.[99]

NOTES

1. καὶ τὸ εἶναι τε καὶ τὴν οὐσίαν ὑπ' ἐκείνου αὐτοῖς [sc., τοῖς γιγνωσκομένοις] προσεῖναι, οὐκ οὐσίας ὄντος τοῦ ἀγαθοῦ, ἀλλ' ἔτι ἐπέκεινα τῆς οὐσίας πρεσβείᾳ καὶ δυνάμει ὑπερέχοντος (*Rep*. 509B).

2. See the review by Sinaiko 1965, 301n.9: "The statement that the Good is 'beyond essence' (ἐπέκεινα τῆς οὐσίας) is one of the most famous (or perhaps infamous) remarks in the dialogues of Plato and, indeed, in the whole tradition of Western thought."

3. Cf., for example, Hartmann 1909, 264f.; Ferguson 1921, 136; Gadamer 1931, 61; Festugière 1935, 202; Joseph 1948, 23f.; Schulz 1960, 274; Berger 1961, 111f.; Sinaiko 1965, 142, cf. 136f.; cf. Proclus, *In Remp*. I, 276, 6f.; 279, 22f.

4. Cf., for example, Natorp 1921, 195f.; Hartmann 1909, 266ff.; then Stewart 1909, 51f.; Nettleship 1929, 222, 225; Stenzel 1931, 114, 119; Cornford 1939, 132: "whereas you can always ask the reason for a thing's existence and the answer will be that it exists for the sake of its goodness, you cannot ask for a reason for goodness; the good is an end in itself"; then Cherniss 1945/1962, 98n.142 (= Cherniss 1966, 116n.142); Shorey 1946, 106n.; cf. ibid., xxxvi; Heidegger 1953, 150; Wolff 1957, 188; Gauss 1958, 201f.; Luther 1965, 488.

5. Cf., for example, Adam 1902, 170f.; Natorp 1921, 192 (ultimate justified principle "of all particular being," "beyond all particular being," that which "first makes possible . . . all particular knowledge and objecthood [*Gegensätzlichkeit*]"); Robin 1935, 250; Hartmann 1957, 61; Hirschberger 1940, 229; Schmitz-Moormann 1959, 80; cf. Krämer 1959, 6; Krämer 1967, 474, 549n.121; Krämer 1966, 68n.2.

6. Cf., for example, Szilasi 1946, 189ff.; Heidegger 1929, 41; Baumgartner 1965, 89ff.

7. 508Ef.

8. On the meaning of these passages as signs of a purposive reservation on the part of Plato, cf. Gomperz 1930, 430 (cf. Gomperz 1953, 123); Festugière 1935, 191n.2; cf. Diès 1932, lxxxvif.; Cornford 1941, 208f.; Gauss 1958, 198, 21n.1; Krämer 1967, 289ff.; Krämer 1964, 154ff.; Krämer 1968, 130f. It is important to note that Plato does not let Socrates express his opinion (τό γε δοκοῦν ἐμοί) (506E2; cf. 509C3) about the good not for substantial reasons, but only for "now" (506E1; cf. 509C9f.), which excludes that this is done for the reason of its inexpressibility.

9. Cross and Woozley 1964, 261 (on 509B): "but what he does say is so brief and so obscure that most commentary tends to become speculation"; cf. the skepticism in Murphy 1951, 184f., and Bröcker 1967, 271.

10. Merlan 1953, 96ff., proved that Speusippus is the author of the fragment, and defended this thesis successfully against critical voices (128ff.); the thesis has largely been accepted. Concerning the beyond-beingness [Überseiendheit] of the one, the Speusippus fragment that has been preserved in Proclus (see above text) provides important corroboration. Iamblichus, who knew at least one work by Speusippus (Περὶ Πυθαγορικῶν ἀριθμῶν) seems to have directly adopted the systematic excerpt in *De comm. math. sc.* IV from Speusippus (see Merlan 1953, 103).

11. *De comm. math. sc.* 15, 7ff.: τὸ ἕν ὅπερ δὴ οὐδὲ ὄν πω δεῖ καλεῖν, διὰ τὸ ἁπλοῦν εἶναι καὶ διὰ τὸ ἀρχὴν μὲν ὑπάρχειν τῶν ὄντων, τὴν δὲ ἀρχὴν μηδέπω εἶναι τοιαύτην οἷα ἐκεῖνα ὧν ἐστιν ἀρχή. Cf. *De comm. math. sc.* 18, 5; 7 (the one is placed after the primary elements). In light of *Rep.* 509B, the expression that the derivative essences would stand after the ἀρχαί and πρῶτα in terms of πρεσβεία and ἁπλότης is also noteworthy (15, 1f.).

12. On the transmission, see note 32 below.

13. Concerning the attribution of the Platonic Academic doctrine to the "Pythagoreans" by Plato's students, cf. the discussion by Frank 1923, 136ff., 252ff. (where Speusippus becomes central); Burkert 1962, 55ff. (also on the abovementioned Speusippus fragment); Krämer 1967, 53ff.

14. Speusippus fr. 35a, 48a–c, 49 Isnardi Parente; see Iamblichus, *De comm. math. sc.* 15, 11f.; 18, 4.

15. Cf. Burkert 1962, 19n.33, esp. 56f.; Gaiser 1963; Gaiser 1968, 531 ("eine Äußerung Speusipps über die platonische Prinzipienlehre," included there as *TP* 50); Krämer 1964, 359.

16. Plato lets Socrates describe the proposition about the beyond-beingness of the good as well as what has been concealed as τὰ ἐμοὶ δοκοῦντα (509C3; cf. τὰ δόγματα, τὸ δόγμα at 506B9 and τὸ δοκοῦν ἐμοί at 506E2), which fits very well with the apparently terminological use (τὰ λεγόμενα!) of the title ἄγραφα δόγματα in Aristotle (*Phys.* 209b15).

17. *Met.* A.6, 988a11: τοῖς δ' εἴδεσι τὸ ἕν [*sc.* τοῦ τί ἐστιν αἴτιον].

18. E.g., Aristotle, *Met.* A.8, 989b18, M.7, 1081a25, 1083b23f., N.4, 1091a25; Alexander, *In Met.* 56, 19f., 26ff.; Simplicius, *In Phys.* 454, 6f. (according to Porphyry and Alexander); Sextus Empiricus, *Adv. Math.*, X.277. See Speusippus apud Iamblichus, *De comm. math. sc.* IV, 16, 17f. as well as Xenocrates fr. 68H = Plutarch, *Mor.* 1012E.

19. *Met.* A.6, 988a14f.: ἔτι δὲ τὴν τοῦ εὖ καὶ τοῦ κακῶς αἰτίαν τοῖς στοιχείοις ἀπέδωκεν ἑκατέροις ἑκατέραν; which is in agreement with M.8, 1084a34f.; N.4, 1091b14f.; Aristoxenus, *Harm.* II, 40, 2. Shorey's assertion that *Rep.* 509B cannot be related to the presentation of the Platonic doctrine in Aristotle's *Met.* A.6 is unfounded (Shorey 1946, 106n; Shorey defends his own, purely ethical interpretation: Shorey 1895, esp. 225 ff., 239).

20. Cf. esp. *Rep.* V, 475E4, 476A, 476E10f., 477B, 478Af., 479A, 479Cff.; cf. *Rep.* II, 380Df.; *Phaedo* 65Cf.; 78Cf.; on κατὰ ταὐτὰ ὡσαύτως, see Parmenides DK28B8, 29f.: "it remains the same in the same place and remains fixed to its spot" (ταὐτόν τ' ἐν ταὐτῶι τε μένον καθ' ἑαυτό τε κεῖται χοὕτως ἔμπεδον αὖθι μένει).

21. The expressions that are used in the allegory of the sun: ὄν, οὐσία, εἶναι, ἀλήθεια, γνῶσις, ἐπιστήμη, have all been anticipated in book V.

22. See Jowett and Campbell 1894, III, 307: "Referring to the history of philosophy we may translate this as: 'the idea of good reaches a step beyond the Eleatic being.' "

23. The refutation of multiplicity (εἰ πολλά ἐστιν) is in Zeno, DK29B1–3 = Lee 94–11 (Lee 1936/1967); furthermore Plato's *Parm.* 127Ef. (= DK29A12); Aristotle, *Phys.* A.3, 187a1f. (= DK29A22); Aristotle, *Soph. El.* 170b19f. (= DK29A14); cf. Simplicius, *In Phys.* 134, 2f. D. (= DK29A23); Philoponus, *In Phys.* 42, 9ff. V. (= DK29A21 = Lee 8); Elias, *In Cat.*, 109, 15f. B. (= DK29A15): the refutation of multiplicity for the purpose of proving the unity of being in the sense of Parmenides. Themistius, *In Phys.* 12, 1f. S.; Simplicius, *In Phys.* 139, 19f., 27f. D.; Philoponus, *In Phys.* 80, 23f. V. (= Lee fr. 1–3): for proofs of the unity of being, cf. Lee 8f., 22f., 111 ff., 120f.; Fränkel 1960, 211, 222, 225, 230, esp. 233f. Melissus, DK30B8 = Simplicius, *In De caelo* 558, 19f. H. (ἕν-πολλά), on fr. B5–7 and B9 (ἕν); cf. Pseudo-Aristotle, *De Melisso* 974a1f. (= DK30A5): ἓν ὄν–not πολλὰ ὄντα, passim; cf. Aristotle, GC A.8, 325a2f. (= DK30A8): ἕν-πολλά, also DK30A6–7, A12f. Cf. also Gorgias, Περὶ τοῦ μὴ ὄντος ἢ περὶ φύσεως, who picks up the Eleatic antithesis of ἕν and πολλά and attempts to refute both parts (DK82B3 = Sextus Empiricus, *Adv. Math.* VII.73–74; cf. Pseudo-Aristotle, *De Gorgia* 979a16f., 979b35f.; cf. Bröcker 1958, 434f.; also Gigon 1936, 204 f. See the account on the deviation of the Atomists from the Eleatic philosophers in Aristotle, GC A.2, 325a29f. (= DK67A7): "being is not one, but the manifold is infinite" (ὄν οὐχ ἕν, ἀλλ' ἄπειρα τὸ πλῆθος).

24. See Kullmann 1958, esp. 158, 165f., 171, 172 (pluralism is already presupposed as an alternative position in Parmenides' statement).

25. *Rep.* 476A, 478B, 479Af.

26. Parmenides says at 137B: "Shall I begin with my own hypothesis, asking whether, when one is posited, it is one or does not exist?" (ἀπ' ἐματοῦ ἄρξωμαι καὶ τῆς ἐματοῦ ὑποθέσεως, περὶ τοῦ ἑνὸς αὐτοῦ ὑποθέμενος, εἴτε ἕν ἐστιν εἴτε μὴ ἕν). Parmenides' statement, on the other hand, mentions the unity of ὄν in one place only (DKB8, 6: ἕν). See Boeder 1968, 41.

27. The line of argument in *Phaedo* 74Af. corresponds with the first part of the *Parmenides* (128Ef.), even in the choice of its examples (ξύλα–λίθοι; ὅμοιον–ἀνόμοιον). The same train of thought is present in *Rep*. V, 479Af. and *Symp*. 211A. Zeno's argument is presupposed everywhere here.

28. See the summary at 245B7f.: "being . . . does not appear to be the same as one, and all things will be more than the one" (τὸ ὄν . . . οὐ τἀυτὸν ὂν τῷ ἑνὶ φανεῖται, καὶ πλέονα δὴ τὰ πάντα ἑνὸς ἔσται); and 245C8: "all things become more than one" (καὶ ἑνός γε αὖ πλείω τὰ πάντα γίγνεται).

29. 245A8f.: "according to the right account, what is truly one must indeed be called entirely without parts" (ἀμερὲς δήπου δεῖ παντελῶς τό γε ἀληθῶς ἓν κατὰ τὸν ὀρθὸν λόγον εἰρῆσθαι). See *Parm*. 158A5f.

30. *Rep*. 476A, 479A, 507B; cf. 478B10f.; *Parm*. 131B5, 131C9f., 132A1f., 132B2, 132B5, 132C4, 133B1, 135B3f., 135C9f.; and esp. the *Philebus* 15A6, 15B1 (ἑνάδες, μονάδες); cf. *Crat*. 439C, 440B; *Meno* 72C7, 72D8, 75A5; *Euth*. 5D3f., 6D11. That the expression ἑνάδες was already employed by Zeno to characterize the many ("the many are a manifold of units" [τὰ δὲ πολλὰ πλῆθος εἶναι ἑνάδων]) (Simplicius, *In Phys*. 99, 13f. D., according to Eudemus [fr. 37a], Philoponus, *In Phys*. 42, 12f. V. = DK29A21; a more detailed account in Lee 1936, 6, 8; Philoponus, *In Phys*. 80, 23f. V. = Lee 3; see also Simplicius, *In Phys*. 97, 13ff.; 138, 32ff. D. = DK29A21 and 16 = Lee 5 [ἕν], see also Lee 26f., 32f.) has been refuted by the philological criticism of Burkert 1962, 265–267.

31. *Parm*. 157Cf.; *Soph*. 245B; Aristotle, *Met*. A.6, 987b21; Alexander, *In Met*. 56, 30f. H. and ap. Simplicius, *In Phys*. 455, 6f. D., as well as Porphyry, ibid., 454, 15 according to Περὶ τἀγαθοῦ; see Sextus Empiricus., *Adv. Math*. X.261f. This thought also seems to have been considered by the Eleatic philosophers: the analogy between ἓν ὄν and multiple individual things often appears in Zeno (DK29B2 = Simplicius, *In Phys*. 139, 19 D.: "each of the many is the same as itself and one" [ἕκαστον τῶν πολλῶν ἑαυτῷ ταὐτὸν εἶναι καὶ ἕν]) and Melissus (B8 §2: "for if there were many things, they would have to be such that I could call each 'one'" [εἰ γὰρ ἦν πολλά, τοιαῦτα χρὴ αὐτὰ εἶναι, οἷόν περ ἐγώ φημι τὸ ἓν εἶναι]; §6: "if there were many things, they would have to be just as the one is" [εἰ πολλὰ εἴη, τοιαῦτα χρὴ εἶναι, οἷόν περ τὸ ἕν]) (regarding the continuing effect in Atomism, cf. Furley 1967, 57, 67ff.) and is sometimes continued to the point of dependence (Gorgias, DK82B3 §74: "for if the one does not exist, the many do not either; for the many is a composition of ones, so that, if the one were destroyed, it would take the many with it" [εἰ γὰρ μή ἐστιν ἕν, οὐδὲ πολλά ἐστιν: σύνθεσις γὰρ τῶν καθ' ἕν ἐστι τὰ πολλά, διόπερ τοῦ ἑνὸς ἀναιρουμένου συναναιρεῖται καὶ τὰ πολλά]).

32. Klibansky and Labowsky defend the following theses about the transmission in their commentary (Klibansky and Labowsky 1953, 86; cf. Praefatio, xli). These theses are supposed to be justified in a special treatise: "1° fragmentum pertinere ad Speusippi Περὶ Πυθαγορείων ἀριθμῶν, 2° Proclum non ipsum Speusippum legisse, sed has sententias repperisse apud Nicomachum, Neopythagoreum qui dicitur philosophum . . . Nicomachum verba Speusippi more Neopythagoreorum aliqualiter variavisse veri simile est." As long as the justification is lacking, one cannot properly discuss these theses, e.g., about the mediating role played particularly by Nicomachus (and not Iamblichus). The interventions of the mediators could certainly not

have been superficial, cf. n.39. Klibansky attempts to restore the Greek original of Proclus as follows: τὸ ἓν γὰρ βέλτιον τοῦ ὄντος ἡγούμενοι καὶ ἀφ' οὗ τὸ ὄν, καὶ ἀπὸ τῆς κατ' ἀρχὴν ἕξεως αὐτὸ ἠλευθερῶσαν. νομίζοντες δὲ ὡς εἴ τις τὸ ἓν αὐτό, χωρὶς καὶ μόνον θεωρούμενον, ἄνευ τῶν ἄλλων καθ' αὐτὸ τιθείη—μηδὲν ἄλλο στοιχεῖον αὐτῷ ἐπιθείς—οὐδὲν ἂν γίγνοιτο τῶν ἄλλων, τὴν ἀόριστον δυάδα εἰσήγαγον (the last phrase, ἀρχὴν τῶν ὄντων, has been left out accidentally).

33. τὸ ἀπορῆσαι ἀρχαικῶς (Aristotle, *Met.* N.2, 1089a1; Krämer 1967, 119f.; see also Merlan 1953, 123, 139).

34. Conj. Klibansky-Labowsky (codd.: *suadere*, apparently in the Greek original τιθείη has been rendered as πείθειν).

35. Conj. Klibansky-Labowsky (codd.: *inducens*, Gr.: εἰσήγαγον–εἰσαγαγῶν). "They held that the One is higher than being and is the source of being; and they delivered it even from the status of a principle. For they held that given the One, in itself, conceived as separate and alone, without the other things, with no additional element, nothing else would come into existence. And so they introduced the indefinite duality as the principle of being" (trans. Klibansky-Labowsky).

36. "It seemed to them that all things that are would be one (viz., Being itself), if one did not join issue with and refute the saying of Parmenides: 'For never will this be proved, that things that are not are.' They thought it necessary to prove that which is not is; for only thus—of that which is and something else—could the things that are be composed, if they are many" (trans. Ross). Cf. 1089a19, 21, 31 (πολλὰ τὰ ὄντα), and further parallels *Met.* B.4, 1001a29f., esp. b19f.: "if someone supposes, as some (the Academics) say, that number comes from the one itself and something other than the one (against Parmenides)" (εἴ τις οὕτως ὑπολαμβάνει ὥστε γενέσθαι, καθάπερ λέγουσί τινες, ἐκ τοῦ ἑνὸς αὐτοῦ καὶ ἄλλου μὴ ἑνός τινος τὸν ἀριθμόν"; K.2, 1060b6f. (ἕν/ὕλη). Cf. *GC* A.8, 325a2f., 23f.; *Phys.* A.3, 187a1f. (the Atomists and Academics against the Eleatic philosophers).

37. Elsewhere Aristotle occasionally introduces the ὄν besides the ἕν as the first principle and "highest genus" (πρῶτα γένη; τὰ ἀνωτάτω τῶν γενῶν) of Plato "and the Pythagoreans" also in the Academy (*Met.* B.1, 996a6, 3, 998b9f., 18f., B.4, 1001a9f., 29f., K.2, 1060a36f., Γ.2, 1004b27f. [cf. 1003b33f.], K.3, 1061a15f.). When looked at superficially, the equation of ἓν αὐτό and ὂν αὐτό could seem to contradict the supreme position of the ἕν. However, if we can trust the scarce sources, it appears that we are dealing with an "ontological difference." However, according to this ontological difference the ground of being [*Seinsgrund*] is indeed not determined, but is the still undetermined (most general, devoid of content) being (cf. Merlan 1953, 102). It is also clear that this fact itself does not suffice to explain Plato's paradoxical beyond-beingness, because it does not differ in any way from the relationship that is common in the generalized doctrine of ideas between general kinds and the essences that participate in them, e.g., between the good itself or the beautiful itself and the individual good and beautiful things. That the ὂν αὐτό partakes neither in εἶναι nor in οὐσία cannot be expected in light of the self-predication of the Platonic idea (concerning this still ongoing discussion, cf. the contributions by Vlastos, Geach, Allen, Robinson, Runciman, and Marten 1967, 209ff.), nor in light of the *Sophist* (see Marten 1967, 224: "That being is one of the persistent dianoetic determinations is according to the *Sophist* itself only an instance of being"; cf. 226). The transcendence

of being exists based on the importance of the contradiction between the ἄγραφα δόγματα, which is prevalent in the testimonies, and the ἕν and the πλῆθος of the Eleatic school. Hence this contradiction creates a tension between ὄν and ὄντα and establishes a basic ontological difference between them.

38. First, it appears contradictory that the one fulfills the function of a principle of being (*a quo le ens*), while at the same time being "freed" of the status of a principle (*ab ea que secundum principium habitudine ipsum liberaverunt*). The end of the account (*entium principium induxerunt*) shows, however, that here we are dealing with the individuating principle of matter (see Gaiser 1963, 531n: "that means: for Plato the 'indefinite dyad' is the real *principium individuationis*").

39. The "ontological" way of questioning that comes from the Eleatic philosophers is also clear in the account given by Speusippus.

40. Cf. esp. *Soph.* 237A, 241D, 258D; Krämer 1967, 531n.76; Merlan 1953, 123.

41. Klibansky, 1961 86: "Ad argumentum quod respicit Speusippos cf. Plato, *Sophistes*, imprimis 252C2sqq." (The expressions εἶναι, χωρίς, τῶν ἄλλων, καθ' αὑτό, which Plato puts in the mouths of his opponents, indeed return in Speusippus: ens–ὄν, seorsum–χωρίς, sine aliis–ἄνευ τῶν ἄλλων, secundum se ipsum–καθ' αὑτό. Most of them are, however, also present in the *Parmenides*; cf., for example, 159Bf.; and cf. note 44 below).

42. The account of Plato's system of principles, numbers, and dimensions from Plutarch's *Quaest. Plat.* III, 1001f., also belongs to these accounts. It explicitly requires the derivation of an opposing principle: "for *one* does not produce number if it is not joined to the indefinite dyad" (οὐ γὰρ ποιεῖ μονὰς ἀριθμόν, ἂν μὴ τῆς ἀπείρου δυάδος ἅψηται).

43. Before the new Speusippus fragment became known, Merlan 1953, 101f., attempted to hypothetically justify the ontological priority of the Speusippean one (in Aristotle and Iamblichus) by drawing on the *Sophist* (it is claimed that the indeterminate ὄν would stand above the determinate ὄν = ταὐτόν, similarly to how an indeterminate μὴ ὄν would have to stand above the determinate μὴ ὄν = ἕτερον as an opposing principle). This in and of itself implausible (see note 37 above) and unwarranted consideration is not confirmed by the new fragment, but rather becomes superfluous: it provides an account of Plato's *own* doctrine of principles; and there is no reason to sever the mentioned beyond-beingness of the one and ascribe it to the interpretation of the author. The possible dependence on the *Sophist* in terms of the question of dualism is no refutation, because it would not be an interpretation but an application of the *Sophist*. Besides, it would only be important for historical reasons, but not for an evaluation of the systematic character of the Platonic doctrine.

44. Concerning the "hypomnematic" character of the late dialogues, cf. *Phaedr.* 275A5, D1, 276D3, 278A1; concerning the preliminary nature and incompleteness of the *Sophist* with respect to ὄν and μὴ ὄν, see 254C. Both passages point toward similar yet further-reaching oral discussions in the Academy. This interpretation is confirmed through a decisive parallel: Solmsen 1960, 187f.; and Owen 1961, 92ff. (see Düring 1966, 299, 325), have independently shown that the fundamental concepts of the theory of the continuum in Aristotle's *Physics* (bks. V and VI) had been anticipated in Plato's *Parmenides* (esp. 148Df.: ἅπτεσθαι, ἐφεξῆς, ἐχόμενον, μεταξύ, χωρίς). But

since the *Parmenides* (DK28, B8, 6; 23; 25) nevertheless lacks an anticipation of the central concept of the continuum itself (συνεχές, see Kullmann 1958, 169ff.), and since the terms, on the other hand, are put into a chain of increasing unity by Aristotle, Solmsen 1960, 198, and similarly Owen 1961, 101, have rightly inferred that Aristotle is drawing less on the *Parmenides* and more so on the philosophical discussions in the background of the Academy, whereby he dialectically called into question and differentiated the Eleatic concept of the continuum. Here the line of development leads primarily from the Eleatic philosophers through the Academy to the students of Plato, and one can legitimately assume that the same is true for the development of the doctrine of principles.

45. The foundational character of the big and small and the more and less has been anticipated in many ways by the Eleatic philosophers as a defense against multiplicity. Cf., e.g., *Parm*. DK28B8, 22f., 44f. (μᾶλλον–χειρότερον; μᾶλλον–ἧσσον); Zeno B1 (μικρά–μεγάλα); Anaxagoras 59B3; Melissus B7 §8 (ἀραιόν–πυκνόν); and Plato, *Symp*. 211B4 (μήτε τι πλέον μήτε ἔλαττον of καλὸν αὐτό).

46. See Krämer 1967, esp. 502ff., 512ff.; and also Merlan 1967, 121.

47. Expressions for multiplicity (πλῆθος, πολλά) are missing in Speusippus' texts, but multiplicity is sufficiently provided through the "dyad" (*dualitas*), the principle of multiplicity, which stands opposed to the one.

48. Since my review of the relevant literature has been published in Krämer 1966, 35n.2, further voices have acknowledged and appreciated the importance of the unwritten doctrine for an understanding of Plato's philosophy: Muth 1966, esp. 249ff., 256f.; Düring 1966, 183f. ("the complete breakthrough of the doctrine of principles we find for the first time in the *Rep*. at 508D–509B"), 194ff., 438; Schneider 1966, 26, 42; Dempe 1967, esp. 524ff. ("It seems certain that Plato's lecture on the good was not a singular achievement of the age . . . , but that it represents an engagement with the highest philosophical questions at least since the time of the *Republic* and its production. It has been continued throughout the production of the dialogues."); Jäger 1967, 9f.; Pépin 1968, 76ff.; Boeder 1968, 61ff.; cf. the investigations by Untersteiner 1966, 246, about the importance of *Republic* X; Oehler 1966, 453ff. Loewenclau 1965, 120n.24; 122n.62; Wippern 1965, 149n.52, 156n.104; Ostwald 1965, 824. I discuss the more recent remarks from the opposing side in Krämer 1968, 20ff.

49. The occasional equation of ἓν αὐτό and ὂν αὐτό in the testimonies of the oral doctrine (see note 37 above) are not important, because in any case we are dealing with Plato's unwritten doctrine of the Eleatic provenience.

50. The analysis of Festugière 1935, 202ff., among others, comes to the same conclusion.

51. Hence, the chronological dating of the doctrine of principles to the period of the late Eleatic dialogues (*Parmenides*, *Sophist*), as it has been attempted by Merlan 1967, 121, is incorrect and can no longer be defended (see Krämer 1968, note 101 and note 77).

52. This is explicitly stressed as a particular aspect of the Platonic one in Aristotle, *Met*. A.6, 987b22f.; cf. B.1, 996a6f.; B.4, 1001a9f.; K.2, 1060b7; N.4, 1091b14.

53. See Krämer 1968, 141ff., on the "functional multivalence" of the Platonic principles within the framework of Platonic dialectic.

54. The one principle of ἀρετή: Aristotle, *Met.* A.6, 998a14f.; Sextus Empiricus, *Adv. Math.* X.264, 266f., 268 on 272, 275; *Div. Arist.* 68c. M., 23c M., 27 D. L. (= *TP* 44A–B), also Hermodorus ap. Simplicius, *In Phys.* 248, 2f. D., cf. *APA* 283-298; cf. *Polit.* 283Cf., and 284D1f.; *Phil.* 26Af., 64Df.; on making inferences concerning the early work ("order"), see Krämer 1967, 323f., 456f., 476f. On the one principle of being, see Aristotle, *Met.* A.6, 988a11, N.2, 1089a6; Alexander, *In Met.* 56, 30f. H.; Sextus Empiricus, *Adv. Math.* X.260f., 277. On the one as the principle of knowledge see note 85 and note 86 below; on the limiting basic function of the one, see note 18 above.

55. Krämer 1967, 137 f., 473 ff., 536 f.; Krämer 1964, 86, 92; Krämer 1966, 36f., 70.

56. Baumgartner 1965, 89–101.

57. Ibid., 101.

58. Ibid., 92.

59. Ibid., 101.

60. Ibid., 101, see 96: "the ἕν thus once again stands subordinate to the question of the good."

61. See the testimonies above.

62. Ibid., 100: "knowing and being, ἕν and ἕτερον, ἐπιστήμη and οὐσία . . . , they only exist for the sake of the good, to which they owe their existence."

63. See above. On the evaluation of Baumgartner, see Jäger 1967, 63.

64. Bröcker, 1966.

65. See note 54 above.

66. See note 18 above.

67. Fritz 1966, esp. 135 ff.; Fritz 1967.

68. Indeed, von Fritz regards such a doctrine as a "concealed doctrine [*Geheimlehre*]." As Plato's self-portrayals show, however, it is really characterized primarily by its being unwritten.

69. It is difficult to understand why von Fritz makes insufficient use of the remarks of the *Seventh Letter* in approaching the question of an "esoteric" philosophy of Plato. Cf. Fritz 1966. He disregards the fact that in the *Seventh Letter* Plato wants to keep unwritten that which Dionysius and others have put into writing, i.e., that which can be written. This invalidates von Fritz's denial of an unwritten doctrine that has purposefully not been written down (Fritz 1966, 145 ff., 152 f.; Fritz 1967, 256f., 259n.1, 268). The clear justification that Plato provides in the letter concerning his reluctance remains unacknowledged, just as do the many individual references to the ἄγραφα δόγματα (see Krämer 1968). It is also impossible to grasp von Fritz's *a priori* argument that the ἄγραφα δόγματα could not have any addressees due to the intellectual inferiority of Plato's circle of students (Fritz 1966, 143). Plato himself remarks at 345B in the letter, which is taken to be genuine by von Fritz, that there are "competent critics" (πάμπολυ κυριώτεροι κριταί) of his unwritten doctrine. He could only have meant the inner circle of his students (cf. 327B1: Dion). Von Fritz does not discuss the *Phaedrus* (esp. 278Bf.), although he nevertheless tries to explain the passages that express Plato's reluctance in the dialogues by saying that we are dealing in each instance with a suspension or postponement that is to be taken up at a later time (Fritz 1966, 139: "rather, it is asserted in each instance that problems

have been left unsolved and that these should be discussed at a different point in time"). This interpretation, however, has been refuted by myself in a different work (Krämer 1964, 155 f.): many records do not point to a "later point in time" but abstain from any further discussion (*Meno* 76Ef.; *Rep.* 611Bf.; *Phaedr.* 246A, 274A; *Soph.* 254C; *Tim.* 28C, 48C, 53D). But what appears to be "postponed" is almost never picked up in the written work, so that, in fact, a far-reaching difference in content has to be assumed between what has been written and what has been left unwritten. Concerning the significance of these points, see below.

70. To prove that the assumption of a purposefully unwritten doctrine "leads to the most absurd consequences" (Fritz 1966, 153), von Fritz provides the following arguments (139ff.): the argumentative *aporias* of the early Socratic dialogues (e.g., *Laches*, *Protagoras*) are said not to be resolved by way of a spoken "doctrine"; the incompleteness of the later dialogues are only intended to lead the reader toward further intellectual thinking; and Plato did not possess an audience for a more sophisticated or special spoken doctrine, because his students were not on his level. Yet difficult and paradoxical arguments are nevertheless contained in the late dialogues. The engagement with an "unwritten" doctrine is said to be self-contradictory, because it has only been transmitted in written form and as such could have been written by Plato himself. Because of their indirect and fragmentary character of transmission, the ἄγραφα δόγματα are said to be inferior to the dialogues and that they can in no way compete with them ("pieces taken out of context," "the whole of Plato's philosophy of which we know" is "nearly" identical with the dialogues [ibid., 147]). These criticisms in part disappear in light of Plato's self-portrayals (see note 69), and in part they only touch the periphery of the problem (such as the special role of the early dialogues) or they miss their target (what is at issue is not some difficulty, but particularly the difficulty of profaning the ultimate of things, which for this reason are also not touched upon in the late dialogues; the written discussion of originally unwritten doctrines is no contradiction, because the modern historian needs to share neither Plato's method of teaching nor his philosophy). The rejection of the unwritten tradition seems perplexing in light of the work that has been done in this field during the twentieth century as well as the corresponding transmissions in other domains of ancient philosophy. It indeed fails to grasp the point that the lesser degree of quality of the indirect tradition is balanced by its primacy of content (see the correction in Krämer 1968). Von Fritz's suggestion to replace the thesis of an unwritten, special doctrine with an "extrapolated filling in of gaps between the dialogues" (Fritz 1966, 146f., 148, 152) means to exchange what is secure with what is insecure by way of replacing an ancient tradition with the hermeneutic no-man's-land of uncontrollable harmonization. Indeed, one example of a too rapid introduction of modern issues is von Fritz's own discussion of the allegory of the sun.

71. Fritz 1967, 255ff. Von Fritz refers to the contributions of Gadamer 1964 and Oehler 1965, and mitigates his criticism, at least insofar as he values the indirect transmission of Plato and its importance for the dialogues much more highly. In taking up Gadamer (supra, 31), he now only raises doubts concerning its schematized form ("schematism"). In this matter, von Fritz holds on to the trend of situating the ἄγραφα δόγματα late in Plato's development ("teachings in old age"), by way of attributing it to the later dialogues. Von Fritz repeatedly claims (Fritz 1966,

152n.65; Fritz 1967, 259n.1, 262; cf. 255) that K. Gaiser was the first one who, in the case of the *Timaeus*, seriously attempted to establish a relationship between the dialogues and the ἄγραφα δόγματα, and that in so doing he acknowledges that the latter have a certain importance, while I allegedly only "pointed to" the existence of the ἄγραφα δόγματα (Fritz 1967, 258; similarly Fritz 1966, 135f.), and allegedly violently separated the written work from the oral doctrine through a "sharp division" and "attempted to neglect and devalue the dialogues." None of these claims are true. Merely "pointing to" the existence of an unwritten doctrine of Plato would be quite superfluous after the detailed works by Robin, Stenzel, Ross, Gentile, Merlan, Wilpert, de Vogel, et al. Far from it, it was the expressed intention of my book on Plato (cf. for example Krämer 1967, 28f., 37, 301f., 455, 457, 461, 469f., 471f., 481ff., 537ff., 554) to achieve what for the most part would be the first comparative and encompassing reading through a close examination of the dialogues and the indirect transmission of Plato. Thus, the whole first half is exclusively dedicated to the interpretation of the dialogues (*Republic* I, the *Gorgias*, *Republic* II–X, the *Statesman*, *Philebus*, and large portions of the *Laws* and the *Symposium*; hence the summary statement at 471f.: "The fact that the universal way of being of everything existent, which derives from the one [ἕν] and many, is present in the κόσμος–τάξις doctrine of being in the *Gorgias*, in the structure of the soul and that of the state in the *Republic*, in the norm of τέχνη in the *Statesman*, in the structure of ethical and natural value in the *Philebus*, and in the political and ethical measure of the *Laws* . . . is the interpretive and systematic main conclusion of this investigation.") Apparently, von Fritz missed my remark concerning the question of a "philosophical system" of Plato (Fritz 1966, 152n.65; 1964, 69ff.).

72. Fritz 1967, 260n.2.

73. This was first developed in Fritz 1961, 616; after that it has been repeated in Fritz 1967, 148ff.

74. See, for example, Ferguson 1921, 133: "It is a mystery . . . how a formal cause like the good can also be a cosmological cause"; Ross 1963, 41f.: "It is, therefore, difficult to see what Plato can have meant when he says that the Idea of good accounts for the existence and the knowability of the world of Ideas"; Murphy 1951, 168: "it is not easy to think of valid reasons for connecting their [the ideas] intelligibility with goodness . . . but 'goodness' applied to uncreated forms does not seem . . . to explain why they should be what they are"; ibid., 194: "but why dialectic should see everything in the light of the good Socrates refuses to explain except by an elaborate set of parables"; ibid., 195: "the goodness of ideal forms which it is hard to explain and which may in fact come from a false track of thought"; Field 1952, 59: "But his hints are extremely opaque and it is difficult to get a clear idea how he thought [of the idea of the good in the *Republic*]"; Gould 1955, 165: "the controversy continues and we must suppose that no wholly satisfactory account has been suggested"; Stahl 1960, 449: "This complex aspect of the idea of the good has created difficulties again and again"; ibid., 450: "These considerations show how for us sometimes many logically inconsistent components are combined in Plato's idea of the good and its consequences"; Cross and Woozley 1964, 260: "unfortunately too, from what he does say, it is very difficult indeed, to form any clear idea of

what was in Plato's mind, and he himself, it will be remembered, at 506E leaves the question of what the Good is in itself and offers only 'the offspring' of the Good"; ibid., 261: "There are puzzling hints about the position of the Form of the Good in the world of Forms; for example, it is the source of being of the other Forms, but itself . . . beyond being in dignity and power. Here again, though all sorts of suggestions have been made, . . . Plato does not say enough to enable us to state at all clearly and discuss what he means"; Hare 1965, 38: "In the *Republic* we have little more than a tantalising prospectus." Thus, it is not difficult to understand that occasionally one spoke of the "semi-nonsense [*Halbunsinn*]" of this passage (Krämer 1959, 473, see also Hartmann 1909, 274, on 509B: "the suspicion of ingratitude and thus also that of nonsense is inevitable"; Natorp 1921, 191, 509B: "For us, too, there is something here to be amazed about"). Von Fritz, on the other hand, does not agree with his opponents that the passage could be better understood in light of the unwritten doctrine, but reverses their position and claims that those who do not understand this passage do not have the prerequisites "to pass the qualifying examination and enter the circle of the followers" of the ἄγραφα (Fritz 1967, 260; cf. Fritz 1966, 148f.).

75. 506D–E, cf. 509C.

76. Fritz 1966, 150.

77. Fritz 1967; cf. Fritz 1961, 616–617: "What is primarily meant by this is that there can only be a determinable or identifiable being in a certain sense, and thus a form of knowledge where, in a certain way, a regular, ordered form is singled out from the chaos of impressions . . . that in both domains [i.e., the ethical and the scientific] the ordered and formed has precedence over that which is unordered, chaotic, and that which has no beginning."

78. Fritz 1966, 151.

79. Marc-Wogau 1941, esp. 40ff. Apart from "determinacy," the thought of "unity" also comes into focus (43).

80. Festugière 1935, 202ff.

81. Stenzel, 1931, 123: The "effect of the idea of the good . . . [is] that it makes everything that falls under it into an εἶδος and thus allows one to think the unity of everything real."

82. Fritz 1966, 150f.

83. There seems to be a certain proximity here to the so-called Southwest School (or Baden School) (Windelband, Rickert) of Neo-Kantianism.

84. νοῦς can only refer to νοητά, i.e., εἴδη, and thus essentially excludes any selection from "the chaos of impressions." (Von Fritz's belief that the "good" has been introduced here, also as the principle of a spatio-temporal object, does not correspond to the wording of the text. It is only through the detour of the concept of ἀρετή that the context shows how the good is also the principle of the perceivable world: cf. *Rep*. 506Af., 517C, 540A; Krämer 1967, 149f., 144.)

85. Aristotle, *Met*. Δ.6, 1016b20f.: "the one is the principle of the knowable in each case" (ἀρχὴ τοῦ γνωστοῦ περὶ ἕκαστον τὸ ἕν); *Prot*. fr. 5 p. 32, 14ff. Ross = B33 Düring, ὡρισμένα and τεταγμένα, which are more knowable, are explained through a system of dimensions (Hermodorus ap. Simplicius, *In Phys*. 248, 4f. D.),

with ὡρισμένα in the Platonic division of being leading up to the ἕν (Alexander, *In Met.* 56, 19f., 26, 29, 31); or according to Περὶ τἀγαθοῦ: ὡρισμένον of ἕν; cf. *Phil.* 64Ef. (from ἀλήθεια to μετριότης and συμμετρία).

86. Aristotle, *DA* A.2, 404b22 = *TP* 25A (νοῦν μὲν τὸ ἕν: apparently, this refers to the intuitive-holistic conception of νόησις, which is referred to by Aristotle with the expression θιγγάνειν, and is distinguished from the other forms of knowledge); cf. *Theaetetus* 184D3 ("unity of consciousness" within the soul); also, cf. the (number-oriented) λόγος structure of the thinking soul in the *Timaeus*, and in this context the connection of the συμμετρία of the soul with the ability to access ἀλήθεια: *Sophist* 228C; cf. Krämer 1967, 474ff.

87. Fritz 1966, 149.

88. *Rep.* 546Aff.

89. *Legg.* 894A.

90. Especially the signposts that allude to further-reaching issues that are present in almost all of the major dialogues (cf. Krämer 1967, 389ff.; Krämer 1964, 154ff.; note 69 above).

91. See note 44 above.

92. Significantly, the μέγιστον μάθημα of the idea of the good is introduced in *Republic* VI as something that is already known (504E8, 505A3).

93. Cf., for example, *Rep.* 511B7, 516B10f., 517C1ff., 518C9f., 526E3f., 532A7f., C5f., E2f., 534B8f., esp. 540A (the ἀγαθόν was only opened up fifteen years after the end of the course in dialectic!).

94. 509C1.

95. *Rep.* 505Bf., 506B2f., 508E3f., 509A6f. This demarcation is present even in the allegory of the sun, whereas the conception of the good as φρόνησις is included in the proper solution, and at the same time surpassed, insofar as the good is not cognition, but rather the *ground* of knowledge that is "even higher" than knowledge itself (ἄλλο καὶ κάλλιον ἔτι τούτων, ἔτι μειζόνως τιμητέον). The introduction of the good as the principle of knowledge is thus intended as polemical, and is aimed primarily at non-Academics. The subsequent statement about the principle of being should be understood clearly as parallel, representing at the same time an augmenting and conclusive continuation.

96. One can respond to von Fritz's attempt to question Plato's comportment "as a human being and philosopher" who conceals important thoughts and misleads his readers by emphasizing that the moral and philosophical motives that are stated in the *Seventh Letter* are not at all "concealed."

97. This has already been pointed out by Gomperz in his undeservedly forgotten article (Gomperz 1930, 430f.; and also in English in Gomperz 1953, 123f.). See Crombie 1963, 450f.

98. Krämer 1966, 35ff.

99. Addendum: Kuhn has recently presented in a collection of essays (Kuhn 1968, 151ff.) a criticism of the "Tübingen position," which, although connected to the conference discussion, is quite independent. I hope to respond to it in detail. This much will suffice for now: the criticism does not seem to be philologically sustainable, and his position is systemically [*Systembegriff*] inaccurate. (Implicitly, the preceding contributions to the mentioned volume already disconfirm this conception.)

THREE

PLATO'S UNWRITTEN DOCTRINE

Hans Joachim Krämer

1.

When a lecture with the same title was announced on a different occasion, someone wrote the following question under the announcement: "Was Plato illiterate?" This term's lecture series has sufficiently shown that this is not the case. Today we will not be concerned with *the* teachings of Plato, but with his unwritten philosophy, which existed *alongside of* what has been laid down in writing. Certainly, there are still further misunderstandings that need to be dismissed: I do *not* intend to claim that Plato, just like every other writer, failed to put all of his thoughts to paper simply because every articulation necessarily proceeds by selecting and editing what is written. In that case the reader and interpreter would be able to read between the lines and add for themselves what had been left out. This meaning of the term "unwritten," however, would not only be trivial, but also it would not be proper to Plato's philosophy: it applies to every act of expression, not just the oral one. Just as little would I want to say that Plato conceived of certain topics as being less important, thus deferring them and leaving them unwritten. In that case the task would be to provide a philological reconstruction of what is less important, and, for reasons of completion, add it to the corpus in a similar way as it is done with an author's literary remains [*Nachlaß*]. Soon it will become apparent why this interpretation is false as well. Before that, however, I need to dismiss one further possible interpretation that is quite common: According to it, Plato had to refrain from writing down certain thoughts because they could not be presented in propositional form, and therefore could not be articulated. If this were the case, then we would have better things to do than waste our time with this lecture: we could not expect to gain any substantial insights concerning that which is essentially unsayable. At most, we could expect to arrive at explanations as to *why*, for Plato, they remained unsaid, and hence for us are not even comprehensible in thought.

The correct meaning of "unwritten" can be derived from a passage in Aristotle's *Physics*, from which the expression "Plato's unwritten doctrine" has been borrowed.[1] This passage should be interpreted in connection with Plato's criticism of writing in the *Phaedrus*,[2] and, insofar as one takes it to be genuine, also from the *Seventh Letter*.[3] Based on these sources, Plato *purposefully and deliberately* avoided fixing certain aspects of his philosophy into written form. He passed these aspects on exclusively by word of mouth. Moreover, based on Plato's interpretation of his philosophical activity in the *Phaedrus*, we can dismiss three further alternatives: Plato did not hold back parts of his doctrine in order to let the reader of the dialogues derive, by way of his own theoretical efforts, what had been left out; rather, he claims, it explicitly requires the intervention of the author himself, who, if necessary, must orally "come to the aid" of his own writings.[4] Secondly, the *Phaedrus* joins Plato's *opus magnum*, the *Republic*, in the criticism of writing;[5] the unwritten doctrine can thus not be mitigated and neutralized by situating it as a chronologically later piece [*Spätdatierung*]. And thirdly, in the case of that which is unwritten, we are not dealing with something arbitrary and accessory, but with something essential and of central importance; Plato even refers to it as being "more valuable" (τιμιώτερα),[6] when measured against that which is philosophically presented in his written work.

All of this appears very strange if one presupposes a *modern conception of literature*, as it is usually done. Is it not the case that Plato is a classic figure of world literature, whose collected works we possess in the original Greek, which have been translated into all the major languages and with which we deal in the same way as we deal with the works of other philosophical and literary classics? This great author invested so much energy in his literary work and even organized it into a comprehensive system by dividing it into trilogies or tetralogies. Could it really be the case, then, that he relativized his work in such a bold fashion without having expressed what is most essential to it? This assessment is very reasonable within a culture such as ours, which excessively relies on the written word. This prioritization of what is written dates back to late antiquity, and has been amplified even more through the canonization of the holy scriptures during Christianity and through the modern printing press. This assessment is also expressed in modern research concerning Plato that attempts to diminish Plato's critique of writing, or even deny that it is present in his writings at all. Friedrich Schleiermacher's *Dialogtheorie*, which prefaces his complete German translation of Plato[7] and has thus determined the study of Plato far beyond the German-speaking world, is seminal and representative of this line of interpretation to the present day.

In the course of the twentieth century, however, the modern culture of writing, of books and reading, has itself been called into question, and its claim to ultimate authority has been increasingly limited. Other electronic and acoustic media, such as the radio, telecommunication, cinema, television, and video, have led to a new kind of *orality*, which goes hand in hand even with illiteracy and in many cases has displaced the earlier culture of writing and reading. In this sense, philology and linguistics are increasingly focused on the relationship between the oral and the written in both the past and the present. These disciplines have developed a refined understanding of the transitions, coexistence, and interconnection of the spoken and the written word, especially for periods in which oral culture was predominant. In this context I would like to mention, summarily, the series *ScriptOralia*, which encompasses sixty volumes and is being edited by the special research group *Übergänge und Spannungsfelder zwischen Mündlichkeit und Schriftlichkeit*, which has existed since 1985 at the University of Freiburg.[8] The anthology by Assmann and Hardmeier, which appeared in 1983,[9] concerning *Schrift und Gedächtnis* (writing and memory), and the work by Gentili and Paioni on *Oralità, Cultura, letteratura, discorso*, from 1985,[10] the new book by Assmann, *Das kulturelle Gedächtnis*, from 1992,[11] and finally Jack Goody's *The Logic of Writing and the Organisation of Society* (1986) as well as Walter J. Ong's *Orality and Literacy* (1982)[12] also deserve to be mentioned. The books by Marshall McLuhan[13] and Neil Postman,[14] which trace the hegemony and one-sidedness of certain media and forms of communication within human civilization up to the present, operate within an even greater horizon. A seminal contribution by Vittorio Hösle, which addresses Plato's criticism of writing in particular, appeared in 1996.[15] Some important articles by Richard Harder in his *Kleine Schriften*,[16] which receive too little attention today, as well as the substantial seminal writings by Eric A. Havelock, which are condensed in the volume *The Muse Learns to Write* (1988),[17] and finally the anthologies *Les savoirs de l'ecriture en Grèce ancienne* (1988)[18] and Kullmann and Reichel's contribution to *ScriptOralia* (1990), under the title *Der Übergang von der Mündlichkeit zur Literatur bei den Griechen*, should also be mentioned.[19] The older works on oral poetry can be seen as anticipating these more recent investigations.[20]

All of these research approaches shed more light on the relationship between the oral and the written, both historically and systematically. This is true for the novel establishment of writing within a previously oral culture, the latter of which is found even today in Asia and the Caribbean. This clarification also applies to the interference and mutual influence of writing and continuously existing spoken language. For adequately understanding and situating *Plato*, it is important to keep three things in mind. (1) The phonetic alphabet, which had been used consistently by the Greeks, was applied exclusively to *spoken language*, which it divided into its abstract, a-semantic elements, in contrast to the Asian and Egyptian instances of pictographic writing, which was able to represent [*abbilden*] the world through bypassing spoken language (Derrida's rehabilitation of *writing* against "phonocentrism" thus stands in line with *this* tradition, and not with that of the Greeks). (2) The primacy of written culture only begins to assert itself in the middle of the fourth century, i.e., only thenceforward was language conceived of primarily from the perspective of written language. Until then, written language primarily fulfilled only a derivative function of preserving the spoken word. Thus, Plato is prior to the line of demarcation constituted by the "inner turn toward writing" [*inneren Verschriftlichung*][21] of the Greek language, and should be placed within the period of "inner *orality* [*inneren* Oralität]," to alter Harder's fitting expression. This is to say that Plato still regarded language and writing primarily from the vantage point of the spoken word. (3) In contrast to the era of Christianity, Greek antiquity never had a corpus of sacred, authoritative scriptures, and the internal turn toward writing never reached the point where the spoken word was fully dismissed (thus, when alone, one did not read silently as we do now, but rather one read aloud with the aid of the voice).

Hence, Plato's concept of literature stands essentially within the tradition of "inner orality," and needs to be clearly distinguished from modern conceptions. *In concreto*, this yields a number of consequences: *on the one hand*, writing for Plato does not primarily function as a means to communicate a message and instruct someone, but rather serves the purpose of *storing* and *preserving* what has already been orally transmitted or come to be known in a different way. The function of mere *remembrance*, which Plato attributes to writing in his fundamental treatment of this topic in the *Phaedrus*,[22] contradicts the modern task of *philosophical communication* that Schleiermacher's theory of dialogue attributes to Plato.[23] Nietzsche, who was a professional philologist, already defended this point against Schleiermacher in his lecture on Plato. Nietzsche states: "The hypothesis of Schleiermacher is only possible in a *literary* age. . . . [Schleiermacher has] presented him [Plato] like one of our great classics. . . . This whole hypothesis," however, "conflicts with the assertion in the *Phaedrus* and is supported by a false interpretation. . . . According to Plato, writing does not have a didactic and educational purpose at all. . . . [T]he assertion of the passage from the *Phaedrus* presupposes the existence of the Academy; for the members of the Academy, the writings are a means for the purpose of remembering."[24] Hence, Plato's writings primarily have the character of *documentation*[25] and not that of direct or indirect communication. If today we necessarily use them according to the latter function, then we are dealing with what Plato himself regarded as a questionable substitute. *On the other hand*, Plato obviously knew that these writings could also fall into other hands. Recent formal comparisons have shown that he at least partially *also* thought that the writings serve a protreptic, advertising function, which was intended to attract outsiders to the Academy.[26] *Thirdly*, however, Plato did not just preserve inner orality in an archaic form, but justified it with arguments: according to Plato, orality, after being written down, has the traits of personality, persistence, and of reconnecting understanding [*Rückkopplung*] with communication.[27] Based on these insights, Plato went one step further, bringing him into proximity with his teacher Socrates, as well as the Pythagoreans: The most significant, most valuable, and most difficult topics are excluded from documentation and storage for the purpose of recollection, and instead are reserved exclusively for orality. Plato gives two reasons for this: one does not need documentation for these topics, because once they have been grasped, they cannot be forgotten;[28] and secondly, it is possible that, if they were written down and made publicly accessible, they could be mocked and ridiculed in a way that would derogate their dignity.[29] Inner orality in Plato thus steps beyond the secondary function of writing toward a *substantive* [inhaltlichen] difference between spoken and written language. Based on its *methodological* primacy, spoken language possesses a substantive surplus. This is the justification of the ambiguity or duality [*Zweigleisigkeit*] that is present in the transmission of Plato's thought, with which we have to deal today. After all, Plato pointed to this *unwritten surplus value* not only in his methodological reflection in the *Phaedrus*, but also in detail throughout almost all of his major writings but without fully revealing what it amounts to. These points of reference, or better, points of concealment,[30] were intended to remind the insider of the connection to *what was said beyond* what is written in the text without repeating the contents of that beyond, in contrast with the recollected topics. The outsider was obviously unable to do anything with that information, as is also the case with modern interpreters of Plato. What the outsider could do, however, was to see a far-reaching *protreptic*, which led him to suspect that, given the proper circumstances, he could be led not only to something more explicit, but also to further-reaching matters. *In Plato's case, inner orality thus creates a complex and multilayered construction in his written works*.

If we want to understand Plato's philosophy historically and as a whole, we have to try to reconstruct the relationship that Plato attributed to the written and the unwritten, and we have to mutually elucidate both by means of the figures in his hermeneutic circle. Plato's unwritten doctrine is schematically preserved in the accounts [*Referate*] of his circle of students, who, as Aristotle, for example, does, stand on this side of the divide with respect to writing, or at least enabled the unwritten as well as other topics to be remembered by way of the written word. In this preliminary part of my lecture, I hope to have shown that it is not legitimate to misinterpret Plato from the vantage point of a later, modern conception of literature, only to then distinguish and create a contradiction between his literary work and the existence of an unwritten doctrine. The incompatibility[31] of such an attempt is already entailed in the unhistorical premise that commits Plato to too strong and emphatic a conception of self-sufficient literature, which does not do justice to the complicated context of the fourth century BCE.

2.

In what follows, I will attempt to provide examples of how Plato's written work is complemented by his unwritten doctrine. In particular, it needs to be shown how Plato's philosophical method of *dialectic* fully appears in its executed and materially fulfilled form. For a long period of time modern research has not dealt appropriately with this method in treating it as a mere propaedeutic, or as the sketching-out of a program, and in the end only as a petrifaction, indeed, as a mythological concept that lacks all functionality. The task is, however, not to cite dialectic in an evocative way, but to make it apparent in its execution and to comprehend its composition in detail. The difficulties that arise at the point when Plato prematurely suspends the dialectical movement in his writings can be solved if one "comes to the aid" (λόγῳ βοηθεῖ)[32] of his writings from the vantage point of the unwritten doctrine according to his methodological reflection in the *Phaedrus*, and thus fully brings the dialectical endeavor to its end.

In *Metaphysics* A.6, Aristotle discusses Plato's doctrine of principles, which provides justification for the ideas, since the ideas ground perceivable objects: "the forms are the cause of the essence of all other things, and the one is the cause of the essence of the forms; and it is evident what the underlying matter is, of which the forms are predicated in the case of sensible things, and the one in the case of forms, namely that this is a dyad, the great and the small. Further, he [Plato] has assigned the cause of good and that of evil to the elements [i.e., the principles]."[33] The latter is more explicit in *Metaphysics* N.4: "the one itself is the good itself; but they thought its substance lay mainly in its unity."[34] Theophrastus, who was probably still a student of Plato, describes this multilayered construction more precisely in the third chapter of his *Metaphysics*: "Now Plato in reducing things to the ruling principles might seem to be treating of the other things in linking them up with the ideas, and these with the numbers, and in proceeding from the numbers to the ruling principles, and then, following the order of generation, down as far as the things we have named."[35] Aristotle confirms this double movement of regression and progression in *Nicomachean Ethics* A.4: "Plato, too, was right in raising this question and asking, as he used to do, 'are we on the way *from* or *to* the first principles?' "[36] The distinction between an order of knowledge and an order of being obviously clarifies what we learn from the allegory of the divided line and the allegory of the cave in the *Republic*. Other accounts continue to fill in this scheme, while partially mathematical and partially categorical types of reductions play a role as well. (Please excuse my use of non-Platonic terminology for the sake of brevity; what I am referring to are the ultimate genera in the later dialogues, which have recently also been referred to as "meta-ideas.") According to various accounts,[37] Plato traces these back to *unity* and *multiplicity*, namely, by subsuming identity, equality, and similarity under *unity*, and difference, inequality, and dissimilarity under the *multiplicity*. In this context, Plato also introduces the even and the uneven, which in the allegory of the line in the *Republic* serve as a simple example of basic mathematical concepts (together with the kinds of angles). These concepts are to be understood dialectically from the principle of the good. How this is supposed to be possible remains notoriously obscure in the text of the *Republic*, and Plato, in the beginning of the allegory of the line, explicitly states that he has left out much that cannot be stated at this point.[38] That we are dealing with a hierarchical construction of the realm of ideas becomes clear in the passages following the allegory: in the discussion of entities, which are said to be "attached" to the principle of the good,[39] or in discussing the "stars," which stand outside of the cave, i.e., in the ideal realm *between* the ideas of things and the good, the latter of which is symbolized by the sun.[40] It is evident that Plato here alludes to a general synopsis that ascends from the ultimate genera as they appear in the later dialogues, to unity on the one hand and multiplicity on the other. Multiplicity was determined more specifically in the secondary accounts as the principle of multiplication and *gradation*, i.e., as the large and small. (That whose parts relate to each other as larger and smaller is the unequal.)[41] It can be presupposed that, in book VII of the *Republic*, namely, in the context of the ascendance to the good and its dialectical definition that distinguishes it from all the other ideas, the reference is to this synopsis.[42] This reference is also present in the discussion of the mathematical sciences, which refers back to the allegory of the line.[43] Moreover, this has consequences for our understanding of dialectic in the *Parmenides* and the *Sophist*. There, the synopsis is not performed quite so well, and the ultimate genera are left in parataxis. But Plato does make it sufficiently clear that there is more that remains unsaid, or rather unwritten: *Sophist* 254 states that the essence of what is and what is not cannot be clarified at this point. In this regard, he generally refers to the project of composing a dialogue with the title *The Philosopher*, which, significantly, remained unwritten (because it would have contained the unwritten doctrine). From the vantage point of contemporary thought, one might object that such a logic of subsumption could not have been the ultimate conclusion. This is a modern conclusion, similar to Hegel's disparagement of Aristotelian logic. It ignores the difficulties classical Greek philosophy had to face in light of the confusion of sophistry. Plato, it should be noted, expected *more* than formal logical skills. He expected that one should practice and grow accustomed to the concept and intuition of pure unity itself.

A second, related conclusion follows from the division of being in the *Republic* into being itself and its opposing properties. (Note the example of a finger, which always remains a finger even if it takes on different and opposing properties.)[44] In the late dialogues, instead of opposites, there are differing quantities that relate to each other in a correlative way and can be determined and limited through a mediating measure (e.g., in the *Statesman* and the *Philebus*). In an accentuated passage that occurs precisely in the middle of the *Statesman* and its methodological excursion, Plato alludes to an as of yet missing *exhibition of the exact itself*, which remains not realized in his written works.[45] However, from the unwritten doctrine we learn that Plato retraced the kinds of being to being in itself and relative being, which breaks down into opposites and their correlatives, and to the principles of one and the indefinite dyad. He performed this task in the form of a dialectical synopsis, which again contains the species of the equal and the unequal.[46] Here, too, it would be improper to regard this attempt only in terms of formal logic and not as a practice of gaining dialectical access to unity itself. Additionally, the one is conceived of here in an axiological manner as the good, because the positive opposites, together with the middle between their correlatives, are also retraced to it—an explication based on the implied axiological account of the previously mentioned account in Aristotle's *Metaphysics* A.6.

Here is a further example: again and again throughout the written works there is an insistence on the proposition that (dialectical) knowledge can only relate to both sides of an antithesis (as is the case with the doctor who knows what health is, and who therefore also has to know what disease is, and vice versa). The main part of the *Parmenides* confirms this on an epistemological as well as an ontological level with respect to the one and the many as the other of the one: both stand in a relationship of mutual implication. That this alludes to the bipolarity of Plato's *theory of principles* in the form of a historical self-description, which goes beyond parody, polemics, formal education, formal logic, Neoplatonic or even Hegelian metaphysics, as well as a mere apology for the theory of ideas, can only be brought to mind by somebody who is familiar with the unwritten doctrine. Today we can draw on Aristotle's *Metaphysics* N.2[47] and the similar account of Speusippus in Proclus.[48] In the *Parmenides*, the further dialectical context concerning the regression *to* and the progression *from* the principles is admittedly also lacking. According to Plato's conception, it is only such an account that can secure the systematic evidence of the axiom of opposition at the level of the highest principles.

We can reconstruct a further aspect of Platonic dialectic from the middle section of the *Timaeus*, where Plato breaks away twice from a complete dimensional analysis of the elementary triangles according to "even higher principles" (*Tim*. 48C, 53D). This account is completed in the unwritten doctrine, first, through the so-called "indivisible lines" (understood as the minimal magnitudes of extension),[49] then through primary arithmetic to the *ideal* magnitudes and numbers, which are thought of as generated from the principles of unity, and the large-and-small. This side of Plato's mathematics-oriented philosophy is also governed by the *dialectical method* in that it deals with the categories of part and whole and their relevant relations. Indeed, besides the theme of genus and species, Aristotle also attributes that of the part and the whole to the *dialecticians*, i.e., Plato and the Academics.[50] *Both* of these can be subsumed under the categories of ontological *priority* and *posteriority*,[51] which play a central role in the unwritten doctrine and to which we shall return later. (It has already become clear that genus is ontologically prior to species, as is the part to the whole, e.g., the lower number compared to the higher one, or the line compared to the surface, and the triangle compared to the square, etc.) Plato's unwritten doctrine formulates a general prohibition of hierarchies within each ontological realm,[52] which is analogous to the theoretical-type solution to the modern problem of antinomies. The problems with participation that are addressed in the first part of the *Parmenides* are thus definitively removed due to the alternative between equivocation and univocity with self-predication and regress, in favor of a form of univocity that is free of such regress.

Concerning the much misunderstood *theory of the idea-numbers* in the unwritten doctrine, one has to distinguish between ideal numbers, and the other ideas that participate in idea-numbers by way of mathematical relation, just as mathematical numbers do. (Hence it would be better to talk about ideas that are numerically determined, or of idea-numbers, instead of ideal numbers.) First of all, it is clear that there should be a dialectical synopsis of the relation between the ideal numbers and all other types of numbers. Furthermore, the arithmetical structuring of the domain of universals, as an unfolding of the Greek concept of logos and as a *precise determination of dialectic*, should assign each member an exact and determinable place within the whole. One can find modern parallels to this concept much more in Leibniz or in coherence theories of truth than in logistics. I am of the opinion that the mathematical structuring [*Relationierung*] of the domain of universals in Plato has not been developed beyond programmatic initial points. But this is not the reason why it was reserved for orality. The reason, rather, lies in the difficulty of dealing with this topic, which would have required a similar level of reflection on dialectic even in its more developed form.

If one can say that the principles, considered in light of universality, are the highest genera, *genera generalissima*, then in light of the categorization according to the elementary categories of part and whole according to the order of being, the principles are the first elements: *elementa prima* (Greek: στοιχεῖα). Both of these aspects are present in the accounts of Plato's inner-Academic teachings. Here, Plato also started with a definition of the one-good, which was suggested but not developed in book VII of the *Republic*.[53] Unity could not be defined as a species of a higher genus, because this would have led to an infinite regress. It is possible, however, to explain unity analytically as an element and *measure* of multiplicity, which is generated through it. This is possible because we are dealing with the first and last, absolutely undivided unity as an *exact measure*, with epistemological, ontological, and axiological connotations. Since this determination is based on many presuppositions and completes the dialectical process, and since it stands in a relationship of mutual conditioning [*Bedingung*] supported by the evidence of intellectual intuition (νόησις), it is clear why Plato reserved this determination primarily for orality.[54]

So far we have for the most part discussed the dialectical *via cognitiva*, regression, and the synopsis of ascendance according to the *order of cognition* [Erkenntnisordnung]. Now let us trace the theory of principles in the unwritten doctrine to the progression in the *order of being* [Seinsordnung], and thus, most importantly, elucidate the allegory of the sun in the *Republic*. In so doing, it will become clear that these mysterious passages can be fully explained, both systematically and historically—something that until now has not been achieved in full by any immanent interpretation. It is advisable to keep in mind the fact that Plato furnished the order of allegories with a threefold barrier and thus mystified it for the outsider in a virtually unsolvable way: it is not just the case that the "greater (*dialectical*) way" is not being taken,[55] but additionally, Plato evades the outsider by using an image, which he does not even complete.[56] The suitableness and responsibility of dialectic is already presupposed in the case of the order of being, as it was in the case of the order of knowledge through the categorical structure of ontological priority and posteriority. We have to presuppose as the *basic conception of the unwritten doctrine* that the principle of unity, determinacy, identity, and persistence *determines* or, as it is said in the accounts, "limits" the opposing principle of indeterminacy, multitude, difference, multiplication, and increase. What does this amount to concerning the axiological, ontological, and epistemological function that is attributed to the idea of the good in the allegory of the sun?

First of all, the philosophers of the ideal state have to know to what extent that which is just and right is also good: the state then will be *in order* and *unity*—a formula that recurs again and again from books V through IX.[57] This *also* applies to the soul of an individual. The unwritten doctrine, which explicitly retraces justice, prudence, and other virtues as *orderings* [Ordnungen] through *numbers* to *unity* itself, shows that, especially here, we are not dealing with a mere logic of subsumption.[58] Ordering, indeed, is uniformity [*Einheitlichkeit*] within multiplicity that participates in pure unity, and thus can alternate in the *Republic* with the concept of uniformity in the state and the soul. That the middle and measure of the later dialogues is to be understood as derivative of unity as well has just been shown in our discussion of categorical reduction. One has to add that the unwritten doctrine suggests that the ordered is also limited and determined.[59] This is significant when pursuing the question, as we do now, to what extent the good is the ground of being [*Seinsgrund*], or the *causa efficiens* of the ideas, and then of everything else as well. We have to keep in mind that unity, as the principle of determination, posits identity, self-sameness, persistence, and singularity. The accounts state that every thing, insofar as it is determined and limited, is *one*.[60] In book V of the *Republic*, on the occasion of introducing the doctrine of ideas, Plato points out such a direction with a play of words: everything is, he states there,[61] either "one thing or no thing," i.e., that which is not nothing has to be one thing, namely, a unified something [*ein Einheitliches*]. Plato is here dealing with different degrees of being: the ideas are more unified than things, but they are not as uniform [*einheitlich*] as is pure unity itself. From the qualification of beings as something *determinate*, it also follows that the question concerning the essence of being, which is left open in the *Sophist*, should be answered (Plato himself provides a hint in the *Sophist* at 245Af.). But what should we think about the identification of the good as the ground of *truth and knowability*? The accounts of Plato's inner-Academic teachings connect knowability again to determinacy and being ordered.[62] We can make sense of the latter by drawing on modern *Gestalt* psychology. A special theory of truth connected to the unwritten doctrine has not been passed down, but we can infer it through an analogy with knowability. Plato obviously has the truth aspect of the Greek concept of being in mind, just as he is following the ontological connotations of the concept of ἀρετή. The axiological, ontological, and epistemological aspects can thus converge in the basic conception of the determination of the indeterminate through unity as determining. It can rightly be said that with the theory of principles, Plato largely anticipated and at the same time justified the thesis of the conversion of the later doctrine of transcendentals—*ens, unum, bonum, verum convertuntur.*[63]

One additional note on the power of thought in the soul, which is also grounded in the good and is related to the latter according to the principle that the equal ought to be known through the equal. The *Timaeus* already shows that the soul that has reason is mixed and numerically structured according to the divisible and the *indivisible*, i.e., unity, as well as according to difference and *identity*. The justification through the theory of principles results from the derivation according to these categories. The unwritten doctrine adds that noetic-intuitive cognition proceeds unitarily and holistically insofar as it is subordinated to unity—in contrast to the dynamic structure of discursivity.[64]

Having said as much, one can easily understand that unity as the determining ground of being *qua* being determined, cannot itself be a being, but must rather stand "beyond being and beingness" [*jenseits des Seins und der Seinsheit*], as it is stated in the *Republic*[65]—a perfect case of dialectical priority and posteriority (together with an allusion that is striking to the insider: Ἄπολλον, "*Apollon*," the surprised interlocutor answers,[66] which can also be understood etymologically as not-many, i.e., one, according to the Pythagorean symbolization of unity through Apollo). Furthermore, it becomes clear why the idea of the good can blind the eye, just as the sun can blind the eye when looking directly at it:[67] it is very difficult to conceive of pure unity as lacking parts, and at the same time as thinkable as intuition.

At this point, I have to refrain from inferring consequences from the *Republic* concerning the preceding dialogues, such as the *Phaedo* and the *Symposium*. I think Reale's interpretations are correct in this regard.[68] (Concerning the *Symposium*, I am referring to an as of yet unpublished contribution by Reale, which goes far beyond my own interpretation here.)[69] Meanwhile, it should be clear by now that, overall, the written and the unwritten doctrine for Plato stand in a relationship of implication and explication that is comparable to the relationship of *Realphilosophie* and logic in Hegel.

POSTSCRIPT: ON THE HISTORY AND RESEARCH OF PLATO'S UNWRITTEN DOCTRINE

The testimonies of the unwritten doctrines (ἄγραφα δόγματα) of Plato have been collected in Gaiser 1968 (443–557). An extended and annotated bilingual edition was for the most part completed by Gaiser in 1988; I provided additional editing of the collection, which appears in Krämer 1982 and Krämer 1990. An almost complete bilingual edition (Greek and French) is included in Richard 1986 (243–381). Selections are provided in Findlay (1974, 413–454) (English translation with a brief commentary) and Krämer 1982 (370–417) (Greek and Italian), and respectively in the English edition, Krämer 1990 (199–217) (English translation). A critical edition of the testimonies is to be published as volume VIII of the *Supplementum Platonicum* that was founded by K. Gaiser and is expected to encompass nine volumes to be edited by Th. A. Szlezák. The more important research literature up to 1990 is documented in Krämer (1990, 287–300). While the unwritten doctrines have been developed further in the Old Academy (by Plato's students), and more or less combined with the dialogues, their tradition remained intact during the Hellenistic age only in doxographic form, primarily in Peripatetic sources. Middle Platonism and Neoplatonism included this doxographic tradition in (allegorical) interpretations of the dialogues such that they created a fusion with it, and it could no longer be recognized in its specificity. Modern interpretations of Plato that have asserted themselves since the seventeenth century have increasingly dismissed the Neoplatonic tradition that operates according to the hermeneutical slogan *sola scriptura*, but did not appropriately acknowledge the indirect tradition, especially since the investigation of the "inner form" of the Platonic dialogues by Schleiermacher. Around the middle of the nineteenth century, after the first collections of testimonies by Chr. A. Brandis (1823) and A. Trendelenburg (1826), back-dating [*Spätdatierung*] came into existence and became prominent for more than half a century ("Altersvorlesung": K. F. Hermann, E. Zeller). The extensive collection and commentary of the testimonies by Robin (1908), or the philosophical and mathematical analyses by Stenzel (1924), W. D. Ross, O. Toeplitz, M. Gentile (1930), and Wilpert (1949), presuppose that the indirect tradition belongs to the late phase of Plato's philosophy. First Gomperz and then independently I raised objections (Krämer 1959) to this, as did J. N. Findlay, who presupposes a double track of literary production and unwritten doctrine in Plato. Because both strains of the tradition need to be systematically brought into relation, and because the dialogues need to be read anew in this light, Giovanni Reale has diagnosed a paradigm change within Plato research, which, after the Neoplatonic and Romantic, led to a third model in Platonic studies (Reale 1994; Reale 1993). Meanwhile, a critique of transmission [*Überlieferungskritik*] that was presented by H. Cherniss (Cherniss 1945) and his circle of students called into question the authenticity of the unwritten doctrine. Their work became prominent in Anglo-American and in part also in continental scholarship. However, it seems that this direction, which itself has been submitted to a metacritical analysis by W. D. Ross, C. J. de Vogel, H. J. Krämer, et al., became recently less influential, including the United States, where it originated. In contrast, the referential character of the dialogues, and their pointing toward an unwritten doctrine, has been further uncovered and discussed during the last decades, especially in the works of Szlezák (1985), Szlezák (1993), and Reale (1993). After Gaiser, the mathematical presuppositions and aspects have been again the object of detailed debate (by Annas [1976]; by Duranti in several works, most recently: Duranti [1994]; by Hösle [1994]; Cattanei [1996]; also, cf. the proceedings of the VIth Symposium Aristotelicum [1984]; Graeser [1987], and Napolitano Valditara [1988]). Bonagura (1991) analyzes the impact of the unwritten doctrine on the pedagogic considerations of Platonic philosophy, and Halfwassen (1992) draws out the consequences for the novel determination [*Neubestimmung*] of the relationship between ancient Platonism and Neoplatonism. Apart from the works already mentioned, the following are informative for a new determination of the function of literary work in Plato's practice of oral teaching: Schmalzriedt (1969); Gaiser (1984); Erler (1987). The further tasks of Plato research that would take the unwritten doctrines into consideration, might be the following: (1) further commentary on the dialogues in light of the inner-Academic teaching of Plato as assumed in the background of the dialogues; (2) conversely, commentary on the indirect transmission, primarily with an eye to Plato's literary work; and (3) further philosophical interpretation and investigation of particular topics that might be reformulated anew from a perspective of a more complete and unified image of Plato.

NOTES

1. Aristotle, *Phys.* Δ.2, 209b14f. = *TP* 54A.
2. Plato, *Phaedr.* 274B–278E.
3. Plato, *Ep.* VII 341B–344E.
4. Plato, *Phaedr.* 278C.
5. Plato, *Phaedr.* 276E2f. (cf. Plato, *Rep.* 376D, 501E).
6. Plato, *Phaedr.* 278D8.
7. Schleiermacher 1804.
8. Raible 1987–.
9. Assmann, Assmann, and Hardmeier 1983.
10. Gentili and Paioni 1985.
11. Assmann 1992.
12. Goody 1986; Ong 1982.
13. McLuhan 1964.
14. Postman 1985.
15. Hösle 1996.
16. Harder 1960, 57ff., 81ff., 98ff.
17. Havelock 1982, Havelock 1988.
18. Detienne 1988.
19. Kullmann and Reichel 1990.
20. Cf. the parallel development within Indian civilization: Hinüber 1996.

21. Harder 1960, 79.

22. Plato, *Phaedr.* 275A, 275D, 276D, 278A. Cf. the monograph by Thiel 1993 (following Derrida and converging with Havelock) concerning Plato's theory of recollection.

23. Schleiermacher 1804, 4, 25, etc.

24. Nietzsche 1913, 239–241. It is, however, not the case that Nietzsche anticipated the new program of Plato research that integrates the unwritten doctrine. Nietzsche does not mention an unwritten doctrine of Plato, i.e., the substantive difference between orality and writing. Accordingly, neither does he take into account the allusion to that which is "more valuable" (*Phaedr.* 278D). Zeller, for example, makes essentially the same claim as Nietzsche, i.e., that Plato's written works fulfill the function of helping one remember something after a preceding oral instruction (Zeller 1844, 485n.1).

25. The aesthetic and artistic qualities of dialogues such as the *Symposium* or the *Phaedrus* do not contradict the function of remembering; rather, they serve to enliven and deepen what is to be remembered. Thus, these qualities take on a special psychagogic task within the framework of the basic hypomnematic function. This is also true of the relationship between these qualities and the additional protreptic function of the Platonic writings (addressed above). This has recently been proven quite convincingly by Giovanni Reale for the *Symposium* (Reale 1996).

26. Gaiser 1959. Cf. Gadamer 1968.

27. Plato, *Prot.* 329Aff.; *Phaedr.* 275D, 276B, 276E, 277Ef.; *Ep.* VII 341C, 343Cf. 343E, 344B.

28. Plato, *Ep.* VII 344D9–E2.

29. Plato, *Phaedr.* 275E; *Ep.* VII 341E, 344C, 344D.

30. Plato, *Prot.* 356E8–357C1; *Meno* 76E3–77B1; *Phaedo* 107B4–10; *Rep.* 506D2–507A2, 509C1–11; *Parm.* 136D4–E3; *Soph.* 254B7–D3; *Polit.* 284D1f.; *Tim.* 28C, 48C, 53D; *Legg.* 894A.

31. Some efforts are being undertaken to resolve this "contradiction" by stating that, in truth, the unwritten doctrine is, after all, entailed by the dialogues (most recently, Sayre, Hitchcock, et al.). However, this is incompatible with Plato's own self-descriptions (*Phaedrus*; *Seventh Letter*) and the related references to what remains unsaid (see note 30). Nor is it consistent with the external testimonies about "*unwritten* doctrines," which substantively depart from the written texts. If there were indeed no substantive difference, then the controversy about the authenticity of the indirect tradition would be incomprehensible; furthermore, modern Plato research would have failed beyond imagination if it could not have deciphered the dialogues without drawing on the—allegedly not far-fetched—unwritten doctrine. (The fact that one now claims to be able to do so retrospectively and circularly based on—"concealed"—prior knowledge of the unwritten doctrine, obviously lacks the force of argument.) Finally, one needs to be aware that the Academic term of the so-called "unwritten doctrines" derives from the same Platonists for whom the dialogues were written for the sake of memory and in cases where someone needed to know whether or not there were unwritten doctrines of Plato, i.e., doctrines that were not approved for written remembrance. Furthermore, the fact that the oral teachings of Plato are transmitted in the past tense by those who report them

(in contrast to the present tense when citing the dialogues) once again underscores the substantive difference between both traditions (cf. Aristotle, *Met.* A.6 passim, A.9, 992a20f.; Δ.11, 1019a1f.; Λ.3, 1070a18f.; *NE* A.4, 1095a32f.; A.4, 1096a17f.). It is telling that not even Schleiermacher fully questioned the difference between both traditions.

32. Plato, *Phaedr.* 275E, 276A, 276C, 277A, 278C.

33. Aristotle, *Met.* A.6, 988a10–15.

34. Aristotle, *Met.* N.4, 1091b14f.

35. Theophrastus, *Met.* III, 6b11–15.

36. Aristotle, *NE* A.4, 1095a32f.

37. Cf. the *TP* 22B, 32, 39–42; 35B.

38. Plato, *Rep.* 509C.

39. Plato, *Rep.* 511B8.

40. Plato, *Rep.* 516A8f., 532A4.

41. The unlimited number of non-right-angled angles of geometry (*Rep.* 510C4f.), which Plato obviously summarizes as the acute and the obtuse, are indeed different from one another according to differences of more and less. Cf. Marković 1965, esp. 310ff., concerning the derivation of the acute angle from equality and unity and the other kinds of angles from the indefinite dyad of the large and small in the tradition following Plato.

42. Plato, *Rep.* 534Bf.

43. Plato, *Rep.* 531D, 537C. Cf. the proper interpretation in Gaiser 1986 (see chap. 4 of this volume).

44. Plato, *Rep.* 479Af., 523Cf., *Sophist* 255C. Concerning the prehistory cf. the *Dissoi Logoi* VS 90 c. 5, 1f., together with Plato, *Phaedr.* 263A; *Alcibiades I* 111B.

45. Plato, *Polit.* 284D1f.

46. *TP* 22B, 32, 43 (cf. 31).

47. Aristotle, *Met.* N.2, 1089a1f.

48. *TP* 50.

49. Aristotle, *Met.* A.9, 992a21f.; M.8, 1084b1.

50. Aristotle, *Met.* Γ.2, 1005a16f. and B.1, 995b20f.; cf. *Divisiones Aristoteleae* n. 65 *Cod. Marc.*, p. 64 Mutschmann.

51. Most important for Plato is the report in Aristotle's *Metaphysics* (Δ.11, 1019a1–4 = *TP* 33A; cf. also Aristotle, *NE* A.4, 1096a17–19; *TP* 22B, 23B, 32, 34); the relations of genus–species and part–whole are subsumed under ontological priority and posteriority (with examples), *Div. Arist.* Nr. 65 C. M. p. 64, 15ff. Mutschmann.

52. Aristotle, *NE* A.6, 1096a17–19.

53. Plato, *Rep.* 534Bf.

54. For more details on this subject, cf. Krämer 1966. Cf. also Krämer 1990, 102.

55. Plato, *Rep.* 504C9f., 506D3f.

56. Plato, *Rep.* 506E, 509C5f.

57. For example Plato, *Rep.* 443D, 500C, 506A, 540A (order); 422E, 423A, 423D, 443E1, 445C, 462Af., 551D, 554D, 560Af., 568D (unity).

58. Aristotle, *EE* A.8, 1218a16–23; Aristotle, *Protreptikos* frag. 5a Ross = B 33 Düring.

59. See note 58 above.

60. For example, *TP* 22B; 23B; cf. *TP* 32, §261.

61. Plato, *Rep*. 478B10f. (cf. 476A, 479A).

62. *TP* 34 = Aristotle, *Protreptikos* frag. 5a Ross = B 33 Düring.

63. The integration of the ideas of the bad, unjust, and so forth, only seems to create difficulties, because all ideas, such as non-being in the *Sophist*, are limited and existent. However, the idea of the bad, in contrast to those things that participate in it—and according to the differentiation into types (see above, note 52)—is not itself bad. In other words, unity implements itself in the intelligible world more forcefully than it does in perceivable reality. Primarily in the latter, however, there are differing degrees of being and goodness.

64. *TP* 25A = Aristotle, *DA* I.2, 404b22f.

65. Plato, *Rep*. 509B8f.

66. Plato, *Rep*. 509C1.

67. Plato, *Rep*. 516Af., 517C1, 532Bf.

68. Cf. Reale 1996, and in a more detailed form in Reale 1993, chaps. 5 and 7. The questioning of the hypothesis of ideas through an overarching hypothesis, which is alluded to in the *Phaedo* (101D), presupposes a two-step justification, which, on the one hand, refers to the good from 97Cf., and on the other hand, to the unwritten theory of principles.

69. Cf. note 68 above.

FOUR

PLATO'S SYNOPSIS OF THE MATHEMATICAL SCIENCES

Konrad Gaiser

This essay was presented at several occasions where there was an opportunity to convey the "Tübingen Plato interpretation" and discuss the question of how it should be represented.[1] Hence, here again we are pursuing the attempt to relate Plato's literary dialogues, which were intended for the public, to the "esoteric" doctrine that was present within the school. Furthermore, we will establish a connection between the students' testimonies about Plato's theory of the principles and the relevant allusions in the dialogues.[2] Most importantly, I want to draw on a particular and central Platonic motif in order to reevaluate and prove that there is a close connection between his literary statements and the testimonies concerning his oral doctrine.

The guiding question shall be that of determining in what sense Plato expects mathematics to provide a crucial aid for the cognition of ideas, especially cognition of the "idea of the good." This question is addressed in the *Republic*, yet it also touches upon the core of the "unwritten doctrine," because the "idea of the good" is the highest cause of all being. According to the accounts given by his students, Plato referred to this idea from a mathematical perspective as "the one."

Most of what Plato says about the imperative of mathematical studies for the philosopher has often enough been rightly interpreted and is generally familiar. However, it seems to me that what he says about a "synopsis" [*Zusammenschau*] of the mathematical sciences, which is supposed to be especially instructive for dialectic, needs further explanation.[3] I would like to try to analyze passages from the texts of the dialogues more precisely and completely than has been done so far in Tübingen and elsewhere.

1. PLATO'S DEVALUATION OF THE PRACTICAL UTILITY OF MATHEMATICS

When one is asked today what good mathematics serves, what first comes to mind is its eminent importance for natural science and technology. One might also mention that to become aware of the theoretical beauty of mathematical structures causes pleasure. During antiquity such practical interest was also more dominant. All of early mathematics prior to the Greeks—Babylonian and Egyptian—was oriented to purpose and application. Even the Greeks valued the science of numbers, geometry (i.e., "the art of land measurement"), and astronomy because of their importance for trade and transportation, architecture and underground engineering and other technical constructions, and creating calendars; naturally, music for them was primarily not a theoretical science.

However, already before the time of Plato mathematics approached the level of a theoretical science in two ways. On the one hand, it played an important role within religious speculative traditions, especially in the Pythagorean mathematical ideas that in part were kept concealed as mysterious wisdom. On the other hand, there were already Greek thinkers prior to Plato who carried out mathematical research and formulated some universal mathematical propositions—presumably Thales, who is credited with having discovered the proposition concerning a right angle inscribed in a semicircle, and this is certainly true of mathematicians such as Hippocrates of Chios and Theodorus of Cyrene. In Plato's case, both tendencies coincide: on the one hand mathematics was included in a comprehensive interpretation of the world, and on the other hand it was developed to the point of full scientific autonomy.[4]

What is new in Plato is a conscious reflection on the importance of mathematical sciences within the larger context of an interpretation of being [*Seinserklärung*] and approaching the question of how to lead one's life [*Lebensgestaltung*]. In particular, one must mention the conception, which was also firmly defended by later thinkers, that the proper value of mathematics does not lie in its practical utility but in its ability to lead thinking on the way to true knowledge.

Plutarch tells us that Plato even rejected the use of mechanical tools for solving geometrical-stereometric problems. Archytas, Eudoxus, and other mathematicians had constructed devices in order to solve the problem of doubling the cube (i.e., for the purpose of finding the cube root of a given magnitude). These devices made it possible to represent the curves of a higher degree by performing the required operation of rotation. Thus, Plutarch notes (*Vita Marcelli* 14, 5–6):

> However, since Plato grew reluctant and accused them of destroying and debasing geometry by directing it away from immaterial and theoretically knowable things toward sense-perceptible bodies and those that require a great deal of lowly manual labor, mechanics was removed from geometry and has since been despised by philosophy, and for a long time belonged to the domain of military techniques.

In a different place in Plutarch (*De genio Socratis* 7, 579B–D) we find a story about the Delians, who were told by the oracle that they and the other Greeks would be relieved from their current suffering if they doubled the altar of Apollo.[5] Plato allegedly told them:

> the god plays with the Greeks because they care too little for their education: he scorns our ignorance and demands from us that we do not just casually concern ourselves with geometry. . . . This task [the "Delian problem" of doubling the cube] will now be solved by Eudoxus of Cnidus or Helikon of Cyzicus. However, they should not believe that this is what the god desires; instead he commands all Greeks to refrain from participating in war and vice, and to dedicate themselves to serving the Muses and tempering their passions through the sciences, especially mathematics, and treat each other not in a harmful, but in a beneficial manner.

However, we do not need to depend on such late accounts in order to learn about Plato's opinion concerning the value of mathematics. Plato himself speaks explicitly about this issue in his dialogues, especially in books VI and VII of the *Republic* and book VII of the *Laws* (817E–822C). There he states that mathematics is necessary for education not so much for its practical use, but mainly because with its help it is possible to gain a deeper understanding of the reality around us, particularly concerning the movements of celestial phenomena, and it gives us access to the world of pure ideas.

Plato also mentions the effects of what we would call the "formal educational value" of mathematics: a general awakening, inspiration, and clarification of thinking.[6] Hence Plato was the first to call for training in the mathematical disciplines for all free citizens (in the *Laws*), and within the Platonic curriculum these μαθήματα (which initially meant nothing other than "objects of learning") become the "subjects of teaching" par excellence and the "mathematical" sciences necessary for every form of higher education.[7]

What is even more important for Plato is what the best philosophers gain through mathematical studies for the knowledge of being. It is possible to distinguish three functions: (a) through mathematics the soul is transformed and detached from the appearances of the sensible world and raised to supersensible, purely thinkable, spiritual, ideal objects; (b) the individual mathematical sciences elaborate structures that can serve as models for describing certain aspects of the structure of being; (c) the mathematical sciences enable a systematic synopsis, which is especially helpful for the cognition of all reality and the highest principles of being. Each of these functions will be discussed in turn; the third function, whose far-reaching importance has been discerned the least so far, will therefore be discussed in the most detail.

2. THE SOUL'S TURN TO TRUE BEING

In the well-known example from the *Meno* (80D–86C) of doubling the square, Plato wants to demonstrate that through mathematics the soul is made to recognize a supersensible truth. The human soul, Socrates explains in a myth, has already seen the ideal original forms of the order of being [*Urformen der Seinsordnung*] before entering its present corporeal life. This former knowledge has now been forgotten and covered up, but through a form of remembrance (ἀνάμνησις) this knowledge can be revived if we come into contact with those appearances that point beyond themselves to the reality that can only be grasped in thinking. Socrates regards the fact that the slave is able, in a number of steps, to identify the diagonal line of the original square as the sought-after side of the double of the square as proof that such knowledge has been acquired prior to his birth.

Indeed, this simple mathematical fact points to a supersensible truth, for the given ratio holds true not just for some square drawn in the sand, but for all squares that can possibly be conceived. When one is asked to state how long the diagonal is in relation to the side of the square, then one is directed beyond the world of sense perception. By that time it was well understood—and Plato alludes to this point in the *Meno*[8]—that the two magnitudes are incommensurable, i.e., that there is no common measure for them. This, however, can only be made intelligible through theoretical investigation; it can never be perceived through the senses.

Plato apparently regarded the fact that mathematical propositions can only be verified in thought, and that they are at the same time particularly evident and intersubjectively binding, to be a strong argument for the existence of supersensible "ideas." He repeatedly elucidates the essence of the idea through mathematical examples. In the *Phaedo* (74A–75D) he states that there is nothing that is absolutely the "same" in the domain of concrete, sensible, perceivable things: strictly speaking, sameness cannot be seen but only thought. In the *Republic* (VI, 510D–E) he states that the mathematician is not interested in the square that is drawn, but rather in the "square itself," the true, perfect square. However, "things themselves," which Plato refers to as "ideas," are similarly distinguished from visible things, namely, through a precision and perfection grasped only in thought. Moreover, in the *Seventh Letter* (343A–B), it is stated that every circle we draw will always merely represent the idea of the circle incompletely.

In the so-called "allegory of the line" in *Republic* (VI, 509D–511E), there are four domains of reality that are distinguished:

A. Ideas (with the idea of the good at the top)
B. The objects of mathematics (μαθηματικά)
C. Appearances (with the sun as the highest cause)
D. Copies of appearances (mirror images and shadows)

The lowest level, or the domain of mirror images and shadows, elucidates the mimetic relationship [*Abbildungsverhältnis*], which is said to be universal, in a particularly clear way: the μαθηματικά (B) are images as well, namely, of ideas (A); and the entire super-empirical world (A + B) relates to the sensuous world (C + D) as the original relates to the copy.[9]

Accordingly the position of the μαθηματικά is here presented as intermediary between ideas and appearances.[10] (a) The mathematician orients himself with the help of visible appearances, especially drawn figures; but concrete, visible figures are mere copies with respect to the true objects of mathematics. (b) On the other hand, the μαθηματικά are not the highest originals, but instead are themselves subject to the ideas. The philosophical dialectician traces the mathematical facts and basic presuppositions (ὑποθέσεις)[11] of the mathematical sciences back to ideas, and in the last instance to the idea of the good.

The allegory of the cave also gives an account of the domains from the allegory of the line, as Socrates makes clear in his interpretation (*Rep*. VII, 514A–521B; 532A–D).[12] The humans in the cave initially only see shadows on the wall: these are copies of appearances. When they are then freed from the chains and guided upward they see objects being carried: these are the appearances in their entirety. When a human exits the cave, he initially only sees mirror images and shadows of things in the light (516A): these are mainly mathematical objects. Only then he is able to see the things themselves on the ground and in the sky, and finally he sees the sun: these are the different ideas, with the idea of the good as the highest cause.

According to the allegory of the cave, the μαθηματικά therefore also mediate between appearances and the ideas; and the allegory makes particularly clear that because these μαθηματικά correspond to the mirror images and shadows of true things in daylight: they are copies of ideas.[13] This is why the mathematical sciences are capable of helping us acquire knowledge of the ideas. As is stated metaphorically again and again in the discussion of the individual mathematical disciplines and dialectic (521C–534E), they possess the power to "transform," "elevate," and "lift up" (μεταστρέφειν, περιάγειν, ἀνάγειν, ἕλκειν) one's soul from illusory images to the truth.

Mathematics can lift up or "purify" and "enliven" (572D–E) the knowing part of the soul because, even though its objects can be concretely visualized, its essence is not empirical or sensible and it can only be grasped in pure thought. Plato does not establish a fundamental difference between arithmetic, plane geometry, stereometry, and the other mathematical sciences, and those which are generally regarded as being directed toward empirical states (phenomena), i.e., astronomy and musicology. It is also supposed that the latter two sciences depart from empirical data, and that they acquire their theoretical insights [*Erkenntnisse*] in a purely theoretical way. Plato with all resolve postulates that the regularity of planetary movements and harmonic intervals rests on simple mathematical forms and proportions that cannot be measured empirically with any precision yet are still theoretically necessary and certain.

As indispensable as the μαθηματικά are on the path to acquiring knowledge, the mathematician does not yet reach the whole truth. Only the dialectician, whose gaze is directed at ideas and principles, can reach the truth. In light of the entire way in which knowledge is acquired, the mathematical sciences are no more and nothing less than a "prelude" (προοίμιον, 531D; 532D). According to the *Republic*, the value of mathematics lies precisely in the fact that, despite all of the exactitude and certitude of its knowledge, it seems to start with hypothetical presuppositions; thus, it points beyond itself toward the problem of a philosophical "ultimate justification [*Letztbegründung*]."

3. MATHEMATICAL STRUCTURAL MODELS OF ONTOLOGY

The mathematical sciences, however, do not just indicate the direction for philosophical thinking. For if the μαθηματικά provide images of the world of ideas, then the structures that mathematicians study must therefore be instructive for the knowledge of being. Thus the Platonic dialogues sometimes state that mathematical laws serve as models for the description of the structure of being.

(a) The domain of numbers, which is the object of arithmetic, is constructed by multiplying the one, its decisive measure. The investigation of the eventual transition from oneness to an indefinite multiplicity is also the task of philosophical dialectic, as Plato shows most explicitly in the *Philebus* (14C–18D).

(b) The properties of regular and irregular plane and solid figures, which are the objects of plane geometry and stereometry, respectively, also have ontological meaning for Plato. The five regular solids that were theoretically constructed and completely investigated by Theaetetus from the perspective of Plato's system are also called the "Platonic solids." This is because, in all material things, matter is reduced to atomic tetrahedrons (pyramids), octahedrons, icosahedrons, and hexahedrons (cubes), while the dodecahedron is associated with the form of the cosmos (*Tim.* 53C–56C).

In the *Laws* (VII, 819D–820C), plane geometry and stereometry are presented in terms of measurable and immeasurable. At the same time the difference between commensurability and incommensurability (or rational and irrational magnitudes) is still understood within the framework of the dimensions (plane lines and solid lines).[14] The different kinds of non-rational magnitudes can be classified and systematized in relation to those that are rational. In the system of irrational lines, which was theoretically elaborated by Theaetetus, Plato saw a model for clarifying ontological relations: the participation and separation (μέθεξις and χωρισμός) between ideas and appearances.[15]

(c) In book VII of the *Republic* (529D) Plato states that astronomy determines the temporal and spatial proportions of the planetary movements (speeds and paths of motion), while music theory investigates the numerical system of harmonic intervals (531C). As he does in the final myth of the dialogue (X, 617B), Plato here alludes to a close connection between astronomical and musical proportions in the sense of the Pythagorean "harmony of the spheres"; but he looked for the ground of this connection in the structure of the world-soul and the order of the world of ideas.

4. THE SYNOPSIS OF THE MATHEMATICAL SCIENCES IN THE DIALOGUES

4.1 The problem

Although Plato does not elaborate the ontological meaning of particular mathematical structures in the *Republic*, he does clarify what is decisive as a point of transition from the mathematical sciences to the dialectic of ideas. He mentions a summary or synopsis of the μαθηματικά twice, but only after such a summary has been undertaken will it be certain that mathematical studies are valuable for the philosopher.

In the first passage (VII, 531C–D), Socrates explains that the study of concordant numbers (in harmonic intervals) is instrumental in searching for the beautiful and the good (πρὸς τὴν τοῦ καλοῦ τε καὶ ἀγαθοῦ ζήτησιν). He adds:

> "[I]f the inquiry [μέθοδος] into all the things we have gone through [= arithmetic, plane geometry, stereometry, astronomy, music theory] arrives at their community and relationship with one another [ἐπὶ τὴν ἀλλήλων κοινωνίαν . . . καὶ συγγένειαν], and draws conclusions [ἐὰν . . . συλλογισθῇ] as to how they are akin to one another [ᾗ ἐστὶν ἀλλήλοις οἰκεῖα], then the concern with them contributes something to what we want, and is not a labor without profit, but otherwise it is." (Trans. Bloom)

The second passage (VII, 537B–C) is a description of the curriculum [*Bildungsganges*] that is supposed to lead the most talented guardians of the state to the highest knowledge:

> "Then, after this time," I said, "Those among the twenty-year-olds who are given preference will receive greater honors than the others. And the various studies acquired without any particular order [χύδεν] by the children in their education must be integrated [συνακτέον] into an overview [σύνοψιν] which reveals the kinship of these studies with one another [οἰκειότητός τε ἀλλήλων τῶν μαθημάτων] and with the nature of that which *is* [καὶ τῆς τοῦ ὄντος φύσεως].
>
> "At least, only such study," he said, "remains fast [βέβαιος] in those who receive it."
>
> "And it is the greatest test," I said, "of the nature that is dialectical and the one that is not [διαλκεκτικῆς φύσεως καὶ μή]. For the man who is capable of an overview is dialectical while the one who isn't, is not [ὁ μὲν γὰρ συνοπτικὸς διαλεκτικός, ὁ δὲ μὴ οὔ]."

Until they are thirty, i.e., for ten years, those who are chosen because of their talent are supposed to engage in the synoptic summary of the mathematical sciences and the whole order of being. After that they ought to engage in the dialectic of ideas for five years. The long time invested in mathematical synopsis already shows how important the latter is for philosophical education.

Admittedly, the demand for a synoptic vision is still rather vague in terms of content. It remains open as to what the "similarity," "relationship," and "affinity" among the μαθηματικά consists in. Thus it is difficult to understand what is supposed to be "subsumed," "theoretically related," and "brought into synopsis," and to what end.

In their own way, Neoplatonic interpreters intensively attempted to fulfill Plato's demand of a *mathesis universalis*, as is documented in Iamblichus' book on the κοινὴ ἐπιστήμη of mathematics (*De comm. math. sc.*, esp. chaps.

3–5, cf. 12–20) and in Proclus' commentary on Euclid (*In Eucl.* 7.15–10.14). They both state that what is "common" consists of general opposites, such as equality and inequality, which appear in all of the mathematical sciences and are interpreted as manifestations of the most general principles of being. For our present purpose I will ignore these ancient interpretations in order to avoid being dependent upon Neoplatonic systematization.

Modern interpreters have only rarely taken up or attempted to solve this problem. Most of the work dealing with mathematics and dialectic in Plato, including the most recent, does not pursue the question of the "commonality [*Gemeinsamkeit*]" that is supposed to connect all of the μαθηματικά to one another and to the "nature of being." It seems to me that this is why Plato's remarks on the "idea of the good" in these works remain opaque and enigmatic, or else exposed to arbitrary modern interpretations.[16]

Some interpreters have at least provided important insights for understanding the synopsis of the mathematical sciences: it has been convincingly shown (especially by F. M. Cornford, 1932) that the common ground of the μαθηματικά rests on a certain unity [*Einheitlichkeit*], and that this points to the idea of the good as the highest unity. The good can therefore also be understood as unity, because unity is the ground of "order" (and thus of the well-formed [*Gut-Beschaffenem*]).[17] H. J. Krämer has advanced the furthest, as is shown in his article "Über den Zusammenhang von Prinzipienlehre und Dialektik bei Platon" ["On the Connection between the Doctrine of Principles and Dialectic in Plato" (1966)], where he writes:[18]

> What are these terms, κοινά and οἰκεῖα, according to which the μαθηματικά relate to one another? One could think of some of the highest kinds, such as even-uneven, equal-unequal, similar-dissimilar, which mediate between mathematical beings [*Wesenheiten*] and principles. However, a different interpretation seems more plausible. According to the teachings within the Academy, the different domains of mathematical beings relate to one another through the analogy of composition [*Aufbau*]. . . . Each domain is composed of a specific, monadic, and basic element. Such separate elements and measures (στοιχεῖα and μέτρα) . . . are, for example, μονάς for numbers, the indivisible line for the forms of extension, the movement of a circle for motion, the quarter tone for music, and the moment (νῦν) for time. . . . Hence, from this perspective the transition from beings to the ground of being appears to be an abstraction that moves beyond all individual "monads" and "magnitudes" and is a pure grasping of the original-monad, the original-element, and the original-magnitude.

Apart from the uncertainty as to whether or not we are dealing with the most general pairs of opposites or instead analogically connected and elementary units of measure, one aspect of Krämer's interpretation, which overall I take to be correct, remains problematic: his interpretation is primarily based on testimonies from Plato's oral doctrine, i.e., testimonies whose relevance for the *Republic* can be doubted either because it is possible to place them at a later stage in Plato's development, or because one could raise doubts concerning their authenticity.

It seems to me that one must first interpret this data in the context of the two passages I have already referred to, i.e., the discussions concerning mathematics and ontology from the *Republic*. Parallel passages from later works (the *Laws* and the *Epinomis*) may then prove helpful for corroboration and specification.

My interpretation of the text will attempt to bring together and create a "unified vision," so to speak, based on connections in the text of the dialogue that Plato does not explicitly relate to one another. Thus, I presuppose that the Platonic text contains unexpressed systematic relations that the reader may discover by pursuing the author's allusions. If one does not want to give up on the possibility of a meaningful interpretation altogether, then I do not see any other method. The resultant common ground of the μαθηματικά may seem all too trivial and simple, yet this impression only arises if one ignores the fact that what is most essential is not contained in simple expressions, but rather in the abundance of insight that such expressions entail. The idea, which is obviously a misconception, that these simple statements can communicate the subject matter itself is the reason why Plato avoids making such statements in his written work, while nevertheless employing them in oral conversations on the systematic theory of principles. An interpretation of the relevant passages in the dialogues will necessarily lead us to testimonies concerning the theory of principles that Plato discussed orally.

4.2 Republic

If I am not mistaken, while presenting the schema of the line and providing details about the particular mathematical sciences in the *Republic*, Plato makes hidden remarks about essential characteristics [*Wesenszüge*] that can be grasped synoptically. Taken together, they also reveal something about the common ground of reality as a whole. What the μαθηματικά share in common is revealed along two lines:

(a) On the one hand, the relationship between the mathematical sciences (or their objects) exhibits an internal connection, a systematic order.

(b) On the other hand, the simplest presuppositions of the mathematical sciences reveal a tension that is created through the opposition between a moment of unity and a moment of disunity.

The systematic interconnection of the mathematical sciences is emphasized when Socrates emphatically insists that it is necessary to situate stereometry between geometry, which deals with lines and planes, and astronomy (VII, 528B–C). Saying that this arrangement is necessary is justified because arithmetic, which deals with non-spatial numbers, is followed by the dimensional space of plane geometry (the domain of the linear-plane), the latter of which is followed by stereometry (the domain of the three-dimensional solid), which in turn is followed by astronomy and music theory as sciences that deal with the (visible and audible) movements of bodies. The principle of their configuration is consistently the same: a constant progression from the simple, unextended, and limited, to the spatially extended, multiple, and changing. The totality of the μαθηματικά can be seen together or "synopsized" [*zusammenschauen*] from this perspective. At the same time, a "synopsization [*Zusammengehörigkeit*] with the nature of being" emerges as well, for the entire structure of reality exhibits a gradation that is analogous to the mathematical sequence of dimensions (number–line–plane–solid) because it stretches from the non-spatial ideas through an intermediary domain (the soul's) down to multiple and moving corporeal things.[19] Hence the dialectician can conceive of the systematic connection among the μαθηματικά that is determined by the order of dimensions as a model for the entire order of being.

The basic opposition, which we have tentatively referred to by using the concepts of "unity" and "disunity," displays different grades when describing the mathematical sciences. These different *modi* of unity and disunity can be depicted as follows:

"unity"	"disunity"
equal (ἴσον)	unequal (ἄνισον)
similar (ὅμοιον)	dissimilar (ἀνόμοιον)
identical (ταὐτόν)	different (ἕτερον)
mean (μέσον)	more-or-less
indivisible, whole	divisible
consistency (σύμμετρον, σύμφωνον)	inconsistency

In the allegory of the line (*Rep.* VI, 510C) the following examples of basic mathematical presuppositions (ὑποθέσεις) are listed: the odd and the even (τὸ περιττὸν καὶ τὸ ἄρτιον), figures (τὰ σχήματα), the three types of angle (right, acute, and obtuse), "and whatever else is related to them in every investigation."

When discussing even and odd numbers, Plato presupposes the Pythagoreans' structural conception of numbers, according to which uneven numbers are constructed evenly in a straight line, whereas even numbers are constructed unevenly.[20] If one regards numbers as lines of points that are each distributed on two sides (in the form of the gnomon), this results in equal sides for the uneven numbers. When we continue to apply the gnomon we get squares (according to the proposition that the sum of uneven numbers is always a square number). In the case of even numbers, however, we get unequal sides and finally varying rectangles (according to the proposition that the sum of even numbers can never be a square number).

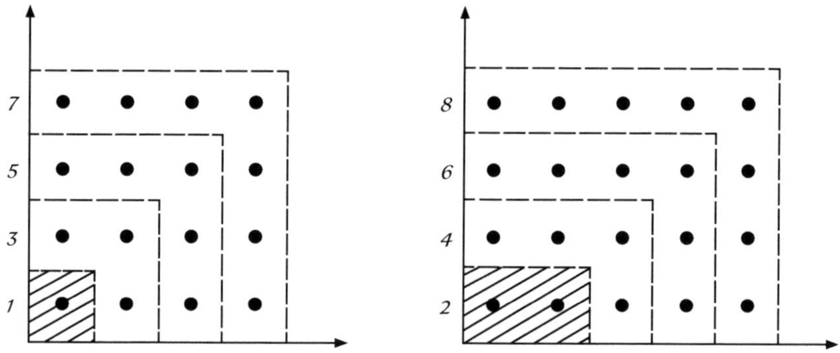

In the case of (planimetric and stereometric) figures, it is true by analogy that their major differences result from the opposition between unity and disunity. One may think, for instance, about the opposition between the form of the circle and the infinitely many possible rectilinear shapes into which it can be inscribed as its limit (triangle, quadrangle, etc.), or between equal sides and figures (infinitely many in appearance) with unequal sides, or the infinite variety of curves that are neither circular nor rectilinear.

Finally, the three kinds of angles are particularly good examples of these contraries, because the right angle is always equal and in the middle, while the acute and obtuse angles diverge from it in the infinite multiplicity of the greater and the less.

The corresponding kinds of opposites appear in book VII of the *Republic* during the discussion of the individual mathematical sciences: forms of unity (equality, consistency), which are contrasted to the appearances of disunity (inequality, inconsistency).

In the section on arithmetic (VII, 522C–526C) the mean is primarily contrasted to its deviations, which are relatively larger or smaller. This is followed by an explanation of how mathematics traces these relations from sense perception up to the domain of purely thinkable being. While in sense perception what is large is always also (relatively) small and what is small is always (relatively) large, i.e., it is two different things at the same time, thinking can distinguish clearly between large and small. Plato presupposes the possibility of an absolute measure or mean (or equality), and largeness and smallness as such, i.e., beyond perceivable things that appear only relatively larger or smaller. In terms of numbers, Plato then distinguishes between the countable concrete objects of the world of appearances, which are divisible and unequal, so that one thing is also, and pure mathematical unity (αὐτὸ τὸ ἕν), which is indivisible and equal (ἴσον) to every other mathematical unity.

The section on astronomy (528E–530C) describes faster and slower movements in definite temporal and spatial forms as the objects of this science. The true ratios, which cannot be derived from appearances, are supposed to exist in the "symmetry" of different movements. This may be the case either through equality (ἴσον) or in a numerically determined proportion, and also in the unchangeability of the orbits (ἀεὶ ὡσαύτως). The opposite of this symmetry and persistence consists in what cannot be accurately determined numerically: the irregular movements of visible celestial phenomena. Philosophically understood, the harmonies (530C–531C) determine the concordant and non-concordant numbers and the ground for their opposition.

This fundamental opposition shows itself, as the text shows, also in the "commonality" of the various sciences; it consists in the tension that can be characterized, among other ways, by the universal concepts of "unity" and "disunity" [*Einheitlichkeit und Uneinheitlichkeit*]. The general opposition between unity and non-unity [*Einheit und Nicht-Einheit*] corresponds to the basic presuppositions of the individual mathematical disciplines. This is also the case for the systematic order of the μαθηματικά, which corresponds to the progression of the dimensions and advances from the limiting (simple) to the multiply extended [*Vielfach-Ausgedehnten*].

Plato apparently assumed that the general tension of this relationship is not just an intelligible abstraction, but that in principle it grounds and causes different manifestations and occurrences. This also means that it is not the mere singling out of a more general opposition, but the study of the diverse and gradual transition from the dominance of unity (proportionality) to the dominance of disunity (disproportionality), in which such fundamental tension becomes manifest.

Hence we reach the conclusion that Plato's demand for a synoptic summary of what the μαθηματικά and the order of being have in common is aimed at the basic opposition between unity and indefinite multiplicity, which constitutes the whole system of the μαθηματικά and the structures in the individual mathematical sciences, as well as reality at large (from corporeal appearances to the ideas).

4.3 The Structure of the World-Soul in the Timaeus

Part of the synopsis of the μαθηματικά put forth in the *Republic* can be found, as it seems, in the later *Timaeus*. The world-soul is characterized as a mathematical structure in a passage that has always been regarded as opaque and difficult (35A–36D). The difficulty consists primarily in the fact that the arithmetical and geometrical as well as the musicological and astronomical proportions are said to be located in the structure of the soul. We can assume that the numbers are being referred to as the "indivisible and always self-identical Being," which is opposed to the corporeal-extended, divisible form of Being. The domain of linear-planes mediates between those two. The sequence of the first even number (2) and the first uneven number (3) to the third power (1–2–4–8 and 1–3–9–27) needs to be understood in terms of a spatial structure that does not extend beyond the third dimension. In this context, Plato performs a classification according to the numerical ratios of musical intervals; and all this is supposed to serve as an explanation of the celestial movements.

I think that the Platonic meaning for this peculiar characterization of the world-soul lies in the summary of the different mathematical orders.[21] Plato also focuses here on the common ground and inner agreement of the mathematical sciences. What is common to them is manifest in the basic opposition between unity and disunity: on the one hand, there is identity, indivisibility, sameness (of proportions, parts and intervals), and unity. On the other hand, there is diversity, divisibility, relatively more and less, inequality, and irregularity. Here, too, their commonality consists in the collaboration of a structuring principle of uniform organization and an opposing principle of formless extension.

Of course in the *Timaeus* a synopsis is not mentioned, for the intention is not to bring together the initially divided mathematical disciplines, but rather to bring about their differentiation based on a uniform and unified vision [*einheitliche Gesamtschau*]. Such a holistic vision guides the divine demiurge, which, keeping in mind the order of the world of ideas, constructs the cosmos with the world-soul at its center. Human cognition approaches the μαθηματικά, which are grounded in the order of being, from the opposite direction, i.e., through the synoptic summary of its different manifestations [*Ausprägungen*].

That the μαθηματικά are contained in the soul (of the cosmos and thus also of the individual human being) is, in accordance with the fundamental presuppositions of the Platonic ontology, as reasonable and necessary as is the soul's being an intermediary domain between ideas and bodily appearances as the realm of μαθηματικά.[22] Apparently Plato's conception as it is expressed in the *Timaeus* is that the soul and all of the μαθηματικά within it analogically reproduce the structure of the whole in concentrated form through a step-by-step transition from the unitary to the polymorphous and amorphous.

4.4 Laws XII

The "synopsis" of the mathematical sciences is explicitly mentioned again in Plato's later work. He states in an illuminating passage from book XII of the *Laws* (967D–E) that the philosophical and religious education of the statesman must combine the following:

(1) the insight "that the soul is the oldest [most original] of all things that partake of generation, and is immortal, and rules over all bodies," (trans. Bury)

(2) the insight that a divine reason of the world (νοῦς τῶν ὄντων) presides over the regular motions of celestial bodies,

(3) the acquisition of the "necessary objects of learning that precede these (insights)" (μαθήματα = arithmetic, geometry, astronomy, harmonics),

(4) that one gives a synopsis of that which, according to the Muse, represents what these (mathematical teachings) have in common (τά τε κατὰ τὴν Μοῦσαν τούτοις τῆς κοινωνίας συνθεασάμενος),

(5) that, afterwards, the latter is applied in a corresponding manner (συναρμοττόντως) to the institutions and laws (τὰ τῶν ἠθῶν ἐπιτηδεύματα καὶ νόμιμα) concerning the right way to lead one's life, and

(6) that for everything for which there is an explanatory justification one can give an explanation thereof.

Without a doubt, what Plato means by the phrase "necessary μαθήματα" are the mathematical sciences that we know from the *Republic*, whose "necessity" is emphasized in book VII of the *Laws* (817E–822C), and where a "synthesis" is called for that is supposed to synoptically synthesize what is common to those sciences. The "muse" who is supposed to play an important part in this synthesis most likely represents the universally true proportions that are the basis for the harmonies in music. Their universality also contributes to the required "synopsis" of "the common ground."[23]

Philosophical dialectic and the ideas, including the idea of the good, are not mentioned here, which is justified insofar as the *Laws* is an intentionally exoteric work directed toward the political public even more so than the other dialogues, and at no point explicitly deals with philosophical justification, which would lead to transcendence. But here dialectic, which ascends from the synopsis of the μαθηματικά to the idea of the good, is clearly in the background. Prior to the passage above, it is explicitly stated (XII, 960B5–966B) that the more exact education of the philosopher, which belongs to the "Nocturnal Council," has a particular purpose: that of unity within the multiplicity of the beautiful and the good, which can be known through a comprehensive synopsis, the one ἀρετή in its different manifestations. It has also already been remarked that, due to this final synopsis of the politician, the practical as well as the theoretical and instructive mediation of the good can be achieved. In the passage cited above, this fact is apparently recapitulated, whereby a necessary relationship between the synopsis of the μαθηματικά (4), ethico-political action (5), and its acquittal (6) is asserted: the politician is supposed to set up concrete rules for living based on and according to this synopsis, and should provide as good a justification as possible for those rules. This effect of the synopsis is only reached if it leads to an understanding of moral norms and ultimately to an understanding of the idea of the good as the absolute normative cause [*Ursache*]. Furthermore, this understanding is only ensured when its knowledge is reached through the logos of dialectic that allows for instructive communication.

4.5 The Epinomis *of Philippus of Opus*

The synopsis of the μαθηματικά, which is only touched upon in book XII of the *Laws*, is discussed in the *Epinomis* in more detail. This "addendum to the laws" derives from Plato's student Philippus of Opus, who edited the *Laws* after Plato's death. In the book that Philippus himself added, he attempts to answer the question concerning the highest philosophical knowledge and the way to reach that goal, at least to the extent that this is possible given the literary form; and it is precisely this question that Plato does not answer in the *Laws*. While the leading scholars today assume that Philippus rejected Plato's doctrine of ideas and defended his own views,[24] I think that he essentially tried to clarify what Plato himself all too briefly alludes to in the dialogues, including the *Laws*. According to this interpretation, Philippus explicates in more detail what Plato otherwise only spelled out through oral communication.[25]

The section in the final part of the *Epinomis* (990C–992A), which has often been commented upon because of its difficulty,[26] starts with an overview of the mathematical sciences and ends with the demand for a unitary synopsis of these sciences; this passage may be translated as follows:[27]

> "For this reason [= to prepare talented young people for the knowledge of the celestial order] we need the mathematical sciences."
>
> I. *The mathematical sciences and the structure of being* [φύσις]
>
> 1. *Arithmetic*
>
> The most important and first science is that of numbers themselves; not of those numbers that are corporeal [= those present in concrete things], but of the whole origin and potential [δύναμις] of the odd and the even, and the greatness of their influence on the nature [φύσις] of being.
>
> 2. *Geometry (plane geometry)*
>
> When one has learned this, there comes next what they call by the very ridiculous name of "geometry" [the art of land-measuring], when it proves to be a manifest likening of numbers that are not like one another by nature in respect of the province [the structural property] of planes; and this will be clearly seen by him who is able to understand it to be a marvel not of human, but of divine origin.
>
> 3. *Stereometry*
>
> And then, after that, the numbers thrice increased and like to the solid nature, and those again which have been made unlike, he likens by another art [τέχνη], namely, that which its adepts called stereometry.
>
> 4. *The order of the dimensions and music theory*
>
> And a divine and wondrous thing it is to those who envisage it and reflect, how the whole of nature [φύσις] is impressed with species and classes according to each analogy [proportion], as power [δύναμις]

[of unfolding] and its opposite [the power of division] continually turn on the double and its opposite.

Thus the first analogy is of the double in point of number [= the geometric mean], passing from one to two in order of counting [λόγος], and that which according to power [δύναμις] is double [2 : 4]; that which passes to the solid and tangible is likewise again double, having proceeded from one to eight [1 : 2 : 4 : 8].

Yet the [analogy] of the double has a double mean [= the arithmetic mean], as much more than the less as it is less than the greater, while its other mean [= the harmonic mean] exceeds and is exceeded by the same portion of the extremes themselves. Between six and twelve [=1 : 2, an octave] comes the whole-and-a-half [3 : 2] [= the fifth] and whole-and-a-third [4 : 3] [= the fourth]: turning between these very two [= 6 and 12], to one side or the other, this power assigned to men an accordant and proportioned use for the purpose of rhythm and harmony in their pastime, and has been assigned to the blessed dance of the Muses.

In this way then let all things come to pass, and so let them be.

5. *Astronomy*

But as to their crowning point, we must go to divine generation [γένεσις] and therewith the fairest and most divine of nature [φύσις] of visible things [= to the contemplation of the heavens], so far as the god granted vision of it [φύσις] to men; a vision that none of us may ever boast of having received at his leisure without the conditions [mathematical] here laid down.

II. *Dialectic*

1. *The elenchic method*

And besides these requirements, one must refer the particular thing to its [more general] generic form in various discussions, questioning and disproving what has been wrongly stated; for it is rightly found to be altogether the finest and first of tests for the use of men, while any that pretend to be tests, without being so, are the vainest of all labors.

2. *The cosmological hierarchy*

And further, we must mark the exactness of time, how exactly it completes all the processes of the heavens, in order that he who is convinced of the truth of the statement which has been made—that the soul is at once older and more divine than the body—might believe it a most admirable and satisfactory saying that all things are full of gods, and that we have never been disregarded in the least through any forgetfulness or neglect in our superiors.

3. *The basic summary*

And our view about all such matters must be that, if one conceives of each of them aright, it turns out a great boon to him who receives it in a right way [κατὰ τρόπον]; but failing this, he had better always call it a god. The way is this—for it is necessary to explain it thus far [ἀνάγκη γὰρ τό γε τοσοῦτον φράζειν]: every diagram, and system of number, and every combination of harmony, and the agreement [ὁμολογία] of the revolution of the stars must be made manifest [ἀναφανῆναι] as one through all [μίαν ἁπάντων] to him who learns in the proper way, and will be made manifest if, as we say, a man learns aright by keeping his gaze on unity [εἰς ἓν βλέπων]; for it will be manifest [φανήσεται] to us, as we reflect, that there is one bond [δεσμὸς εἷς] naturally uniting all these things: but if one goes about it in some other way, one must call it fortune [*den Zufall zu Hilfe rufen*], as we also put it.

For never, without these lessons, will any nature be happy [εὐδαίμων] in our cities; no, this is the way [τρόπος], this is the nurture [τροφή], these the studies [μαθήματα], whether difficult or easy, this the path to pursue.

The second main part, which I entitled "dialectic," suggests diverse methods and insights that belong together, insofar as they are supposed to allow for an understanding of the entire divine order of being beyond the mathematical sciences. That the transcendent ideas are not mentioned in this context needs to be interpreted in a different way than in the *Laws*: Philippus leaves out content that would go too far for a non-philosophical audience.

The elenchic method of generalizing and bringing together (from the individual to the general), which is demanded at the beginning (991C), should already be applied within the domain of mathematics.[28] The statement about useless methods of inquiry probably refers primarily to the attempt at establishing empirical certainty. Plato had already denied the value of such endeavors in the *Republic*, particularly for mathematics. But the method of "eidetic" summary is certainly intended to provide guidance for knowledge of the higher super-mathematical ideas and principles.

Then (991C–D) Philippus reminds the reader of the two main pillars of philosophical knowledge discussed in books X and XII of the *Laws*: insight into the primacy of the soul in relation to the physical domain, and into the primacy of the knowledge of the world's divine reason that becomes manifest in the exact structure of the celestial movements.

Finally (991D–992A), Philippus wants to "say at least that much" about the summary of all μαθηματικά as it is expressed in the propositions on the "one homology" and the "one bond." Apparently, he regards this statement as "necessary" insofar as the direction and aim of the philosophical path to knowledge should be somewhat clear and distinct. Like Plato, however, he confines himself to allusions that mostly indicate the path, rather than present and describe it.

Nevertheless, the *Epinomis* does reveal, more clearly than the passage in book XII of the *Laws* and even a little more clearly than the *Republic*, what is meant by the synopsis of the μαθηματικά. Initially, the overview of the mathematical sciences (990C–991B) accentuates the presuppositions for the synopsis in a stronger fashion. Here as well, arithmetic, plane geometry, stereometry, music theory, and astronomy are discussed, but they are discussed in a way that stresses their connection and common ground. This is the case (I) for the connection of the μαθηματικά to one another, (II) for the opposition between unity and disunity, and (III) for the agreement of the μαθηματικά and the order of being (φύσις) as a whole.

(I) As in the *Republic*, here arithmetic, plane geometry, and stereometry follow one another according to the sequence of dimensions (number–line–plane–solid).[29] This dimensional structure is related to the geometric proportion of numbers 1 : 2 : 4 : 8 (991A1–4). Music theory and astronomy necessarily follow these because their objects are sensibly perceivable, yet are knowable only in light of the structural laws from the preceding sciences. The entire system of the μαθηματικά is clearly characterized by the unfolding of the simple and non-spatial, to the extended in many dimensions and moving.

(II) The individual mathematical sciences are presented such that the basic presupposition of an opposing relationship between unity and infinite multiplicity (regularity and irregularity) comes into focus.

(a) Arithmetic deals with the difference between even and odd numbers in which (as was stated above) there is a conflict between unity and disunity.

(b) For plane geometry and stereometry the art of "making similar" figures (ὁμοίωσις) is supposed to be distinctive, i.e., particularly the transformation of a given rectangle into a square (Euclid, *Elem.* II 14), and more generally the fulfillment of the task that Euclid (*Elem.* VI 25) describes as "constructing a linear figure that is similar to another figure and at the same time equal to a different one." What is required for this is to discover the mean proportional line or geometric mean (Euclid, *Elem.* VI 13) as well as the method of the "application of areas" (Euclid, *Elem.* I 44–45). In each instance, what is most important for ὁμοίωσις is similarity as opposed to non-similarity and equality as opposed to non-equality (of plane and solid numbers).

(c) While the "geometric mean" plays an important role for spatial structure (especially for ὁμοίωσις), the other two analogies (proportions) are important for music theory: the "arithmetic mean" and the "harmonic mean." However, in all of these three proportions the contrast between unity and non-unity is revealed: proportionality means that the moment of unity dominates that of an indefinite more or less, namely, through the equality of its ratios or the distances between its parts, to which the non-symmetrical ratios between indefinite-relative larger and smaller magnitudes stand in contrast. The twofold (διπλάσιον) is generally said to have a normative meaning. The claim is that the "double" appears in the (numerically most simple) geometric proportions (1 : 2 : 4 : 8) as well as the arithmetic and harmonic means (6 : 8 : 9 : 12) at the ground of musical intervals. The general meaning of the "twofold" consists in the fact that the relationship 1 : 2 is the first and most simple case of the relation between unity and non-unity.[30]

If one looks at what is common in the presuppositions of the μαθηματικά being discussed, and if one summarizes this synoptically, then one becomes aware of the basic opposition between unity and disunity. As we have seen in light of the *Republic*, this commonality corresponds to the formative moment of the system of mathematical sciences as their succession is determined through the dimensional unfolding from that which is simple to that which is diverse and changing.

(III) As is briefly mentioned in the *Republic*, the synopsis of the μαθηματικά is also brought together in its connection to the "nature of being" in general (σύνοψιν οἰκειότητος . . . τῆς τοῦ ὄντος φύσεως VII, 537B–C). Similarly, the *Epinomis* emphasizes for each mathematical science the importance of the mathematical structures in the "nature"[31] of the divine order of being.

(a) Arithmetic is supposed to investigate numbers in light of their importance for the nature of being (πρὸς τὴν τοῦ ὄντος φύσιν 990C).

(b) Planimetric ὁμοίωσις—and, of course, the same holds for stereometric ὁμοίωσις as well—is called a "divine wonder" (θαῦμα θεῖον). This suggests that the "making similar" of what was initially dissimilar is not just a special mathematical operation, but that it also helps one to discern the process of formation everywhere within the domain of being, and the process of assimilating it to what has form.[32]

(c) Something "divine and wonderful" is supposed to become visible in the three analogies that are essential for the dimensional unfolding and in the harmonies and rhythms given by the Muses, namely, the geometric, arithmetic, and harmonic means. What is astonishing, it is said, is that the whole of nature shapes form and genus (εἶδος καὶ γένος ἀποτυποῦται πᾶσα ἡ φύσις) according to each of these proportions (καθ' ἑκάστην ἀναλογίαν). This probably refers to what is shown in the description of the world-soul in the *Timaeus* (see 4.2 above): that the world of ideas, which is structured according to the relationship between εἶδος and γένος, unfolds like an image according to the structuring effects of these proportions within the domain of the soul and of corporeal phenomena.

(d) Finally, we read that astronomy deals with the "most beautiful and divine φύσις" in the visible domain. Thus, the mathematical theory of celestial phenomena is supposed also to facilitate knowledge of the divine order of reality in general.

Philippus discusses, a little more clearly than Plato does in the *Republic*, what the results are for the synopsis of all of the μαθηματικά: the goal is to understand their internal agreement (ὁμολογία), which is supposed to come into theoretical focus as one unified and uniting bond (δεσμὸς εἷς).

Following the indications provided earlier in the text, this "one bond" is nothing other than the archetype of the opposition between unity and non-unity (or regularity and irregularity, determinacy and indeterminacy), which occurs in every mathematical domain. It is correct to call it "*one* bond" because the moment of unity is dominant compared to the moment of multiplicity, and it is a "one *bond*" because the tension between unity and multiplicity is included within it. In this "one bond," the opposition between unity and multiplicity is, so to speak, uniformly sublated [*einheitlich aufgehoben*].[33]

While ancient interpreters rightly understood the "one bond" as a comprehensive analogy (proportion) or as a comprehensive principle,[34] more recent interpreters conceive of it according to the mathematical theory of proportions.[35] To me the interpretation of the "one δεσμός" as proportion seems justified (because every proportion establishes unity amid difference), but only if one can rightly assume that Philippus, in following Plato, conceives of a single and all-inclusive proportion of being. This proportion needs to be of a supra-mathematical kind. No mathematical numerical relation, no mathematical analogy can be as comprehensive as the δεσμός envisaged by Philippus. Even the systematic theory of proportions cannot perform what the knowledge of this one δεσμός is supposed to achieve. Philippus makes the emphatic statement that one can reach the highest knowledge only on this path. Otherwise there will be no justified knowledge, but perhaps the help of a god. That the knowledge of the "one bond" is experienced as the "shining forth" [*Aufscheinen*] of truth reminds us of an intuition that suddenly gains comprehension after much effort. The claim that the path entered with the summary of the μαθηματικά would lead to human happiness and happiness of the polis (992A–B) primarily points toward a supramathematical principle. This can only be understood if the synopsis of the μαθηματικά here leads beyond the domain of the mathematical, as it does in the *Republic*, and the entire path points beyond the synopsis of what the mathematical sciences share in common to the idea of the good as its final destination. Εὐδαιμονία, after all, can be reached by no other knowledge than that of the good.

The connection between the μαθηματικά in the "one bond" is probably not the immediate vision and full knowledge of the idea of the good itself. However, the text of the *Epinomis* shows that with this synopsis one has already achieved a goal, which in turn opens up a sure vision of the good as the highest principle.

4.6 *From the Synopsis of the* Μαθηματικά *to the Knowledge of the Good*

Now that we have been able, hopefully, to extract from the *Republic* and the *Epinomis* what Plato means by the synopsis of the mathematical sciences, we have to pursue the question as to how this synopsis prepares one for knowledge of the absolute good.

As our interpretation shows, the synopsis of the μαθηματικά leads to a mutual fundamental opposition [*gemeinsamen Grundgegensatz*] between unity [*Einheitlichkeit*] and disunity. If it is the case, however, that the whole domain of ideas is reflected like an image in the domain of the μαθηματικά, then we can expect the synopsis of the mathematical realm to correspond to a possible complete vision of everything in a highest idea. However, this seems to suggest that the synopsis of the μαθηματικά, insofar as it is a universal comprehension of all things, ultimately leads to the idea of the good in which every opposition between unity and non-unity is wholly integrated.

Indeed, one can claim that the structural representation of the whole accomplished by mathematics decisively shows the dialectician the way toward the highest cause. Although the μαθηματικά only exhibit the structural relations of reality, and not its substantive richness, this reduction still provides the advantage of simplification and universal application. The structural model of mathematics allows for the inclusion of all domains of reality; all things—appearances in nature as well as the relations in the world of ideas—can be ordered and structured by means of mathematics. According to Plato, this is also the case for the classification of biological species in the medical analysis of health and illness, as well as for ethical-political laws. In Plato's description of the good and the non-good in the domain of ethical-political life, structures that can be mathematically formulated had a privileged role that can also be applied to the investigation of natural phenomena and the dialectic of ideas: the "value structure" of the correct mean, according to which the good is seen as the mean or equilibrium between excess and lack.[36] However, if the regularities and normative structures of the individual domains of experience and knowledge correspond to one another—which is particularly true in the case of mathematics—they can be summarized in light of a common primary structure and can ultimately be traced back to the idea of the good.

One can expect from the synopsis of the μαθηματικά that the idea of the good should be understood as absolute unity or—corresponding to the "one bond"—as the unity of unity and non-unity. But what sense does it make to understand the good as absolute "unity"? To make a long story short, Plato reaches this conclusion because he assumes that unity is the ground of regularity and order, and that order as the uniform structuring of the many warrants the efficacy of the good, i.e., perfection (ἀρετή), persistence (existence) [*Seiendheit*], and knowableness as well as the capacity to know.[37]

The fact that the idea of the good, understood as the highest unity, is confronted everywhere in reality by a principle of indefinite multiplicity, raises the dilemma that reality cannot be adequately explained monistically according to one principle, yet it cannot be explained dualistically either, because the dyadic principle raises questions concerning the ground of its coexistence and cooperation. Plato seems to have solved this most difficult problem of his own and probably every philosophy by accepting the principle of unity as the "unity of unity and multiplicity" [*Einheit von Einheit und Vielheit*].[38]

This dialectical solution to the problem of principles will not be discussed further at this point, especially since it transcends the possibilities of language and non-contradictory logic. However, at least the synopsis of the μαθηματικά sheds some light on this fundamental problem of Plato's dialectic. From the perspective of the μαθηματικά, the moment of "unity," and also that of "disunity," exhibits two aspects that should be considered together in each synopsis.

(a) Initially, "unity" stands in total opposition to non-unity or multiplicity. There does not seem to be any mediation between these opposing moments. On the other hand, however, the moment of unity as the ground of order and structure takes priority over that of indefinite multiplicity. Thus unity, in a way, is able to integrate the opposition between unity and multiplicity.

(b) "Non-unity" as extreme opposition is on the one hand negation, through which unity, order, balance, rationality are affected and destroyed; as the cause of differentiation, the moment of non-unity, on the other hand, is the condition for the possibility of unfolding, which for the most part allows for the wealth of complex expressions. Hence, within the succession of mathematical sciences, arithmetic, which deals with numbers that are basic for everything else, is the highest and most pure. On the other hand, astronomy, which deals with complex structures, seems to be more sophisticated and illuminating.

Thus, the way that leads through the synopsis of the μαθηματικά to the idea of the good exhibits two different yet complementary aspects. On the one hand, the ascent moves from the multiple and changing to the uniform and most simple: from moving appearances through the intermediary, the realm of souls and mathematical objects, to the ideas, and finally to absolute unity. On the other hand, this process should not be understood as a "simplification" or abstraction according to which increasingly less remains, but rather as a process of "thickening" [*Verdichtung*] in which increasingly more is integrated. The reverse way of descending then leads to the increasing dissolution and the loss of substantive content [*Seinsgehalts*], while it also leads to the rich differentiation of the fullness of being [*Seinsfülle*], which is included in the principles. At the stage of ultimate knowledge of the good itself, which is characterized in the *Seventh Letter* (341C–D) as a sudden illumination, the apparent difference of these aspects needs to enter into a unified vision of the whole.

5. ELABORATION WITHIN THE ACADEMY

Different testimonies show that Plato's school consistently elaborated what was only alluded to in the dialogues on mathematics as a model and testing ground of dialectic. Albeit exaggerating, Aristotle could thus rightly claim that for Plato and his disciples all of philosophy had turned into mathematics, although they claimed that one had to deal with it for other purposes (*Met.* A.9, 992a32–33). Mathematics was so useful for Plato's theory of ideas and principles because it made possible the systematic summary, i.e., the synoptic clarification of the tension of unity and multiplicity. In the school, this led to the attempt to understand the structure of the domain of ideas "more geometrico" as well, and to the conception of "ideal numbers" as the highest originary forms [*Urformen*] of reality, of the positive principle called "the one" and the opposite principle called the "indefinite dyad" or "great-and-small." Plato's program of reaching the highest unity by way of a synopsis of the mathematical sciences is the essential feature of Academic philosophy among his students and followers.[39]

Viewed by itself alone and presented as a formula, the result of the mathematical and primary-theoretical synopsis—the unity of unity and multiplicity—appears trivial and empty, or enigmatic and opaque. This is why Plato did not explicitly formulate this conclusion in the dialogues, but only pointed toward it. Plato states in the *Seventh Letter* (341E) that the schematic and simple concepts of the theory of principles would have evoked either contemptuous rejection or acceptance based on self-conceit. Within his circle of students he could carefully avoid misunderstandings, and clarify why the formulaic concepts of the theory of principles alone did not lead anywhere. Rather, the principles had to be understood as such, which meant that only he could grasp them who was able to trace their interaction, as well as their action in every particular object and in all realms of reality.

5.1 *Plato's Lecture* On the Good

At one point Plato spoke publicly about the connection of the mathematical sciences to the principle of the good: in the lecture *On the Good* (Περὶ τἀγαθοῦ), which has been discussed much recently. The fragmentary accounts of this lecture by the students show that Plato determined the good from the perspective of mathematical issues as "one" or as "the one." Thus, he must have discussed a synoptic summary of the μαθηματικά as it was laid out in the *Republic*, in book XII of the *Laws* and in the *Epinomis*, and became an important topic of scientific and dialectical investigation in the school.

Because Plato—for whatever reason[40]—lectured publicly, and because such lectures must have been incomprehensible without prior preparation within the school, the audience felt irritated and would leave disappointed. Aristoxenus informs us (*Harm.* II 30) that this fact was often recalled by Aristotle who, unlike Plato, would instruct his audience in advance about the method and aim of a lecture:

> Repeatedly Aristotle reported that most of those who heard Plato's lecture *On the Good* reacted in this way [that they got a false idea of the subject matter]. Everyone came with the idea that he would discover something about what is generally thought of as human "goods," such as wealth, health, physical strength, and all in all wonderful happiness. When the mathematical discussions started—on numbers, geometry, and astronomy—and ultimately the proposition that the good is one [καὶ τὸ πέρας ὅτι ἀγαθόν ἐστιν ἕν], it appeared to them, I think, as something absolutely unexpected and peculiar. Hence, some had no respect for the topic, and others rejected it openly.

After what we initially learned from the *Republic* regarding the synopsis of the μαθηματικά as a condition for the knowledge of the idea of the good, I think that we can imagine what Plato elaborated in the public lecture.

The unprepared and thus frustrated audience had apparently not read the *Republic*.

The *Epinomis*, which was written soon after Plato's death, presupposed this lecture, which Plato probably gave some years earlier. One can assume that Philippus took into account the Platonic lecture *On the Good* in his own condensed and self-contained passage on the mathematical sciences and their synopsis. I think that this text—rather than the individual allusions in Plato's dialogues as well as other, rather abbreviated accounts and testimonies of the students—presents us with a holistic conception of the content and the argument of the lecture. However, we need to add to what is said at the end in the *Epinomis* that the "one bond," which the synopsis of the μαθηματικά reveals, represents the highest degree of order and regularity, namely, the absolute good as the "one." Philippus follows Platonic principles also by not directly stating this in his literary work.

In any case, the severely abbreviated content of the lecture *On the Good* that has been passed down is extremely close to what has been said in the *Republic*, and again in the *Epinomis*, concerning the passage from the mathematical sciences to the knowledge of the highest cause. Most testimonies are derived from the Aristotelian work *On the Good*, which included a report of Plato's lecture.[41] They confirm with respect to Plato's lecture that which we have deduced from the dialogues in order to explain the synopsis of the μαθηματικά:

(a) The sequence of dimensions (number–line–plane–solid) appears as a structural model for the whole composition of being, especially for the structure of the soul (*TP* 9, fr. 3 Ross).

(b) Throughout reality there is a tension that manifests itself in a series of analogous oppositions, mainly those of equality and inequality (ἴσον/ἄνισον), similarity and dissimilarity (ὅμοιον/ἀνόμοιον), and sameness and difference (identity and diversity: ταὐτόν/ἕτερον) (fr. 2.5 Ross).

(c) This opposition is traced back to the primary opposition between unity and non-unity. The principle of unity, which shapes and limits and should be understood as the cause of the good, is called "the one" (τὸ ἕν), while the opposite principle is called the "indefinite dyad" (ἀόριστος δυάς) or "great-and-small" (μέγα καὶ μικρόν), because it causes multiplicity, extension, and relation (*TP* 3–8, fr. 2 Ross).

Thus, the preserved fragments from Aristotle's transcript reveal that Plato discussed in the oral doctrine precisely the issue that has only been alluded to with reservation in the literary works, and has been elaborated more explicitly within the academy, namely, the path from the mathematical sciences by means of their synoptic summary to the idea of the good. What has been transmitted from this central topic of Plato's theory of principles is mutually complementary and illuminating: the allusions in the literary dialogues, the content of the indirect transmission of Plato's lecture *On the Good*, and the inner-Academic dialogues and discussions.

5.2 Plato as the "architect" of mathematical research

If we are justified in trusting the accounts of Plato's collaboration with the mathematicians of his time, then the philosopher was not only the recipient but also a contributor. The question as to what Plato could have contributed to the development of mathematical sciences always raises difficulties for recent scholarship.[42] On the one hand, Plato apparently did not contribute mathematical research and discoveries of his own. On the other hand, it is well-known that very important mathematicians such as Eudoxus, Theaetetus, Menaechmus, and Theudius of Magnesia were present in Plato's Academy.[43] And, in a report from Aristotle's student Dicaearchus, we are told that as the "architect" of such research Plato assigned the mathematicians with the problems that they then pursued:[44]

> It was a great advance in the study of the mathematical sciences when Plato took up the lead as an architect and assigned the problems [ἀρχιτεκτονοῦντος καὶ προβλήματα διδόντος] that were at that time being rigorously investigated by the mathematicians. Hence for the first time mathematical research reached its peak with the [general] theory of proportions [*Maßtheorie*] and the problems of definitions, while Eudoxus completely renewed the original [ancient] attempts and approaches of Hippocrates [of Chios]. Geometry in particular was greatly advanced, for then the method of analysis as well as the determinations of possibility [διορισμοί] came into being. While great progress was made in the science of geometry, neither optics nor mechanics was neglected in any way. A group of freeloading corn-pickers [*körneraufpickenden Schmarotzern*] benefited themselves of the entire fruit of such labor; one could even say that there was a different sort of people from the school who collected their own private piece of the harvest.

This report and other related pieces of information[45] confront us with the following question: What did the mathematicians look for and what did they find in Plato? How should we conceive of his achievement "as an architect"? I believe that the answer is revealed according to what we have discovered concerning Plato's interest in a synoptic summary of the μαθηματικά.[46]

The more complete the mathematical rules that were investigated, and the more systematic the presuppositions that were discovered, the better mathematics could serve philosophical dialectic as a model and domain for establishing certainty. A synopsis could only be achieved if one could already assume common foundations. Thus Plato had to attach importance to the discovery of the elementary foundational presuppositions of individual mathematical sciences. He thus demanded the mathematicians to systematically order the complex structures and to reduce them to simple presuppositions: he demanded the axiomatization of the mathematical sciences. He was not just motivated by the intention to use the μαθηματικά as a model for the analysis of being but mainly by the philosophical conviction that reality as a whole was constituted on the basis of the most simple principles. Thus, a systematic order had to exist in the μαθηματικά (as a subset of reality) by way of ontological necessity.

We can assume that Plato's call for a systematic, definitional, and axiomatic extension of mathematics was not taken by specialists as a senseless or petty paternalism, but rather as an adequate program. This was all the more the case as Plato's expectation was being fulfilled: the systematization and axiomatization of the mathematical sciences quickly followed.

The conclusions for arithmetic and geometry have been included in the relevant books of Euclid's *Elements*:[47] Euclid's definitions, postulates, and axioms methodically and substantively correspond to the Platonic program, and there is general agreement that Euclid took over the preparatory work of the Platonic school.[48] Sources indicate[49] that astronomy also pursues what at that time was a successful reduction of phenomena to simple patterns. These investigations and results were also inspired by Plato: the system of homocentric spheres, which Eudoxus constructed in order to explain the planetary movements, corresponds to Plato's requirement for regular forms of movement, because all appearances are thereby reduced to circular orbits.[50] Based on the mathematical sciences, Plato's methodical program also influenced the research in the Academy in other domains as well: everywhere, one was looking for the structural connection in which the multiplicity of individual appearances is reduced to and deduced from as few regularities and basic presuppositions as possible. This is characteristic of scientific work to the present day.

NOTES

1. I would like to thank my colleagues and students at Tübingen, Herdecke, Braunschweig, Mainz, and Frankfurt for their valuable suggestions.

2. Recently, Thomas A. Szlezák proved the legitimacy and productivity of this hermeneutic approach in Szlezák 1985. Now also the important account by Giovanni Reale (1984) has been published.

3. Since my book, Gaiser 1963, the following important contributions concerning the importance of mathematics for Plato's philosophy (dialectic, the idea of

the good) have been published: Cross and Woozley 1964, esp. 196–228, 230–261; Hare 1965; Krämer 1966(2); Krämer 1972; Fritz 1969; Gosling 1973, 100–119; Ebert 1974, 132–208 (the idea of the good and mathematics); Böhme 1976; White 1976, 89–115; Annas 1981, 272–293; Wieland 1982; Graeser 1983, 151–157; Mittelstraß 1985.

4. Concerning Plato's place in the history of the sciences see Krafft 1971, 295–356. On the topic of praxis, theory, and related themes, see Burkert 1982.

5. All references to the story of the "Delian problem," which probably dates back to Eratosthenes of Cyrene, can be found in Swift Riginos 1976, 141–145.

6. Plato, *Rep.* 526B; *Laws* 819C.

7. In Proclus' "list of geometricians" (*In Eucl.* 65.15–21), Pythagoras is said to have made mathematics into an object of general education. This, however, attributes Platonic concerns to Pythagoras.

8. Gaiser 1964, esp. 257–360; Cosenza 1977, 221–231.

9. The relationship between domain B (μαθηματικά) and C (appearances) is not particularly clear. According to the required ratio these sections are of equal length, which is a fact that, admittedly, is not stated in the dialogue. The interpreters explain this issue differently. One group (including scholars such as Ross 1963, 45–46; Cross and Woozley 1964, 204) believes that Plato does not intend the equality of the middle sections, since there should be a selfsame continuous original–copy relationship. The other group (scholars such as Morrison 1977; Wieland 1982, 201–208) believes that the same magnitude for both sections is well justified: we are dealing with identical domains of objects, which, however, are the aim of different intentions (of the knowing subject) because they function sometimes as originals and sometimes as copies. The latter interpretation denies that domain B essentially includes the μαθηματικά, which are said only to be examples. Both of these interpretations are unsatisfactory. Wieland's conviction, according to which domain B corresponds to a certain activity of the soul that purposefully regards sensuous objects as copies, appears to be the least faithful to the text. Perhaps Fritz 1969, 55–60 has provided a clue to the solution of the problem when he was led, so to speak, to the spiritual constitution of the μαθηματικά through the comparison of the schema of the line and the stages of knowledge in the *Seventh Letter*. It seems to me that the equal length of both sections is meant to show that they do not share the same illustrated relationship that exists between the parts of the schema of line. Although Socrates repeatedly claims (510B, 510D, 510E, 511A) that the mathematicians use certain representations (e.g., drawings and modeled figures) as copies (εἰκόνες), this does not mean that appearances (C) are also created through the representation of the μαθηματικά (B), which is, however, the case with domain D as a copy of C, and domain B as a copy of A. The world of appearances (C) is substantively much richer than that of the ontological level of the μαθηματικά (B); and the visible forms (also those by which the mathematician orients himself) are not created by mathematical objects but by the soul, which mediates between the ideas and appearances (see 4.3 on the world-soul in the *Timaeus* and Gaiser 1963, 91–99). Hence the analogy of the schema of the line in my opinion excludes the ratio of B : C, because between A (ideas) and C (appearances) not only are there the μαθηματικά (B), but there is also the soul as a mediating domain; one that,

while including mathematical figures, cannot be reduced to the latter even if the discussion in the dialogue is limited to addressing mathematical objects.

10. Whether or not the μαθηματικά in the *Republic* possess a middle ontological position (Aristotle attributes this idea to Plato in *Met.* A.6, 987b14–18, among other places) is a controversial question that has been taken up again and again. Krämer reviews the discussion in Krämer 1966 (2), 45–53 (= 1972, 408–409, 420) Guthrie 1975, vol. 4, 342–345, 509–510, 523. Cross recently denies this μεταξύ-position of the μαθηματικά in the schema of the line, Cross and Woozley 1964, 233–238; White 1976 (see note 3 above), 109–110; Mohr 1981, 620–627; Wieland 1982, 212. Annas 1975 attempts to distinguish between the references to "intermediates" in the dialogues and the account given by Aristotle; she remarks (see note 3 above, Annas 1981, 251–273) concerning *Republic* VI–VII: "He has clearly not thought out this problem." In my opinion the criticisms of the interpretation of the section of line B in terms of the "intermediates" are not convincing. With "square itself" and "perimeter itself" (*Rep.* 510D) Socrates does not mean *a* form in the sense of the theory of ideas, but a form of supersensible precision. Accordingly, he seems to mean by *αὐτὸ τὸ ἕν* (*Rep.* 525D–E) the mathematical one, which occurs in infinitely many examples.

11. The concept of "hypothesis," which is used by Plato in different ways (cf. Robinson 1953, 93–179) is also interpreted to mean different things. Some interpreters think of elementary entities, i.e., objects (Hare 1965, 22–24; Fritz 1969, 101; Wieland 1982, 209; et al.), while others think of definitions and axiomatic propositions (e.g., Taylor 1967). Graeser 1983, 152–153 (see note 3 above), meanwhile, remains undecided. The examples used by Plato—uneven and even numbers, figures, the three angles—either show that such simple objects themselves are meant, or that the propositions concerning existence ("there is . . .") or universality ("all numbers/figures/angles are either . . . or . . .") are intended, but not mathematical definitions or axioms. It will be shown that Plato's call for the ultimate grounding of these objects in the "idea of the good" will become clearer by understanding *ὑποθέσεις* in this way.

12. Concerning the widely discussed difficulties in the relationship between the schema of the line and the allegory of the cave, see the summary in Ebert 1974 (see note 3 above), 151–159, and Annas 1981, 252–256. That Plato intends a continuous parallelization is, I think, obvious, even if a variety of aspects are addressed in his discussion. This becomes clear especially in the characterization of the lowest domain, in which the copies of the line correspond to the partial sense perception and subjective, easily accepted views (opinions) of the cave.

13. Initially, the coordination with the line speaks in favor of identifying the domain of the μαθηματικά with the level of reflections and shadows that initially appear when leaving the cave and entering into daylight. However, Socrates explicitly states (*Rep.* 532B–C) that ascending (ἐπαναγωγή) to essential beings through the mathematical sciences (πᾶσα αὕτη ἡ πραγματεία τῶν τεχνῶν ἃς διήλθομεν) leads to the domain that, during the ascent (ἐπάνοδος) in the allegory of the cave, corresponds to the reflections and shadows of daylight. Because the mathematicians do not yet see the true things (ideas), but only their copies, one can therefore say metaphorically that they only "dream" (*Rep.* 533B–C; 534C).

14. In the *Republic* the theory of incommensurable magnitudes is only touched upon, once at 504C, and again when referring to the absolute measure (527A) in terms of the translation and squaring of plane areas in geometry; another reference occurs at 534D in a play on words with the phrase ἄλογοι γραμμαί (the attempt by Erler 1983 to read this expression as meaning the "as of yet unwritten lines" of the writing tablet [*Schreibtafel*] remains uncertain due to there being a lack of any linguistic parallel); finally, a reference is made at 546C to the differentiation between rational and irrational (ῥητῶν and ἀρρήτων) diameters.

15. Theaetetus' theory of irrational magnitudes is included in book X of Euclid's *Elements*. A systematic account of the irrational magnitudes in terms of their relation to numerical ratios was achieved within the framework of the general theory of proportions, which was completed by Eudoxus (Euclid, *Elem*. V). The previous method of "exhaustion" ["*Wechselwegnahme*"] (i.e., ἀνθυφαίρεσις) laid the foundation for this achievement. See most recently Bulmer-Thomas 1983. On the ontological meaning of the theory of irrational magnitudes, see Gaiser 1963, 125–136; as well as Gaiser 1964, 263–264, and Cosenza 1977 (see note 8).

16. Krämer 1966 (2), 44 (= Krämer 1972, 406–408) observed a certain "perplexity" on the part of scholars with regard to the relationship between mathematics and the idea of the good. This scholarship ignored the testimonies concerning Plato's equation of the good and the one. In more recent work one may also see that a satisfying interpretation of the idea of the good will not be reached as long as Plato's demand for a synopsis of the μαθηματικά (aimed at both the good and the one) has not been clarified. Hare 1965, 35–38, understands the idea of the good for the μαθηματικά in that a circle, for example, in order to be a true circle, must be a "good," perfect circle—and criticizes this view, which he attributes to Plato, as being theoretically unsatisfactory. Ebert 1974 (see note 3 above) reduces what for Plato was conceived in ontological terms to those of functional relations. He does so by claiming that the value of the mathematical sciences for knowing the idea of the good consists in their ability to lead one toward gaining insight into the function of the good as the condition of possibility for ideal [*ideativer*] concepts, or normative boundary concepts (see, in particular, p. 208). White 1976 (see note 3) raises important questions but hardly answers them. Santas 1983, 251 reaches the trivial conclusion that "the Form of the good consists or is constituted by the very ideality common to all the other Forms by virtue of which they are the best objects of their kind." Concerning the question of the relationship of mathematics and dialectic with the interpretation, which in any case is not sufficient, he concludes that the dialectician sees "that mathematics must be only about Forms if it is to be knowledge." Annas 1981 only claims (pp. 285–287) that dialectic synoptically investigates the methods and concepts of the other sciences. Wieland 1982, 159–185 also leaves out the issue of synopsis when discussing the relationship of mathematics and dialectic; with his modernizing interpretation, according to which the idea of the good is characterized by the immateriality of non-propositional know-how, Wieland at best captures a peripheral aspect of Plato's argument. Graeser 1983, 156, regarding his attempt to explain the idea of the good that he shares with other interpretations, says "the disadvantage [is] that we do not know what Plato understood by 'being good' *simpliciter*." According to Sayre 1983, 188–206, the good in the *Republic* is too

amorphous to be able to justify knowledge, particularly the presuppositions of the sciences. Finally, Ferber's attempted interpretation, Ferber 1984, is also insufficient, for he interprets the idea of the good as a third element between thinking and being and sees the connection between the mathematical realm and the good only within the extra-temporal (and thus worthy) mode of being of the μαθηματικά. He thus ignores instances of order, measure, and the mean (33–35, 102–105).

17. Concerning the correct attempts on the part of earlier research, see Krämer 1966 (2), 58 (= Krämer 1972, 427–428). Some are correct but still indeterminate, e.g., Adam 1929, vol. 2, 136 (cf. 173): "The apprehension of the 'one in the many' in these preliminary studies prepares us for the dialectical conception of the universe of Thought as an organic and correlated whole." Cornford's contribution (Cornford 1932) was groundbreaking: Cornford regarded the knowledge concerning what the μαθηματικά had in common as "the apprehension of 'the existence of the One' as the single hypothesis from which all mathematical propositions can be deduced" (187). He thought the relevance of the idea of the good lay in the idea of order (harmony, rhythm, symmetry), which manifests itself in ethical values just as it manifests itself in mathematical structures. However, the transition from the synopsis of the μαθηματικά to the ἀγαθόν remains too indeterminate. Guthrie 1975 (see note 10 above), 524–526, follows Cornford: "mathematical order leads to the order of values, for order (κόσμος) is itself good."

18. Krämer 1966 (2) (see note 3 above), 59–60 (= 1972, 429–430). The contribution by Kucharski 1971, 359–386, does not contribute to an interpretation of the two passages dealing with the synopsis in the *Republic*. Kucharski believes that these passages cannot be understood from their context: "Les deux texts en question n'ont apparemment rien de commun avec les procédés 'dialectiques' longuement exposés à quelques pages du VIIe et à la fin du VIe livre de ce dialogue" (370). Kucharski's contribution addresses Plato's changing conception of the synopsis of the many within the one from the *Protagoras* to the *Laws*.

19. On the presentation of the structure of being (body–soul–ideas), compare the analogous relation of the mathematical progression of dimensions (body–line/plane–number) in the dialogues and Plato's oral doctrine, cf. Gaiser 1963; Krämer 1966 (2), 52–56 (= 1972, 418–424). The world-soul, accordingly, is described in the *Timaeus* (34B, 36C) as being a linear-planar limitation of the cosmos-body. The process of generation (γένεσις) is interpreted in the *Laws* (894A) as a dimensional unfolding. From the same basic conception results the idea that all of the μαθηματικά (from numbers to three-dimensional figures) gather in the soul (*Tim.* 35A–36D, cf. 4.3; Aristotle, *DA* A.2, 404b16–27), such that the soul captures its own structure through mathematics, and at the same time acquires a domain in which it finds proof for the certainty and cognition of the entire order of being.

20. Cf. Gaiser 1963, 54–55, 94. As is typical, the *Theaetetus* (185C) refers to the opposition betweeen περιττὸν and ἄρτιον in connection with the basic oppositions between οὐσία and μὴ εἶναι, ὁμοιότης and ἀνομοιότης, and ταὐτόν and ἕτερον.

21. It is thus not very promising to try and solve the specific problems of the individual mathematical sciences based on this passage by Plato, as Kytzler tried to do for musicology in Kytzler 1959, 393–414.

22. Cf. note 9 and note 10 above.

23. In the past one might have connected the expression κατὰ τὴν Μοῦσαν with the synopsis and patterns of musicology (Cornford 1932, 188 = Allen 1965, 93). Cherniss 1953, 377, however, has shown, in reference to *Rep.* 499D, how it is more likely that the expression refers to the Muse of philosophy (Görgemanns 1960, 222, agrees with this interpretation). Although the Muse at this point probably does indeed refer to a comprehensive philosophical synopsis, I think the expression at the same time indicates how this synopsis is possible, i.e., through the common unified order that appears everywhere in harmonies, rhythms, and symmetries.

24. The view that in the *Epinomis* Plato's philosophy of ideas was reduced to cosmology and astro-theology without transcendence is defended by Tarán 1975, 32; and Krämer 1983, esp. 112–113.

25. Neither of the relevant passages (981B or 983D) suggests (as Tarán and Krämer recently assumed) that the author of the *Epinomis* rejects the doctrine of ideas. In both passages Philippus claims that there is nothing "other" or "third" beyond bodies and the soul. I do not think this means, however, that the world of ideas is denied, which is not discussed here. Instead, the context suggests clearly enough that Philippus rejects any further element aside from body and soul for the cosmos and its generation. Thus, he turns against a cosmology that reduces everything to natural forces, such as heat and cold, movement and energy. Philippus explicitly remarks that it would be absurd to assume that certain "swings" (ῥῦμαι) or characteristics of bodies could be the cause of things (983C). He adds that it would be foolish to assume that the heavens could have come into being through "something else" and not through body and soul (983E). In this sense, he rejects an explanation of the world in which the physical realm takes precedence over the soul in which those movements (φοραί) that result from "warmth and cooling and such things" become primary. Such forces were indeed affirmed by a mechanistic cosmology (atomists such as Democritus?). Philippus resolutely rejects the latter view, namely, that all things are caused by forces (and not through the effect of soul on body), that those forces are themselves non-bodily and invisible (981B), and that they collectively pervade every possible thing (κοινόν) (983D).

26. Recent literature on the "mathematical *Epinomis* passage": Lacey 1956; Novotný 1957, 14–20; Novotný 1960, esp. 202–215; Koller 1959, 238–248 (addendum to the latter: Koller 1960); Gaiser 1963, 112–115, 362–363 (nn.89–91); Szabó 1970; Tarán 1975, esp. 329–348; Krämer 1983, esp. 108, 110–112.

27. I have here added the subheadings in order to indicate the structure of the text. [The English translation is modified from Lamb 1967—Ed.]

28. One should call to mind how the definition of the mathematical difference between μῆκος and δύναμις is rendered in the *Theaetetus* (147D–148B).

29. ἐφεξῆς (990D1); μετὰ δὲ ταῦτα (990D6); κατ' ἀριθμόν–κατὰ δύναμιν–εἰς τὸ στερεόν τε καὶ ἁπτόν (991A).

30. On duality as the basic form and shape of multiplicity [*Vielheit*] in Plato and in more recent number theory, see Hösle 1984, 321–355.

31. By φύσις (nature) Plato here means, as he often does, the idea, reason, and soul upon which order is based. Plato explains this spiritual-normative understanding of φύσις (as opposed to a materialistic conception of nature) explicitly in *Laws* 888E–892C.

32. The "adaptation" of the human being to the divine ἀρετή (ὁμοίωσις θεῷ), which is demanded in a central passage of the *Theaetetus* (176B), should also be taken into account here.

33. Plato uses the concept of δεσμός in a similarly normative way in the following passages: *Tim*. 31B–32C (the geometric proportion of the δεσμός, which combines differences as far as possible through unity; cf. 36A, 37A, 43D); *Statesman* 309B–310E (for νοῦς as δεσμός, see *Laws* 632C).

34. The interpretations of ancient authors (Cicero, Eratosthenes, Theon of Smyrna, Nicomachus of Gerasa, Proclus) are mentioned by Tarán 1975, 165–167. Eratosthenes and Theon in particular think of analogy or proportion; Proclus speaks of a collection of principles for the individual sciences and of combining them into a unitary principle (*De prov*. 138). He also considers a three-fold unity of mathematics and dialectic being synthesized in the absolute unity of νοῦς (*In Eucl*. 43–44).

35. Tarán 1975, 31, 68, 94, 345–346, 347, distinguishes the "one δεσμός" of the *Epinomis* from the number of the Platonic synopsis, and interprets it as the general theory of (mathematical) proportions or analogies: "This εἷς δεσμός, however, is neither the separate idea, for the apprehension of which Plato recommends the preliminary mathematical training, nor the unity of virtue which the members of the Nocturnal Council must know according to the *Laws* (961D–966B). For . . . the context shows that this bond (δεσμός) must be number and more specifically the theory of proportions" (345). H. J. Krämer writes in 1983: "The correct way of applying these disciplines lies . . . generally in the unitary conception of planimetry, arithmetic, harmony, and astronomy as a single, large system of relations (δεσμὸς εἷς . . .), for while one should primarily think of the theory of proportions [*Proportionslehre*]" (108). "The theory of proportions, which probably dates back to Eudoxus, has proven to be the only 'bond' which comprehends and integrates [*zusammenschließt*] the individual mathematical disciplines" (111).

36. Concerning the justification of the theory of principles by linking it to the mean structure [*Mesotes-Struktur*], which is often applied in the dialogues, see the detailed discussion in Krämer 1959.

37. Building on earlier observations, Krämer has also adequately presented this central thought of Plato's in Krämer 1959 (see note 17 above).

38. Illuminating discussions on this topic in light of Hegel's philosophy can be found in Hösle 1984, 459–490: "In a certain sense Plato's philosophy can be schematically summarized as follows: *it has thought . . . the unity of unity and multiplicity*; what is important with this statement is the structure, which summarizes a positive and a negative category within the positive" (481).

39. In positioning himself against Plato, Aristotle disputed the possibility of such a synthesis of the different sciences. That the synopsis of the sciences continued to be seen as the program of academic philosophy is shown by a quotation from the "memoirs" of a certain Diodorus who was a student of Speusippus (Philodemus, *Index Acad*., col. T 3–4: γέγονεν ἀπὸ Σπευσίππου). He is reported to have said about Speusippus (Diogenes Laertius, *Lives* IV.2 = Speusippus, fr. 2 Isnardi Parente = Speusippus, fr. 70 Tarán): πρῶτος ἐν τοῖς μαθήμασιν ἐθεάσατο τὸ κοινὸν καὶ συνῳκείωσε καθ' ὅσον ἦν δυνατὸν ἀλλήλοις. If the word πρῶτος also refers back to Diodorus, then we have to assume an additional circle of sciences beyond the mathematical

ones. To me, it seems more plausible, however, that Diodorus is referring to an advancement that was made by Speusippus to what had been laid out by Plato.

40. See Gaiser 1980, 5–37: being under political pressure and in order to defend his theory of principles from being misappropriated, Plato decided (just as Dionysus II of Syracuse did) to go public when he had reached old age.

41. The reflections and fragments of the transcription by Aristotle are included in the *Frag.*, 111–120 Ross.

42. Cf. a critical review by Mugler 1948; Cherniss 1951 (= Cherniss 1977, 222–252).

43. Cf. Proclus in the "catalogue of geometers," which dates back to Aristotle's student Eudemus of Rhodes (fr. 133 Wehrli): *In Eucl.* 66.8–68.4.

44. Philodemus, *Index Acad.*, col. Y 2–23, pp. 15–17 Mekler (1902). For an improved version of the same text and its attribution to Dicaearchus, see Gaiser 1983, 53–62.

45. Proclus (*In Eucl.* 211.19–23) and Diogenes Laertius (*Lives* III.24) report that Plato recommended the method of analysis to the mathematician Leodamas of Thasos (which is also mentioned by Philodemus / Dicaearchus). However, this method was already common in mathematics before Plato, so that Plato could not have discovered it. It is quite possible that he encouraged the application of this method to as many problems as possible, which is probable since he used such a method by tracing appearances back to ideas and the most general ontological grounds: the method of analysis consists in tracing back a complex issue to its most simple and primary presuppositions, conditions, and causes.

46. Recently, Hösle provided an original answer to the question of Plato's contribution to the mathematical research of his day in a fascinating work in Hösle 1982. Based on the evidence in Aristotle and Euclid, he concludes that in Plato's life the unprovability of the parallel postulate (Euclid, *Elements* I, 5) caused a crisis of principles, because this also called into question the proposition concerning the total sum of angles in a triangle and opened up the possibility of "non-Euclidian" systems of geometry. Plato's important achievement consists, according to Hösle, in his affirmation of philosophical-ontological reasons for the validity of "normal" geometry, which then was also presented in Euclid's *Elements*, so that today we call it Euclidian geometry while it should really be called "Platonic." Unfortunately, however, the philological basis for this thesis is hardly sufficient, as Cherniss 1951 (see note 42 above), 405–407 (= Cherniss 1977, 232–234) and Manasse 1976, 541, have already shown, with respect to a similar attempt by Charles Mugler. Neither of the passages referred to by Hösle, namely, the schema of the line in book VI of the *Republic* and 436D from the *Cratylus*, support the assumption that Plato had the uncertainty of the axiom of parallels in mind. The *Republic* passage fails to support this assumption because the ὑποθέσεις of the mathematicians (510C) clearly does not refer to such an axiomatic proposition (see note 11 above), and because Plato's criticism of mathematics does not aim at an unsolved problem but at the essentially "hypothetical" status of all mathematical foundations. However, what is convincing about Hösle's thesis is that it was primarily the unsuccessful attempt to discover a proof for the axiom of parallels that got the attention of the Platonic school (from which relevant remarks by Aristotle are also derived) not only with respect to the

difficulties of mathematical axiomatization, but also regarding the limitations of the deductive axiomatic method in general.

47. According to how individual theorems and constructions result from prior definitions (postulates and axioms only occur in book I), in books I–VI of the *Elements*, Euclid discusses planimetry (with the theory of proportions in book V), in VI–IX arithmetic, in X the theory of irrational magnitudes, and in XI–XIII stereometry.

48. Solmsen 1931 and 1940 repeatedly emphasizes the Platonic character of Euclid's *Elements*, with respect to Euclidian definitions. In his 1931 contribution, Solmsen also wanted to trace Aristotle's κοινὰ λεγόμενα ἀξιώματα and Euclid's κοιναὶ ἔννοιαι (axioms) to Plato's demand for the synoptic discovery of the κοινωνία, συγγένεια, and οἰκειότης of the mathematical sciences. Fritz 1969, 40, 62–63, 83, and 98 evaluates Plato's role as less important, but he also states that one can find Platonic influence in the definition-based foundations of Euclidian geometry and "that further *axiomatization* of mathematics in the discussions in the Academy concerning the essence of mathematical objects and the essence of mathematical proofs were partially in the sense of Plato, and partially against him" (98). In an important contribution by Fritz (1955), the importance of the Platonic school, whose discussions are also presented in Aristotle's methodology, has not been adequately acknowledged. Szabó 1978, 322–329, cites remarks by Zeuthen, Töplitz, and Becker about the decisive influence of Plato on the development of mathematics; however, he himself rejects the idea of a "Platonic reform" of mathematics.

49. Simplicius, *In De caelo*, 488.14–24 = Eudemus, fr. 148 Wehrli = Eudoxus, fr. 121 Lasserre: "Sosigenes claims that Plato assigned the following task to those who were specialists in the field: to rescue those regular and orderly movements, one had to hypothetically presuppose in order to rescue the phenomena that occurred together with these movements." Because the transmission is uncertain (whether the author be Sosigenes, Eudemus of Rhodes, or only Geminus / Poseidonius), it is therefore impossible to ascribe, directly and without reservation, this position to Plato. A further cause of hesitation is that Plato, at least in the *Republic* (529C–530B), rejects appearances as unimportant. One can assume with Krafft 1965 that the expression σῴζειν τὰ φαινόμενα is not Platonic. Still, we can continue to assume that the source of Sosigenes' tracing the astronomical hypotheses for the explanation of apparent anomalies in planetary movement back to Platonic suggestions was justified. Bulmer-Thomas 1984 once again reaffirms the influence of Plato on scientific astronomy.

50. An overview of the development of astronomy in the Platonic school is provided by Gaiser 1980, 68–91. That the "true astronomy" that Plato calls for in *Republic* VII should not be independent of empirical data in spite of the devaluation of visible appearances, is demonstrated by Vlastos 1980. In contrast, Mourelatos 1980 and Mourelatos 1981 relate Plato's demand for a "true astronomy" to a purely geometrical and general kinematics (a theory of circular movements). While the reduction of the stellar movements to circular orbits succeeded at the time (even though some empirical data was neglected) the idea of a harmony of the spheres, i.e., the assumption that the orbits were ordered according to harmonic intervals (*Rep.* 530D, 617B; *Tim.* 36D) contradicted the phenomena. This originally Pythagorean idea rests on the insight that, in the case of sound, movement (frequency) is inversely proportional to the length of the string and directly proportional to

the tone of the pitch. Thus, the expectation was legitimate that in the case of planetary movements (if one conceives of the orbits as curved strings) the speed of an orbit could be similarly related to its length. The phenomena corroborated this expectation because stars close to the earth exhibited a shorter circumlocution, while planets that were further away took a longer time to complete their circuits; but these temporal ratios do not in fact reveal any agreement with the numerical proportions of harmonic intervals.

FIVE

THE IDEA OF THE GOOD AS *ARKHĒ* IN PLATO'S *REPUBLIC*

Thomas Alexander Szlezák

1. SOCRATES' THEORY OF THE PRINCIPLE

The Socrates of the *Republic*—a literary character whom we will not directly equate with its author—says the following about the "highest point of knowledge" in the middle books:

(1) There is for humans a highest object of instruction and learning, a μεγίστον μάθημα (504D2–3, E4–5).

(2) This μεγίστον μάθημα, according to Socrates' view, is the idea of the good (505A2). This idea gives the other ideas their value and usefulness (505A6–7, E3–4) and makes them "sufficiently" (ἱκανῶς) knowable (506A6–7). The knowledge of this idea is on this account necessary for the political leadership of a truly just state (505E4–506A6).

(3) In the sensible world there is something that is "very similar" (506E3) to the idea of the good and represents an (exact) "correspondent" (ἀνάλογον) (508B13) to it: the sun.

(4) The idea of the good brought forth or generated (ἐγέννησεν [508B13]; τεκοῦσα [517C3]) the correspondent (ἀνάλογον)

of itself, such that Socrates metaphorically calls the good the "father" (πατήρ) of the sun (506E3), and the sun the "offspring" or "descendant" (ἔκγονος) of the good (506E6).

(5) Each and every soul does what it does for the sake of the good: the idea of the good is the ultimate *causa finalis* (505D11–E1).

(6) The idea of the good is, at the same time, the cause of the knowability and the "truth" of things that can be (fully) known, i.e., the ideas, and it is also the cause of the cognitive faculty of the cognitive part of the soul (508E1–4, with 508A9–B7; 509B6).

(7) The idea of the good further causes the being of the ideas—it gives them τὸ εἶναι τε καὶ τὴν οὐσίαν, their "being and essence" (509B7–8).

(8) The idea of the good itself, however, is not being (οὐσία), "but exceeds οὐσία in dignity [or rank] and power" (ἀλλ' ἔτι ἐπέκεινα τῆς οὐσίας πρεσβείᾳ καὶ δυνάμει ὑπερέχοτος [sc., τοῦ ἀγαθοῦ]) (509B9–10).

(9) The idea of the good, although above (prior to) the ideas, still appears to affect them, on which account Socrates says that it rules the ideas in the manner of a king, analogously to the royal rule and complete guardianship (πάντα ἐπιτροπεύων) (516B10) of the sun in the sensible world (καὶ βασιλεύειν τὸ μὲν νοητοῦ γένους τε καὶ τόπου, τὸ δ' αὖ ὁρατοῦ) (509D2–3).

(10) Since the idea of the good brought forth the sun (see 4), and the sun "in a certain sense" is the cause of all visible things (ἐκείνων ὧν σφεῖς ἑώρων τρόπον τινὰ πάντων αἴτιος) (516C1–2), the idea of the good is also "in a certain sense" the cause of all things, both visible and intelligible. This comprehensive causality covers knowability and knowledge alike: since the good also created light in the sensible world (517C3), and since light makes it possible that the object's own ability to be seen and the eyes' power of sight are both actualized (507C10–E3; 508C4–D10), then all knowing—sensible as well as intelligible—is caused by the good. In connection with the explanation of noetic knowledge, Socrates calls the idea of the good τὴν τοῦ παντὸς ἀρχήν (511B7). Yet it has this function not only in an epistemological sense, but at the same time also as the ultimate *causa finalis* (see 5), and further as "that which gives birth" (τεκοῦσα) to the

sun and as the origin of the being of the ideas, as well as, indirectly, of the becoming of visible objects. In particular, the idea of the good is "for all things the cause of everything right and beautiful" in the visible and the intelligible world (πᾶσι πάντων αὕτη ὀρθῶν τε καὶ καλῶν αἰτία) (517C2).

(11) Intelligible objects—and, indirectly, therefore, perceptible ones as well (see 4 and 10)—are connected with the ἀρχή in a way that is not further defined: beginning from the ἀρχή the knower comes to the subordinate ideas, "keeping hold of what is directly connected with it" (ἐχόμενος τῶν ἐκείνης ἐχομένων); he came to the ἀρχή in the first place through the interrelation of things—which must at the same time be an epistemological and an ontological interrelation (511B5–C2).

(12) The idea of the good is knowable (508E4, 517B8–C1, with 516B4–7, 518C9–10, 532A5–B2) and its nature can be defined (534B3–D1). Socrates everywhere presupposes the existence of philosophers who are able to have knowledge of the good, without counting himself among them (e.g., 519D1–2, 520A8–B4).

(13) There is only one way that leads to knowledge of the ἀρχή: dialectic (533A8–9, C7–D4). Dialectic is characterized by a double movement of thought: the step-by-step (see 511B6: οἷον ἐπιβάσεις τε καὶ ὁρμάς) ascent to the non-hypothetical starting point, and the ordered (ἐχόμενος τῶν ἐκείνης ἐχομένων [see 11]) descent (see 511B8: καταβαίνῃ) from the highest to the lowest point.

(14) Dialectical knowledge of the good is εὐδαιμονία for humans (498C3; 532E2–3; 540B6–C2; cf. 519C5).

These statements taken together comprise something like a "theory of the principle (sing.)." That they must be taken together to comprise a whole is clear from the fact that they belong to Socrates' answer to the question as to what the μεγίστον μάθημα consists of (504E4–6), as well as that regarding on the basis of which μαθήματα the philosopher-kings should become qualified to safeguard the existence of the state (502C9–D2).

Three reasons could be given to dispute our assessment of these statements as a "theory of the principle":

(a) They are only put forth as the opinion of Socrates, with an admittedly weak truth claim.

(b) They are not substantiated; particularly the central statement that the sun is an analogon and offspring of the good such that, through a description of the sun, we can obtain characteristics of its "father"—this central statement is a mere hypothesis on the part of Socrates.

(c) They do not, to the slightest degree, represent Socrates' complete opinion (506E1–3; 509C5–10; 533A1–4).

Yet what makes a theory a theory is not that the author openly identifies himself with it, or that the character in whose mouth he has put the words constantly praises its correctness, or that all of its proofs are immediately given, and definitely not that the different component parts are exhaustively listed, but rather this: whether its propositions show an inner connection by relating to the same object, and whether they are spoken with the intent of explaining this state of affairs in one or several aspects. Without a doubt, both of these conditions are present here.

One may also, in order not to leave out any qualifying characterization, refer to the present theory as "the theory of the principle put forth incompletely and without a strong truth claim by the literary figure Socrates."

This does not change the fact that in the middle books of the *Republic* we are dealing with a theory of the principle.

2. THE PLATONIC THEORY OF PRINCIPLES IN THE TRADITION OF INDIRECT TRANSMISSION

In the doxographic information provided by Aristotle, Theophrastus, and other authors collected by Konrad Gaiser under the title *Testimonia Platonica* (= *TP*),[1] there is a theory of principles (plur.), whose main characteristics are the following:[2]

(1) There are two ultimate principles from which the whole of reality is to be explained: the one and the indefinite dyad (*TP* 22A, 22B [= Aristotle, *Met.* A.6; Alexander, *In Met.* 55.20–56.35]).

(2) The interaction of these two principles, which is understood as a limitation and definition of the indefinite and the unlimited through the one (and its derivatives), represents a "generating" (γεννᾶν) of reality (*TP* 22A et al.; Aristotle, *Met.* A.6, 987b34: γεννᾶσθαι).

(3) The first products of intelligible "generation" are the ideal numbers (*TP* 22B et al.).

(4) On the whole, the ideas owe their essence (τί ἐστιν) to the one, just as sensible things owe their essence to the ideas (*TP* 22A = *Met.* A.6, 988a10–11). This seems to imply that the one as a principle is above or beyond the ideas in the same way that the idea is above or beyond the individual object. (The word "beyond," ἐπέκεινα, is not used here by Aristotle.)

(5) The positive principle is also called the good and its being (τί ἐστιν) can be defined: it is the one (*TP* 28B = Aristotle, *Met.* N.4, 1091b13–15). The other principle is the cause of all that is negative in the world (*TP* 22A = Aristotle, *Met.* A.6, 988a14–15, et al.).

(6) The one or good is the ultimate *causa finalis*. Even numbers "strive after" or "desire" the good (Aristotle, *EE* A.8, 1218a24–31 = *T* 79 Richard [not in *TP*]).

(7) The Platonic theory of principles tries to explain a comprehensive ontological coherence and continuity of being from the principle to appearances (*TP* 22A = Aristotle, *Met.* A.6, 987b8–20; *TP* 22B, 23B, 26B, 30 = Theophrastus, *Met.* 6a15–b17).

(8) The path of knowledge "toward the principles" corresponds to an opposite path "away from the principles" (*TP* 10 = Aristotle, *NE* A.4, 1095a30–b3; *TP* 30 = Theophrastus [cf. 7]; *TP* 32 = Sextus Empiricus, *Adv. Math.* X.263ff., 276ff.).

It is clear that this theory of principles is not identical to Socrates' theory of the principle in books VI and VII of the *Republic*.

It should also be just as clear that both sketches are very closely related to one another. If the images and metaphors, the manner of thinking and the concepts of the *Testimonia Platonica*, were not held together by being commonly attested as Platonic, but instead held together anonymously or possibly transmitted as the common views of the Πυθαγορικῶν παῖδες (as in Sextus Empiricus, *Adv. Math.* X.270 [= *TP* 32]), then looking at them in an unbiased light we would no doubt say that these "followers of the Pythagoreans" were close intellectual relations of the Socrates of the *Republic*.

For there is agreement concerning such important things as the explanation of the whole of reality from one principle (or one pair of principles), the creation of subordinate levels of reality by the original level (including the use of gender metaphors: "father" at *Republic* 506E6; "male/female" as μιμήματα τῶν ἀρχῶν in *Met.* A.6, 988a7), the causal ability of the first principle *qua* goal toward which all things strive as well as source of their essence, the determinability of the τί ἐστιν of the principle, the coherence and continuity of being, and the two-way path to knowledge: "moving toward" and "moving away from the principle."

Yet the differences are also quite obvious: Socrates speaks only of one ἀρχή, whereas the tradition of indirect transmission speaks of two ἀρχαί. Socrates says nothing about the τί ἐστιν of the good, whereas the *Testimonia* define its nature as the ἕν. The *causa finalis* for everything is the good according to the *Testimonia* but, according to the *Republic*, it appears to be the cause only of human striving. Socrates does not speak of a limitation of the unlimited through the one, while the tradition of indirect transmission knows no special ἀνάλογον of the good in the visible world.

3. HOW ARE THE TWO THEORIES RELATED TO EACH OTHER? DIFFERENT EXPLANATORY POSSIBILITIES

How should the agreements and differences of both theories be settled? Is one of the theories meant to correct the other? Must one of them be given up as being un-Platonic? The following possibilities can be outlined:

(1) Even if Socrates' theory of the principle is completely incompatible with the theory of principles in the tradition of indirect transmission, it would still not follow that we must give up one of the two theories. The view that Plato underwent a development is today not very popular, and indeed the constancy and consistency of the ideas put forth in the dialogues are more impressive than the (for the most part relatively small) inconsistencies that the developmental approach of the last two centuries wants to explain away. On the other hand, wanting to deny, *a priori*, the possibility of any change in Plato's views on the ἀρχή or the ἀρχαί would be simply categorical. There remain the following options:

(1.a) Assuming a development in Plato, Socrates' "monistic" theory would be placed earlier, and the dualistic theory of the ἄγραφα δόγματα later. Since the manner of thinking is the same, the transition from the one to the other version would not be unheard of. We should then accept the position of the ἄγραφα δόγματα as a more mature product of Plato's thought.

(1.b) Without assuming a development, we would—insofar as they are fundamentally incompatible—have to choose between the two theories:

(1.b.1) Whoever supports the thesis of Plato's "anonymity"—i.e., the thesis that Plato does not clearly reveal his own position in the dialogues, on which account no character, not even Socrates, can function as a mouthpiece for the author—will have to prefer the theory of principles of indirect transmission, since this is the only theory that fits with Aristoxenus' report of the lecture *On the Good*, in which Plato spoke in his own name, while the Socrates in the *Republic* cannot be said to represent Plato himself.

(1.b.2) Whoever does not support the "anonymity" thesis, however, will prefer the "monistic" theory of "Socrates," insofar as an "authentic" text of Plato is opposed to an (allegedly) distorted secondary report.

We do not need to choose between these three possibilities (i.e., Plato's development [1.a], the greater authenticity of the ἄγραφα [1.b.1], or the greater authenticity of the *Republic* [1.b.2])—all three of which have their difficulties—provided the following possibility be true:

(2) Considering the intention of the textual testimony more closely, there is no real contradiction between the two theories.

In order to judge this question, it is necessary to look at the context in the dialogue where Socrates puts forth his view of the principle.

4. THE LITERARY FORM OF THE EXPOSITION OF SOCRATES' THEORY OF THE PRINCIPLE

Since Friedrich Schleiermacher's "Introduction" to his translation of Plato in 1804, the importance of form for the meaning of Plato's dialogues has been constantly affirmed. Yet detailed investigations, which really deserve to be called *literary* analyses of the dialogic form, are rare, and they are mostly concerned only with obvious details and do not consider the dialogue as a whole or even what is common to all of the dialogues.

A literary analysis must begin by recognizing the dialogues as *dramas*. The literary peculiarity of drama results from the combination of a multiplicity of elements. Among them, the conception of the *characters* and the dramatic *action* are without a doubt crucial and of the utmost importance.

In a different context, I have already analyzed[3] how the characters as well as the action are conceived in the drama of the *Republic*. "Socrates" is characterized as a man of personal modesty and urbanity, yet represents at the same time nothing less than the superior dialectician who has "descended" from the height of his knowledge—κατέβην is the first word of his report (327A1)—to a discussion with friendly minded and philosophically interested, but admittedly not very advanced, interlocutors. That "Socrates" is to be understood as an image of the dialectician is made explicitly clear when, at the end of the allegory of the cave, the person who has "descended" from the vision of the good (cf. 516E4: καταβάς) is attributed precisely the fate of the thinker with the same name,[4] and who was executed in 399 BCE (517A4–6; cf. D4–E3). The interlocutors are clearly conscious of the difference between themselves and the leader of the discussion: Socrates should conduct the search, they want him to take the lead (427D1–E5; 432C1–6; 453C7–9; 595C7–596A4), and they themselves want to follow and help in whatever way they can, namely, through benevolence, encouragement, and suitable answers (427E4; 474A6–B2)—answers that are tailored to questions that for the most part, on account of their form, already indicate the correct answer.[5]

Whoever pays close attention to the atmosphere of the discussion created by the way in which the characters are drawn up will reject as inappropriate and incompatible with the text the idea that there could be a situation in which the dialectician "Socrates" was not already far ahead of the present state of the discussion.

Still, the same message is more clearly conveyed by the dramatic action. This we have to understand as a "trial of strength," which is all about whether Socrates lets himself be forced by the larger group around Polemarchus to enter into the discussion, which they want, or whether he succeeds in persuading the others to "let him go" (327C1–14). It turns out that the motive for "not letting go" and "forcing" the philosopher is what dictates the action well into the seventh book. Inasmuch as Socrates, in the beginning of the discussion, gives in and lets himself be forced many times throughout the course of the discussion to make further statements, he appears to lose the "trial of strength."[6] Yet with respect to the philosophically important questions—the deeper foundation of the doctrine of the soul, the τί ἐστιν of the good and the types and methods of dialectic—he succeeds in persuading his interlocutors to let him go, i.e., they accept, without pressing him further, his clearly conveyed, conscious limitation of the philosophical discourse. The victor at the end of the "trial of strength" is Socrates.[7] That he himself imposes limitations on the discussion with regard to its content is made clear in the passages where he leaves what I call "deliberate gaps," of which I would here like to remind the reader briefly:[8]

(1) The "longer path" of dialectic (435D3: μακροτέρα ὁδός; 504B2: μακροτέρα περίοδος) is not traveled in the dialogue. The interlocutors explicitly do without it in book IV as well as book VI (435D6–7; 504B5–8; 506D3–6), although there is no doubt whatsoever that it is the longer path alone that leads to the goal of knowledge of the good (504C9–D3; 533A8–10, C7–D1).

(2) Even Glaucon's request that Socrates should deal with the good in the same way he dealt with the virtues (506D3–5)—namely, in the manner of a mere sketch (ὑπογραφή) (504D6) that lacks dialectical exactness but still arrives at a definition of its object, just as the virtues were defined in book IV—even this request is rejected: the report of his "view" (τὸ δοκοῦν ἐμοί) (506E2) on the τί ἐστιν of the good would, in Socrates' opinion, be more than could be reached now with the present kind of approach (506E1–3). Hence his decision: αὐτὸ μὲν τί ποτ' ἐστὶ τἀγαθὸν ἐάσωμεν τὸ νῦν εἶναι ("let's leave aside for the time being what the good itself is") (506D8–E1). This much is clear: Socrates does have his own view on the nature of the good.

(3) Instead of this view, however, Socrates offers the analogy of the sun and the idea of the good, the clarification of the ontological and epistemological implications of this analogy through a diagram, and, finally, an allegory of ascending to the highest form of knowledge. He does not offer this because it is the only way to speak about the good; rather, Socrates makes clear that his similes and allegories can be resolved or translated into conceptual language (533A2–3).

(4) The "image" of the good (509A9: εἰκῶν; 509C6: ὁμοιότης), which Socrates clearly understands as a mere substitute, is not fully drawn out by him. At 509C7 he says to Glaucon συχνά γε ἀπολείπω ("I am certainly leaving out a lot"), referring to the fact that the current discussion will not allow him to say everything: he does not want to leave anything out only with respect to those things ὅσα γ' ἐν τῷ παρόντι δυνατόν ("that are possible at the moment") (509C9–10).

(5) The longer path of dialectic is not only not *passed over* (cf. 1), but Socrates refuses even to give a mere sketch of the "types" and "paths" of dialectic. Yet this is what Glaucon asks of him once again, when he says that Socrates should talk about the "way" or "manner" of dialectic just as he talked about the "prelude" of the mathematical disciplines (ἐπ αὐτὸν δὴ τὸν νόμον

> ἴωμεν, καὶ διέλθωμεν οὕτως ὥσπερ τὸ προοίμιον διήλθομεν) (532D6–7). Socrates' overview of introductory mathematical studies was only an "external" sketch, and not at all an attempt to enter into mathematics itself. An analogous representation of dialectic is again refused by Socrates because he knows that Glaucon would not be able to keep up with him anymore: Οὐκέτ', ἦν δ' ἐγώ, ὦ φίλε Γλαύκων, οἷος τ' ἐσῇ ἀκολουθεῖν, ἐπεὶ τὸ γ' ἐμὸν οὐδὲν ἂν προθυμίας ἀπολίποι ("'You will no longer be able to follow, my dear Glaucon,' I said, 'although there wouldn't be any lack of eagerness on my part.'") (533A1–2). This answer implies that Socrates would definitely be able to give the requested sketch.[9]

5. NO CONTRADICTION BETWEEN THE TWO THEORIES

Whoever is prepared to appropriately appreciate these clear limitations of the philosophical reach of the discussion carried out "now," has to come to the conclusion that there is no contradiction between Socrates' theory of the principle and the theory of principles indirectly transmitted to us, and that it would make little sense to want to correct the Aristotelian and various other reports concerning Plato's theory of principles by using the theory from the *Republic*.

Let us consider the most obvious differences.

(1) Socrates' ἀρχή is the good, whose τί ἐστιν remains open; the positive principle in the tradition of the indirect transmission is likewise the good, whose τί ἐστιν is called the one. A categorical difference is only seen by one who believes he has proof that Socrates' view—which Socrates consciously does not present—on the τί ἐστιν of the good (506E) should have something else as its content than the equation: the one = the good. One, however, who is of the opinion, as is Gadamer,[10] that this equation is behind the text of the *Republic* as well, will prefer to say that "Socrates" offers a (purposefully) abbreviated version, while the indirect transmission offers a more complete representation of the same opinion about the good.

(2) Socrates speaks only of the good; the *Testimonia* speak of the one-good and the indefinite dyad. Monism against dualism? Hardly. Socrates' idea of the good is emphasized as being the cause "of all that is right and beautiful" (πάντων ὀρθῶν τε καὶ καλῶν) (517C2). Is there, according to Socrates' view, nothing bad in the world? Yet in book II, the same Socrates says

that the good is not the cause of all things (οὐκ ἄρα πάντων γε αἴτιον τὸ ἀγαθόν) (379B15), and that one must seek other causes for bad things (τῶν δὲ κακῶν ἀλλ᾽ ἄττα δεῖ ζητεῖν τὰ αἴτια) (C6–7). The search for the causes of bad things is simply not carried out in the *Republic*. Do we want to categorically conclude that Socrates' search would have led to everything possible, but definitely not to the negative principle of the ἀόριστος δυάς? Only if we could prove this, could we speak of two different theories of the principle (or principles).

(3) The indirect transmission speaks of (ideal) numbers as the first products of ontological generation; the *Republic* says nothing of this. Yet what does it mean that the dialectician, in descending from the principle, will proceed ἐχόμενος τῶν ἐκείνης ἐχομένων (511B8)? Only if we can exclude the ideal numbers from τὰ ἐκείνης ἐχόμενα, are we then justified in speaking of two theories.

In short, we must not forget the goals that Socrates imposed upon himself in this discussion. On the one hand, he wants it to be understood why the philosopher-kings must definitely know the μεγίστον μάθημα (504C9–D3; 506A1–3; 517C4–5; 526E4; 540A–B); on the other hand, however, he decided that his own view on the nature of the good and the kinds and methods of dialectic must be left unsaid, because this is something that exceeds "the present kind of approach" (506E1–3; 533A1–2) and that he himself will express his views only incompletely: συχνά γε ἀπολείπω (509C7). This assertion needs to be taken seriously. It is not the intention of the main character of the *Republic* to completely expound his own views (τὰ ἐμοὶ δοκοῦντα) (509C3) on the principles. It is no wonder that we lack certain things from the perspective of the ἄγραφα δόγματα: the negative principle, the definition of the nature of the good, an outline of the ontological coherence of all being, even the way in which the cause of everything works (namely, that the positive principle forms the world through limiting the unlimited and defining the indefinite)—all of this is unnecessary for Socrates' discussion of the best state.

Instead of speaking about two diverging theories, it seems more reasonable, when taking into account the explicit limitation of the topic being discussed, to see Socrates' theory of the principle as an abridged version of the oral theory of principles. The reason for this abridgement is clearly mentioned in the discussion: what is lacking would belong to the longer path of dialectic, which would, at this stage of the game, be much too challenging for his interlocutors.

6. HOW DOES SOCRATES SPEAK? WHAT DOES THE LANGUAGE OF THE ANALOGY OF THE SUN TELL US?

One knows "Socrates" as the thinker who does not attribute any knowledge to himself. One also knows him to be ironic. In our text, while once again not being let go (504E4–6) and being pressed to put forth his opinion on the nature of the good, he asks whether it is correct to speak of something about which one has no knowledge, as if one did have knowledge of it (506C2–5). After telling a lot of things about the good (507A1–517B6), though not revealing his opinion about its τί ἐστιν, he goes on to say that only god knows whether his view is true or not (517B7). And concerning the exposition of dialectic that is requested of him, which, however, he does not communicate, he assures his interlocutors that, through that exposition, one would not see a mere picture anymore, but the αὐτὸ τὸ ἀληθές just as it appeared to him—whether this is correct or not, he does not want to say for certain (533A2–5). Socrates, therefore, clearly reckons with the *possible* difference between his view and the truth itself. On the other hand, the difference between his own view and what he here and now says of it, is for him not only possible, but absolutely certain. The two differences can be expressed in the following manner:

$$\text{αὐτὸ τὸ ἀληθές} \overset{?}{=} \text{τὰ ἐμοὶ δοκοῦντα} \neq \text{ὅσα γ' ἐν τῷ παρόντι δυνατόν}$$

The fact that Socrates adds a question mark to the truth claim of his own view is very often interpreted as if he wants to say: "my δοκοῦντα cannot possibly coincide with the truth itself [αὐτὸ τὸ ἀληθές], for absolutely certain knowledge is in no way possible for humans." Yet there is a big difference between certainty in the modern sense concerning the impossibility of absolutely certain knowledge, and Socrates' unwillingness to raise a strong truth claim. For Socrates, that his δοκοῦντα might hit upon the truth is a real possibility. Playing this possibility down corresponds to Attic urbanity.[11] A disparagement of human cognitive powers is not present, for as we have already seen (see 2), the good, for Socrates, is an object of knowledge in the *Republic*—besides which, in the *Phaedo* it is not Socrates, but rather Simmias, who speaks τὴν ἀνθρωπίνην ἀσθένειαν ἀτιμάζων (107B1). Instead, Socrates confidently promises to reach the point beyond which one will seek nothing more (*Phaedo* 107B9), which is comparable to the end of the journey in the *Republic* (523E3).

But does Socrates not radically debase—and this is a common charge—his δόξαι even before he begins to (partially) express them? "Do you want to see ugly things, blind and crooked?" he asks in 506C11.

Does Socrates really hold his views to be ugly, blind, and crooked? Continuing with the question clears this problem up: "even if you have the possibility to hear from others radiant and beautiful things?" (506C11–D1). What are these radiantly beautiful answers, next to which Socrates' views look ugly, blind, and crooked? We know them already: they are the explanations of the good as "insight" and "pleasure," which Socrates sweeps aside with a light hand (505B5–C11). The statement that his own views are ugly is immersed in the sharpest irony—that is his way of referring to the particular importance of what now follows.

Yet in what way does Socrates express his consciously incomplete views on the μεγίστον μάθημα? Does he humbly approach something inexpressible (ἄρρητον),[12] or, searching for something in an uncertain manner, does he feel his way toward something uneasily, something that, in principle—as is so often claimed nowadays—can only be spoken about metaphorically?

No sign of any hesitation on the part of Socrates is evident in the text. Corresponding to his lowly valued truth claim, he warns his interlocutors once more that his "account of the interest" could be false (507A4–5). Then he recalls (507A6–B11) briefly the theory of the ideas, which he has already expounded very often (507A8); he explains to Glaucon, who for the time being does not understand, why something "third" between the visible object and the eye is necessary for seeing (507C1–508A3); he then comments on the likeness of the eye to the sun and the origin of the sense of sight from the sun (508A4–B11); and finally he propounds his view of the analogy between the sun and the idea of the good, which he does rather self-consciously in a series of imperatives: φάναι με λέγειν, ὧδε νόει, φάθι εἶναι, διανοοῦ, εὐφήμει . . . ἀλλ' ὧδε ἐπισκόπε, φάναι (508B12, D4, E3, 509A9–10, B7). Between these requests for his interlocutors to think of these things in a certain way, there is a clear statement regarding which view of the relationship between knowledge, truth, and the idea of the good, is "correct," and which is false (ὀρθόν, ὀρθῶς appear five times in 508E6–509A4), just as there is the assurance that one must honor the good still more (ἔτι μειζόνως τιμητέον) (509A4–5). The imperatives of the analogy of the sun continue in the analogies concerning the line and the cave: νόησον, τέμνε, τίθει, σκόπει, μάνθανε, λαβέ, τάξον, εἴκασον, σκόπει, ἐννόησον (509D1, D7, 510A5, B2, 511B3, D8, E2, 514A1, 515C4, 516E3; cf. 517B1: προσαπτέον).

What Socrates communicates regarding his δοκοῦντα on the good, he expresses in the form of instructions: Glaucon should comprehend certain ideas if he wants to become familiar with Socrates' opinion. Even though Glaucon is allowed and even requested to say whether or not he understands, one must call the series of the three analogies one of the least dialogical pieces in Plato's dialogues: Socrates is neither interested in Glaucon's agreement nor in finding out his judgment—he only wants to know whether or not Glaucon understands the ideas just as he presents them to him (for example: . . . εἰ κατανοεῖς.—ἀλλὰ κατανοῶ. ["if you understand."—"I do understand." [510A3–4]).

Socrates' extraordinarily certain and self-conscious tone in the analogies corresponds to their message, which, after having been prepared in the similes of the sun and the line, is expressed in the analogy of the cave. Hegel was one of the few who saw that. In the metaphor of the cave, as he says in the *Lectures on the History of Philosophy*, Plato speaks "with all the pride of science. . . . There is in him nothing of the so-called modest attitude of this science towards other spheres of knowledge, nor of man towards God."[13]

This self-conscious and even—according to Hegel—"haughty" exposition of the Socratic δοκοῦντα reaches its first climax in the concluding sentence of the analogy of the sun, where we are told that the idea of the good "still exceeds οὐσία in dignity and power" (509B9–10).

It does not make much sense to want to play down the philosophical importance of this sentence: the careful literary arrangement, which proves that it is the provocative climax of a coherent movement of thought, does not allow it.

Clearly, the literary presentation of the ἐπέκεινα-statement starts already with the long, drawn-out game (504E4–507A6) concerning the alleged worthlessness and possible falsehood of the Socratic δόξαι on the good. For the ἐπέκεινα-statement does not provide the essence (τί ἐστιν) of the good, yet approaches a relatively close understanding of it by using the spatial metaphor of "beyond." We must relate Socrates' downplaying of his own opinion to the obvious linguistic elevation in his manner of speech. Whoever does not see the irony in "do you want to see ugly things, blind and crooked" (βούλει οὖν αἰσχρὰ θεάσασθαι, τυφλά τε καὶ σκολιά) (506C11) may judge the statement about the good's standing "beyond being" as being "ugly, blind, and crooked." Whoever, on the other hand, has a sense for the particularity of Socrates' manner of speech, will admit that we should recognize the ἐπέκεινα-statement—according to the intention of the author—precisely as being "beautiful, clear, and correct."

We are not allowed to consider ἐπέκεινα τῆς οὐσίας in isolation,[14] but rather, in the first place, as an answer to Socrates' typical practice of "self-belittling" or "mock-modesty" (εἰρωνεία) in 506C11 and, secondly, as a clearly recognizable climax in the analogy of the sun. To illustrate this, the following brief remarks may suffice:

After the fundamental claim that the idea of the good "produced" the sun as its ἀνάλογον (508B12–13) and, after the explanation of the function of light and truth for seeing and knowing (508C4–D10), Socrates works on explaining the importance of the idea of the good. He is not anxious to avoid weighty statements on the ontological position of the good: truth and knowledge are exceedingly beautiful (καλά), but the good is, as their cause, "even more beautiful than they" (κάλλιον ἔτι τούτων) (508E6). It is correct to call knowledge and truth "godlike," but not to call them the good, for one must attribute to the good "a still higher position": ἔτι μειζόνως τιμητέον τὴν τοῦ ἀγαθοῦ ἕξιν (509A4–5). Ἔτι, which is used twice with a comparative, does not suffice: the good is ὑπὲρ ταῦτα κάλλει, what Glaucon correctly classifies as an "unconceivable beauty" (ἀμήχανον κάλλος) (509A7–9). Whoever has followed up to this point, must already be deeply imbued with the exceeding beauty and dignity of the good. Yet there is more: the good not only makes the ideas knowable, but it also gives them τὸ εἶναι τε καὶ τὴν οὐσίαν, whereas it itself is not οὐσία, but "still exceeds οὐσία in dignity and power" (509B9). This is the fifth time the unique position of the good has been mentioned in a short passage of little more than twenty lines, where we meet the intensifying ἔτι for the third time. Glaucon has grasped the weight of this intensification: he sees in it a δαιμονία ὑπερβολή (509C1–2), a divine hyperbole.

The view that "hyperbole" here merely means a linguistic exaggeration is not convincing (L. Brisson). By using this word, Glaucon supposedly criticizes the statement concerning ἐπέκεινα τῆς οὐσίας. This criticism is allegedly accepted by Socrates; therefore, Glaucon's reaction, and Socrates' reaction to that reaction, deprive the ontological statement in 509B9 of philosophical relevance.

For ὑπερβολή, as a mere rhetorical *terminus technicus* for exaggeration, is not attested anywhere else in Plato. And even if Plato knew of the rhetorical term, is it possible to consider that he would have referred to a mere linguistic exaggeration—especially if he wanted to criticize it—as δαιμονία ὑπερβολή? A truly "divine" hyperbole or "exaggeration" is present here: the idea of the good is analogous to the sun, and this was introduced in the beginning as a god (θεός) (508A4). But the good is still (ἔτι) higher in dignity and power; it is the ultimate cause of all value, all knowledge, and all being—and also of the being of the sun: δαιμονία ὑπερβολή.

But let us suppose that ὑπερβολή refers only to the language in Socrates' statement, and not to the implied ontological relationship. Is it, then, sufficient to say that in 509C1–4 the relevance of the ἔτι ἐπέκεινα-statement is negated or at least limited?

A properly literary analysis would have to begin here. The crucial question must be: What is the meaning of a linguistic arrangement that now allows the ironist Socrates—who continuously tends to understate, and never overstate, formulations and evaluations—to pick up a "daemonic" hyperbole? And what shall we have gained, if we annul the ἔτι ἐπέκεινα-statement by understanding the hyperbole rhetorically, when four further hyperboles, which are not at all meant rhetorically, remain in the text: ἔτι κάλλιον, ἔτι μειζόνως τιμητέον, ὑπὲρ ταῦτα κάλλει, and ἀμήχανον κάλλος?

Even assuming the (unfounded) rhetorical interpretation of ὑπερβολή, one would need to insist that it must have some meaning when the always sober and critical Socrates celebrates such a linguistic climax. A verbal *celebration* of a puzzling insight, whose incomparable importance ought to be noticed, is without a doubt present in 508E1–509C2. The quasi-religious εὐφήμει ("do not blaspheme") (509A9), and the invocation of the god of light, Apollo (509C1), underline this. The reason for such un-Socratic linguistic behavior can only lie in the fact that a hyperbolic state of affairs clearly must be expressed by hyperbolic linguistic means. Given the "dignity," "rank" (τιμή [cf. τιμητέον] = πρεσβεία), and power (the power of ontological generation) of the good, everything that would be less than a "rhetorical" hyperbole would be too little.[15]

7. SOCRATES' RESERVATION AND THE PHILOSOPHICAL PRACTICE IN THE IDEAL STATE

Why does Socrates not convey his δοκοῦντα without any gaps? The reason has been already mentioned: Glaucon would not be able to follow him; it would be too much, both qualitatively and quantitatively, for the "current course of the discussion" (533A; 506E). Yet it is to be pointed out that Socrates' behavior in the discussion in Polemarchus' house corresponds exactly to the way in which philosophy would be pursued in the ideal state.

In approximately a dozen passages,[16] Socrates emphasizes that only a few people would be suitable for what he likes to call the "true philosophy" (ἀληθινὴ φιλοσοφία).[17] Now it is not the case that most of the people would keep themselves voluntarily out of that which is inaccessible for them. The good name of philosophy (cf. 495D1) lures many who are unworthy. Incompetence and quarrelling are responsible for the fact that many despise philosophy, which annoys Socrates severely—and this is rather clear in the text (487B–497A; cf. 539C–D). Against the tendency of the public to debase philosophers, there is nothing that can be done at present—the few true philosophers, whom people do not recognize as such (488A7–489A2: the allegory of the ship and the state), therefore live in a self-imposed isolation at the fringe of society (496B–E).

This would be different in the ideal state, which would have to do something against the misuse and destruction of the reputation of philosophy. The philosopher-kings would correct the mistake now commonly made in using dialectic (or its distorted opposite, eristic); while today the very young and immature, and even those who have nothing to do with philosophy, use dialectic, one would, in the ideal state, keep these groups from practicing it.[18] This measure of caution (εὐλάβεια [539B1]; cf. ἐπ' εὐλαβείᾳ [539D3]) would be advantageous to the recipient, and would be pursuant to the goal of raising society's respect for philosophy: καὶ αὐτός τε μετριώτερος ἔσται καὶ τὸ ἐπιτήδευμα [sc., τῆς φιλοσοφίας] τιμιώτερον ἀντὶ ἀτιμοτέρου ποιήσει (539C8–D1). These, then, are two major reasons for cautious reservation in philosophical communication.

During his discussion with Glaucon and Adeimantus, Socrates acts in accordance with what he postulates for the philosophical practice of the future ideal state. Although his interlocutor Glaucon is not an immature youth, Socrates refuses to give him more detailed information concerning the enterprise of dialectic (532D–533A), and, being logically consistent, he does not discuss with Glaucon the goal to which the "long road" of dialectic will lead—the nature of the idea of the good (αὐτὸ μὲν τί ποτ' ἐστὶ τἀγαθὸν ἐάσωμεν τὸ νῦν εἶναι [506D8–E1]).

8. PROBLEMS THAT SOCRATES LEAVES OPEN

Until now the discussion has been concerned with the presence of a theory of the principle in the statements of the dialogic character "Socrates," the compatibility of this theory with the theory of principles in the ἄγραφα δόγματα, the manner of its literary presentation, and its agreement with the anticipated practice of philosophizing in the future ideal state. A brief glance at the philosophical problems of Socrates' incompletely reported theory may form the conclusion, which can remain brief since the relevant questions have been dealt with in part by others,[19] and in part by myself in other contexts.[20]

If Socrates had in Glaucon a well-versed dialectician for an interlocutor, he would have to take up, among others, the following questions:

(1) How must the ἀρχή be constituted if it is to fulfill a triple function as the *causa finalis*, the cause of knowledge, and the cause of being?

(2) What does the goodness (cf. 509A3: ἀγαθοειδῆ) of truth and knowledge consist in?

(3) How is discursively running through all of the ἔλεγχοι (534C1–3) related to the "vision" of the good?

(4) What is the precise philosophical sense of the γεννᾶν (508B13) through which the good becomes the "father" of the sun, and in a certain sense the cause of all things?

(1') That it cannot lead to convincing results if one tries to give reasons for the functions that Socrates attributes to the idea of the good in the *Republic* by using the text alone, or by attributing some purely ethical meaning to "good," has been demonstrated by H. J. Krämer several times.[21] Instead of understanding "good" in a modern philosophical sense, we must, as Krämer from his earliest works onward has more than once emphasized, keep to the equation given by Aristotle: ἕν = ἀγαθόν. As the goal toward which everything strives (505D11–E2), the good is the cause of the unity of the person who strives: only living in accordance with virtue helps in overcoming inner conflict and the multiplicity that comes with badness; to be good, for Plato, has the ethical sense of παντάπασιν ἕνα γενέσθαι ἐκ πολλῶν, to become entirely one from many (cf. 443E1). Ἀρετή has only *one* form, clearly because its nature is defined by the good itself, and this in its own nature is the one: therefore, "there is one form of virtue, but an unlimited number of forms of badness" (ἓν μὲν εἶναι εἶδος τῆς ἀρετῆς, ἄπειρα δὲ τῆς κακίας) (445C5–6). The character of the state is conceived analogously to the individual character: the ideal state would be morally better because its leaders know the *one* goal, which must direct all action (cf. 519C3–4). The "good" for the state is that which makes the state a unity (462A–B). At the same time, the one as the fundamental condition of *being* and *knowing* is not a point of contention: what is, is first and foremost *one* being and nothing can be grasped as long as it cannot be grasped as *one* object of knowledge.

(2') Ἀλήθεια and ἐπιστήμη (or γνῶσις [508E5–6]) come from the good and share its character, i.e., are "good-like" (ἀγαθοειδῆ) (508E6–509A5). Both Plato's picture of the way in which νοῦς functions (*Legg.* 898A3–B3) and the indirect transmission (Aristotle, *DA* 404b22: νοῦν μὲν τὸ ἕν) emphasize its character of oneness. Thought becomes identical with its object; for noetic thought (νόησις), this is the idea, the first ontological characteristic of which is to be one (476A5: αὐτὸ μὲν ἓν ἕκαστον εἶναι; 507B6–7: κατ᾽ ἰδέαν μίαν ἑκάστου ὡς μιᾶς οὔσης; 596A–B: εἶδος . . . ἓν ἕκαστον). The objects of pure thought are "good-like" and therefore knowable ("true") in as much as they are "one-like," and the "good-like" ἐπιστήμη grasps them by virtue of its ability to tend toward sameness and unity.

(3') Running through all the dialectically necessary steps would be an enormous task (cf. 534A7–8). For example, the philosophical astronomy called for by Plato would be a much more extensive enterprise than the one now practiced, and yet it would only be one part of the mathematical "prelude," which is itself by far quantitatively exceeded by the "method" (531D7–8: προοίμιον/νόμος). And yet without this "running through everything" it is impossible to find the truth and obtain insight (*Parm.* 136E1–3). One already understands to what extent Platonic dialectic is a matter of living and working together for a long time (*Ep.* VII, 341C6–7). Its very extent—apart from all other reasons—excludes that it could ever become the object of a written account. At any rate, Plato's hints and suggestions, when one considers them together with what was transmitted indirectly, make clear that "running through all of the ἔλεγχοι," in its crucial phase, would lead to a differentiation of the good from the highest dialectical concepts, the μέγιστα γένη, and also to a "definition" of the good or the one as the most exact measure (ἀκριβέστατον μέτρον).[22] It remains difficult to decide a question of great philosophical importance, namely, the question as to how the "running through," which is clearly of a discursive nature (cf. *Republic* 534C2: διεξίων; *Parm.* 136E2: διέξοδος), is related to the sought after vision of the good. The use of mystery-cult terminology (521C2–3; 533D1–3; 534C7–D1) and "erotic" language (485B1; 490B2; 499C2), as well as the clear correspondence between the description of the aspiration of one who truly desires knowledge (ὄντως φιλομαθής) in 490A8–B7, and the climax of Diotima's speech in the *Symposium* (212A), make certain that turning toward the idea reaches its climax in a vision that cannot be discursive anymore. This is certainly true for the knowledge of every idea, inasmuch as it reaches its goal.[23] The knowledge of the idea of the good is repeatedly characterized as a proper stage of the knowledge of the other ideas, which is only consistent with the whole picture insofar as the ideas are οὐσία, and οὐσία is what is actually knowable, whereas for the good this same characterization no longer holds (509B8–9). The discursive "running through" a multiplicity of conceptual relationships is the prerequisite for the noetic "touching" (490B3) or "vision" (*passim*) of the ideas—a process whose adequate epistemological description is notoriously difficult.[24] The description of the step-by-step "ascent" seems to necessitate the knowledge of the uppermost "idea"—which, in contrast to the other ideas, is "beyond οὐσία"—an own level of knowledge that would surpass the noetic knowledge of ideas just as this surpasses διάνοια. The text says nothing as to whether or not this is what Socrates wants to suggest, or how this level would be characterized epistemologically. Whoever might want to assure us that "since it is not in the text, it could not have been in the mind of the author," we must remind him of 509C7: συχνά γε ἀπολείπω.

(4') The good is the "king" and "father" that "engenders" the sun as its visible correspondence. Can a father "engender" without a "mother"? Aristotle testifies to Plato's application of gender metaphors male/female, to the principles (*Met.* A.6, 988a5–7). This tells us, with regard to "engendering," that it must include two factors that act in cooperation—which is no small gain. Since "Socrates" mentions the "father" only, he consequently cannot speak of the ontological meaning of the engendering that is implied in his picture. The Academic search for that which is more fundamental or "prior" (πρότερον, πρῶτον), deals with determining the concepts that are presupposed by other concepts, without themselves presupposing anything (in accordance with the principle of συναναιρεῖν καὶ μὴ συναναιρεῖσθαι). It is, then, easy to understand that the result of this kind of search was the concept of the one as that which is absolutely indispensable for all knowing and thinking, and thus as the foundation of everything. Such a manner of thinking succumbs to the Aristotelian critique that what is logically prior, does not necessarily have to be ontologically prior (*Met.* M.2, 1077B1–2). Plato would presumably have answered this with his version of the Parmenidean equation of thinking and being. The limitation or determination of the undetermined by the determining and limiting was, for Plato, certainly as much an ontological principle as it was a logical one (cf. *Phil.* 16Cf.). In his great monologue, Timaeus leaves not only the nature of the demiurge open (*Tim.* 28C3–5)—and with that the precise ontological sense of the effect of the good on the sensible world (cf. *Tim.* 29E1–3)—but also the number and nature of the ultimate principles (48C2–6; cf. 53D6–7). This is a clear indication that the questions that interest us the most were not coincidentally disregarded by the Socrates of the *Republic* either, but were not meant to be treated in published writings by the author himself.

NOTES

1. Gaiser 1963. For a separate edition of the testimonies (with an introduction by G. Reale and an Italian translation of Gaiser's comments by V. Cicero), see Gaiser 1998. Another collection, expanded by several texts with a French translation of all the testimonies, can be found in Richard 1986, 243–381.

2. The passages given in the following account are very sparse and merely *exempli gratia.* The complete references are in Richard 1986, 171–242.

3. Szlezák 1985 (*PSP*), Szlezák 1992 (*PSF*).

4. I describe the Socrates of the dialogues as "having the same name" as the historical thinker in order to avoid the impression that I would see in him a *portrait* of the historical thinker. The literary Socrates is at most a bold *interpretation* of the historical one, or an interpretation of some of his characteristics with the addition of other characteristics that the historical Socrates lacked.

5. For more concerning the conception of the characters of the *Republic,* cf. *PSP* 290–303 (= *PSF* 375f., 383–390).

6. Cf. 327C9: ἢ τοίνυν τούτων, ἔφη, κρείττους γένεσθε ἢ μένετ' αὐτοῦ.

7. Cf. *PSP* 271–277, 315–316, 325f. (= *PSF* 354–361, 403–404, 415).

8. These passages are interpreted in detail in *PSP* 303–325 (= *PSF* 390–414).

9. On the language of the metaphor of the sun—which is likewise an indispensable part of any literary analysis—cf. §6 below.

10. Gadamer 1978, 82: "That the good is somehow the one, is obviously implied in the construction of the *Republic.*"

11. How would it look if Socrates did not consciously lower the bar for his truth claim? Then his friends could say to him: Ὠγαθέ . . . μὴ μέγα λέγε. Yet such words are reserved in Plato only for the consistently modest Socrates; he uses them against Cebes, who expects that Socrates will solve his problem without much effort (*Phaedo* 95A7–B5). The warning μὴ μέγα λέγε does not hinder Socrates from completely fulfilling Cebes' expectation. Therefore, it is not the trust in Socrates' superior understanding that was exaggerated; it is just that μέγα λέγειν is μή τις ἡμῖν βασκανία περιτρέψῃ τὸν λόγον τὸν μέλλοντα ἔσεσθαι (*Phaedo* 95B5–6). Would this not sufficiently explain Socrates' renunciation of every possible μέγα λέγειν in the *Republic*? As the *Phaedo* shows, such examples of modesty do not allow for any conclusion concerning his inability to find a convincing answer to the problem in question.

12. Gadamer 1978, 21: "To grasp directly the good itself and to want to know it like a μάθημα appears to be impossible on account of its nature. One should take this inexpressibility, this ἄρρητον as soberly as possible." In the text of the *Republic* no ἄρρητον is ever mentioned. Gadamer probably had in mind the *Seventh Letter,* 341C: ῥητὸν γὰρ οὐδαμῶς ἔστιν ὡς ἄλλα μαθήματα.

13. Hegel 1995, vol. 2, 22.

14. L. Brisson considers 509B9 in isolation in Brisson 1993, esp. 23. See also Brisson 2000, which claims to be a literary analysis. In my opinion, literary analysis has to provide more than the explanation of ὑπερβολή in 509C2 as a rhetorical exaggeration (Brisson 2000, esp. 4).

15. To clarify: a linguistic hyperbole is present here, yet δαιμονίας ὑπερβολῆς does not mean the linguistic hyperbole, but rather the ontological relationship in question.

16. 428E5; 476B11; 491B; 494A4; 495B2; 496A11, C5; 499D–E; 503B7, D11; 531E2.

17. 486B3; 490A3; 499C1; 521B2, C7–Dl; cf. 548B8–C1.

18. 539B1–D7; 503D8–9: ἢ μήτε παιδείας τῆς ἀκριβεστάτης δεῖν αὐτῷ μεταδιδόναι μήτε τιμῆς μήτε ἀρχῆς. The "most exact education" is of course the dialectical one.

19. Krämer 1959; Krämer 1969 (see chap. 2 of this volume); Krämer 1989; Gaiser 1986 (see chap. 4 of this volume); Gaiser 1987 (these previous two articles now appear in Gaiser 2004). Reale 1984; Reale 1992; Reale 1993. One could consider Chen 1992 a valuable correction to certain biases in Anglophone Platonic literature since A. Ferguson (1921) and R. Robinson (1953). The commentary and appendices in Adam 1902 are indispensable.

20. Szlezák 1997.

21. See Krämer 1997, 179ff.

22. Cf. Krämer 1989, 41–46, 57–62.

23. Chen 1992 worked out the meaning of the "vision" of the idea in the middle dialogues with exemplary clarity, clearly distancing Plato from some reductionist rationalistic interpretations (Chen 1992, 127–178).

24. Oehler 1962.

SIX

MONISM AND DUALISM IN PLATO'S DOCTRINE OF PRINCIPLES

Jens Halfwassen

Plato's inner-Academic doctrine of principles—of which the most significant twentieth-century interpreter was H. J. Krämer[1]—puts forth, as is now familiar, two final principles: the absolute one (αὐτὸ τὸ ἕν) and the indefinite dyad (ἀόριστος δυάς) of the great and small (μέγα καὶ μικρόν). According to this doctrine, every being can be led back to the interaction of these principles. The question as to "how, according to Plato, these two opposing principles in the end relate to one another," was posed by K. Gaiser in his 1963 groundbreaking book, *Platons ungeschriebene Lehre*, as "the central factual and historical problem" of the Platonic doctrine of principles.[2]

The research into Platonic philosophy during the last century had often treated this very question, which addresses the relationship between monism and dualism in Plato's doctrine of principles.[3] The possible positions range from a pronounced monism (as J. Findlay portrays it in his strongly Hegelianized interpretation)[4] to a thoroughgoing dualism (as P. Wilpert and H. Happ apparently find in Plato).[5]

C. de Vogel and C. F. von Weizsäcker prefer a cautious monism with a clear subordination of the principle of the many according to the model of henology in Plotinus.[6] Gaiser himself tends to a solution akin to the *coincidentia oppositorum* in the absolute.[7] In a similar direction, V. Hösle vigorously develops the belief that an encompassing of the positive by the negative principle in the sense of a dialectical unity of unity and plurality can be found in Plato.[8] In contrast, H. J. Krämer forcefully stresses the dualistic train of Plato's thinking of principles, but, nevertheless, leaves open the possibility of a final monism underlying dualism. In his monumental book, *Der Ursprung der Geistmetaphysik* (1964), for example, Krämer considers a monistic solution. He does not, however, consider a unity of opposites (as understood either by Nicholas of Cusa or Hegel), but, in the tradition of the Neoplatonic interpretation of Plato, instead proposes the reduction of the principle of the many to the one as the all-grounding original principle [*allbegründendes Ur-Prinzip*].[9]

The above discussion of scholarship should warn us not to interpret Plato's unwritten doctrine without qualification as a direct, almost Manichean dualism. Nevertheless, W. Kullmann has recently opposed the "dualism" of the unwritten doctrines to the "monism" of the dialogues as two contextually and hardly unifiable philosophies.[10] Against this view, it should be pointed out that the dialogues (namely, *Timaeus*, *Sophist*, *Philebus*, and *Parmenides*) also reckon with a two-pole structure of reality similar to the unwritten doctrines;[11] on the other side, the testimony of the unwritten doctrines themselves give indications of a final monism in Plato, which, incidentally, the history of the doctrine of principles attests, not only from Neoplatonism on, but also since Speusippus.[12] In the following, I will first examine a few informative passages from the dialogues regarding the relation between monism and dualism in Plato. I will then look into some especially important indications of a final monism of principles in the indirect tradition as well as suggest a previously—I believe—undiscussed solution. Finally, I will support this solution historically through Speusippus and the middle Platonic philosopher, Eudorus, who is dependent upon the former.

1. MONISM AND DUALISM IN THE DIALOGUES

The most informative passage in the dialogues with regard to the understanding of Plato's conception of principles is perhaps the sequence of similes in books VI and VII of the *Republic*, together with the adjacent remarks on the relation between mathematical propaedeutic and dialectic.[13] Plato only reveals his first principle here, which appears as "the good itself" or "the idea of the good," but whose own essence is intentionally held back.[14] That the good, according to its own essence, is the one itself, as Aristotle reports,[15] is unmistakably alluded to by Plato in the *Republic* in his demand for an essential dialectical determination of the idea of the good that defines it by abstracting it from all other things, ἀπὸ τῶν ἄλλων πάντων ἀφελών[16] and removes it from all fundamental determinations of being and thinking.[17] But this ἀφαίρεσις πάντων leads necessarily to the one itself, whose absolute simplicity excludes every manifold determination and thus also explains why the "good"—as the final principle of being, knowledge, and value—must nonetheless lie "beyond being" (ἔτι ἐπέκεινα τῆς οὐσίας).[18] It must lie beyond being because the statement that "the one is" already entails a duality, namely, between oneness and being, from which every other fundamental determination of being is derived, as Hypothesis II of the *Parmenides* shows.[19]

The one beyond being or the good is noticeably called the "unconditioned,"[20] the "unconditioned origin,"[21] or "the origin of the whole [of ideas]."[22] The unconditionality of the one is thereby bound up with its position as the "origin of the whole" and therefore as the all-grounding principle.[23] The dialectical program of the *Republic* clearly describes the ascent to *one* unconditioned and absolute, which functions as the fundamental ground of *all things*. This seems to exclude an irreducible dualism of principles: if the many stands over against the one as an equi-originary and equi-independent principle, then the one would no longer be the principle of *all things* nor the ἀνυπόθετος ἀρχή, because its effectiveness as the origin would be conditioned through its interaction with the principle of the many. Moreover, several unconditioned principles would neutralize one another in their unconditionality, which is why there can only be *one* ἀνυπόθετον that overcomes the plurality of ὑποθέσεις.[24] The statements in the *Republic* speak decisively for a monistic interpretation of the doctrine of principles. Since the ideal numbers[25] and also the μέγα καὶ μικρόν[26] are referred to there, any interpretation that attempts to balance genetically the monistic strain of the *Republic* with the dualism of the indirect tradition (i.e., through their dating) can easily be disregarded.[27] A more plausible monistic interpretation of the doctrine of principles cannot, of course, mean an *elimination* of the thoroughgoing and determinate bipolarity, but only its *relativizing*, insofar as the principle of the many cannot be compared to the one as equally original or powerful and, thus, cannot be held as a second absolute.[28]

This is confirmed in the second part of the *Parmenides*, which perhaps best reveals the unwritten doctrine of principles within the written work of Plato. The one and the many—the two principles of the unwritten doctrine—are examined there in eight arguments or "hypotheses" with respect to their absoluteness in themselves and in their relation to one another. Hypotheses II and III demonstrate the constitution of the being of the world of ideas—of the ontic one—through the interaction of both principles. Hypothesis II characterizes the ontological accounts from the first principle as the unfolding of the one in the many through the dividing but also expanding power of the dyad. Hypothesis III describes the very same ontological accounts, but, from the perspective of the secondary principles, as the limiting of the unlimited through the unity-positing power of the one.[29] In contrast, Hypotheses I and IV thematize the one and the many in themselves independently of one another, i.e., in their unrelatedness. The result is negative insofar as the principles in themselves of every determination of being—which are predicates of the ontic one—as well as being itself, knowledge, and speech are denied.[30] This means, first of all, that the two principles, the one and the many, are not ontic, since they lay before every thinkable determination and, with that, every possible meaning of being. The non-being of the absolute one[31] is more precisely understood as the transcendence of being or as "beyond being."[32] Every other negation of Hypothesis I must accordingly be understood as statements of transcendence, which cut the absolute off from all of its derivatives in the way of a thoroughgoing *theologia negativa*. This is carried out in the *Republic*[33] through the required negative exclusion of the absolute principle.[34] However, the non-being of the pure, unity-less many does not mean "beyond being," but "deficiency of being." The negations of Hypothesis IV, which correspond to this, are therefore to be understood in a privative and not in a transcendent sense.

Both the ontological transcendence of the pure one and the ontological deficiency of the pure many have also been addressed in the reports of the inner-Academic doctrine.[35] These reports, however, elucidate a distinct asymmetry in the relation of the principles to one another: while the one itself in its absolute transcendence of all plurality can and must be taken purely for itself—since it is free in its absoluteness from any relation to another, i.e., to the second principle—the many, on the other hand, cannot be considered purely for itself because, as soon as it gets separated from the one, it also, so to speak, vanishes into the nothing.[36] Only the one posits itself absolutely, not the many, which is in itself nothing. Thus, there is only one absolute. The last hypothesis of the *Parmenides* confirms this by showing that the many, when separated from the one, is no longer many,[37] but nothing.[38] Put positively, this means that the many itself requires the character of unity [*Einheit*] in order to be conceived generally as a principle; and, in fact, Aristotle explicitly attests to this character of unity with respect to the principle of the many in Plato.[39] The many, then, cannot be opposed to the one as equi-originary and equi-powerful. But the possibility of a discursively understandable derivation of the original many from the absolute one is not feasible.

The *Philebus* also indicates a final monism in Plato that does not eliminate but that underlies dualism. In agreement with the *Parmenides* and the indirect tradition, this dialogue posits the one and the many—which show up here in the Pythagorean terms πέρας and ἄπειρον, the limit and the unlimited—as the two constitutive principles of reality on every level of being.[40] Plato stresses, on the one hand, that both principles result in a plurality of aspects and manifestations on various levels and in different realms of reality, but also, on the other hand, that each principle is for itself one (23Ef.).[41] Plato thereby points out the necessary character of unity regarding the ἄπειρον—i.e., the *second* principle—in a completely conspicuous way (25A–C; 23E).[42] If, however, the principle of the many must have the character of unity irrespective of the plurality of its aspects and manifestations—for it cannot be *a* principle or the unifying genus of its own manifold ways of appearing—then it can be neither equally original with nor independent from the one itself as the fundamental ground of *every* unity. Still another indication of a final monism of principles can be taken from the *Philebus*, namely, from the fact that it posits two additional principles of reality besides the πέρας and ἄπειρον (23Cf.): the mixed, μικτόν as the product of the limiting of the unlimited and the cause of mixture, αἰτία τῆς μείξεως as that which coordinates the interaction of the two principles in the limiting of the unlimited (27B, 30A–B). On the level of true being, the μικτόν can, with respect to the *Parmenides*, be identified with the ontic one as the whole of all ideas. In the cosmologically restricted perspective of the *Philebus*, the αἰτία is linked with νοῦς and also, therefore, with the demiurge as the *causa efficiens* of the world.[43] We may, however, suspend this perspectival restriction and question the ground of the interaction of the two universal principles. Insofar as this coordination itself is a kind of unity, only its principle can be the absolute one, which stands for the "ground" as such above the opposition of principles and first makes this opposition possible.[44] Plato himself seems to refer to the one as the final or absolute αἰτία when he calls νοῦς the "king of heaven and earth" (28C) on the basis of its αἰτία-function. This may remind us of the idea of the good, which stands as a metaphor for the all-grounding principle in the *Republic* (509D), and also of the "king of all things" from Plato's second letter (312E), where the one is without question intended. Furthermore, in the *Philebus*, νοῦς belongs to the "genus of the ground of all things" (30D10f.: ὅτι νοῦς ἐστὶ γένους τῆς τοῦ πάντων αἰτίου λεχθέντος),[45] which the dialogue therefore represents as only one of its manifestations. However, the "ground of all things," according to the *Republic*, is the idea of the good as ἀρχὴ τοῦ παντός (511B7),[46] which is the transcendent one itself, whose unity-grounding efficacy νοῦς imitates in the subordinate realm of cosmological being.[47]

2. MONISM AND DUALISM IN THE UNWRITTEN DOCTRINE

Just as the testimony of the dialogues speaks decidedly for a final monism in Plato that does not eliminate the bivalent structure of reality, but instead grounds it in a deeper, comprehensive principle, so too can such an interpretation be found and supported throughout the reports of the unwritten doctrine. Nowhere, in fact, can one find here an actual derivation of the principle of the many from the one. The account given by Sextus Empiricus (*TP* 32, §261), who seems to be the only one to speak of such a derivation, remains unsatisfactory. His description of the self-division of the one "according to its otherness," which is supposed to yield the indefinite dyad,[48] already presupposes otherness and refers to the always repeatable mutual implication of both components of the ontic one in the infinite, as shown in the *Parmenides* (Hypothesis II: 142Ef.). These components are differentiated from and added to one another on the basis of otherness, from which—exactly as in Sextus—the ideal numbers are deduced (143Bf.).[49] This shows the effectiveness of the dyad, in the most originary structure of being, rather than the derivation of the very principle of the dyad itself from the absolute one,[50] which is beyond identity and otherness. By contrast, there are a number of accounts that argue, in principle, for the subordination of the ἀόριστος δυάς under the one without having to be derived from the one, whereby its status as a principle is canceled.

Hermodorus' severely abridged account of the doctrine of principles (*TP* 31), for example, confirms the privative meaning of the non-being of the indefinite dyad in the sense of the deficiency of being,[51] which agrees with Hypotheses IV and VIII of the *Parmenides*. Moreover, Hermodorus denies the indefinite dyad the status of ἀρχή, which can be understood, I think, as meaning that the dyad is not possibly a grounding principle of being, but only the null basis of the unfolding of the one. The comparison to Augustine's characterization of the *malum* as *causa deficiens*, which he took over from Plotinus, is obvious here.

Aristotle also seems to refer repeatedly to an ultimate monism of the inner-Academic doctrine of principles. Specifically, he reports of the thinker who posited the one and the unequal as principles and conceived the unequal as the (indefinite) duality of the large and the small, but spoke of the unequal, the large, and the small as of *one being* (ὡς ἓν ὄντα). Aristotle criticizes this thinker for not distinguishing that these components only form a *conceptual* (λόγῳ) but not a *numerical* (ἀριθμῷ) unity (*TP* 49).[52] This corresponds perfectly with Plato's explicit references to the necessary character of unity with respect to the principle of the many in the *Parmenides* and *Philebus*; however, Aristotle specifies the above distinction in order to make clear that the unity of the second principle has, for Plato, not only a conceptual but also, as a numerical unity, an ontological nature. If, therefore, Plato granted the character of unity to the indefinite dyad both conceptually and ontologically, then his second principle is neither as equally originary nor equally powerful as the one but, according to the criterion of the συναναιρεῖν καὶ μὴ συναναιρεῖσθαι, dependent upon it. As the *Parmenides* shows, the principle of the many is canceled if the one is canceled (Hypothesis VIII), but the one is not, if the many is not (Hypothesis I). In a similar way,

Aristotle's remarks illustrate, strictly speaking, that nothing can be opposed to the one, "but, if at all something, then the many."[53] If the many itself must be a unity conceptually and ontologically—for otherwise it could not be many—then the one is the principle *of all*, even of the many, without and beyond opposition. Nevertheless, both principles form a quasi-opposition[54] insofar as the one can be absolutely separate from the many, but not vice versa. Moreover, Aristotle's assertion that the advocates of the "two principles" doctrine—whom he explicitly calls the friends of the forms—posit another, higher principle (ἀρχὴ κυριωτέρα) can also be understood in the same way.[55] The principle of the ideas thus is the one,[56] which is also the "higher principle" over against the indefinite dyad insofar as it establishes, in the manner of the αἰτία-principle of the *Philebus*, the coordination of both principles as a form of unity—and also, therefore, the participation of the ideas in the principles and the things in the ideas.

It follows from this that Plato's principle of the many is, on the one hand, dependent upon the one as the absolute origin of *all things*, but, on the other hand, cannot be derived from the one itself in its absoluteness; and, even according to the absolute transcendence of the one—which is nothing other than the one itself and which therefore cannot have in itself any latent, undeveloped many—the second principle is neither implied nor predetermined. The ἀόριστος δυάς is evidently a principle, but not in the sense that it stands over against the one as equi-originary and independent, but in the sense that it cannot be discursively derived from the one as the basis of its unfolding: in order to be able to derive anything at all from the one, the indefinite many or dyad must already be presupposed, as Hypotheses II and III of the *Parmenides* show. The ἀόριστος δυάς is therefore not absolutely final or first in the *reductive* ascent to the original ground, i.e., it is not a second ἀνυπόθετος ἀρχή, but rather a discursively non-derivable condition for the deduction of being; for no thinkable determination can be derived from the one itself in its absolute transcendence and unrelatedness. Further, the "it itself" in its pure essence lies absolutely beyond being and the many, and therefore does not yet have any relation to them as a principle,[57] as the conclusion of Hypothesis I of the *Parmenides* illustrates (141E–142A). Speusippus' account of the Platonic doctrine of principles confirms this by openly taking on the difficulty of this relation:

> They [sc., the Pythagoreans to whom Speusippus here ascribes Plato's doctrine] believe that the one is *raised beyond being* and the 'from where' of being, and they have even *freed* the *one from any relational determination as a principle*. But because they mean that nothing comes into being from other things, if one views the one itself, alone in itself, without basing any further determinations,

> pure in themselves, on it and without adding some kind of second element [principle] to it, they introduced the indefinite dyad as a principle of being.[58]

If this interpretation is correct, then Plato's doctrine of principles combines a monism in the *reduction* to the absolute with a dualism in the *deduction* of being. Such a combination of *reductive monism* and *deductive dualism* seems, if looked at more precisely, to be factually unavoidable for a metaphysics of the transcendent absolute. The reverse is impossible; for a dualism in the reduction would always lead to two principles only, neither of which is really an ἀνυπόθετον and whose interaction cannot be established. Conversely, a monism in the deduction would always find the many or, at least, a latent many already in the one itself, which divides itself in itself and therefore no longer lies beyond all things. Also, we find nowhere in Plotinus—whose thinking with respect to a consistent metaphysics of the one is paradigmatic—a discursively understandable derivation of the many from the transcendent one, as Hegel has already shown (and from his standpoint criticized).[59] The coming-forth of the many from the absolutely simple one is only postulated by Plotinus and restated in his well-known metaphors of emanation, but is never made intellectually transparent and graspable in its necessity. Given the one's transcendence of knowledge, this is not at all possible. The many comes forth, rather, *in an unintelligible way* from the transcendent superabundance of the one. Plotinus alludes to the reason why something outside the one, e.g., the many and being, can exist in his notion of the being-positing power and super-abundance of the one. With this, however, only the *that*, but not the *how* or the *why* of the coming-forth of the many from the one is knowable.[60] The decisive Plotinian notion of the 'being-positing power' of the absolute comes from Plato (*Rep.* 509B, *Parm.* 157E–158B); we also find the infinity of the one, understood in the Plotinian sense as the superabundance of δύναμις, in Plato[61] as well as the metaphor of emanation.[62] Whether Plato, like Plotinus, accepted that the coming-forth of the many from the one is ungraspable by discursive thinking, we do not know. We can, however, presume it insofar as the motive of the being-positing πρoόδος from the superiority of the transcendent absolute—held mostly as a specifically Neoplatonic concept—was familiar to the Academy and can also be traced back to it. Speusippus, specifically, spoke of the "coming-forth of the reality of being" from the one that is, likewise, equally effective in every realm of being as a unity-positing principle (fr. 58, 72, 88 Isnardi Parente).[63]

3. OVERVIEW OF SPEUSIPPUS AND EUDORUS

Speusippus does not oppose the principle of the many to the one beyond being,[64] but only to the first derivative, the monad or the ontic one as the principle of numbers, which, together with the many, constitute the numbers themselves. This, for Speusippus, is the highest level of being. The opposition of principles—understood here primarily as the opposition of numerical unity and plurality—remains subordinate to the absolute one as the sole original principle that coordinates, on each level of being, the dualistically opposed principles of each realm (fr. 88 Isnardi Parente).[65] Since Speusippus assumes a gradual coming-forth of being from the one and since the "coming-forth" (προελθεῖν) lays the foundation for the developing plurality of the later levels—which differentiated the ontologically "later" from the ontologically "earlier" level (fr. 58, 72 Isnardi Parente)—he seems to accept a coming forth of the many from the one. This coming-forth, together with the monad, constitutes the first level of being; for, insofar as the numeric monad is generated from the absolute one through the limiting of the many (fr. 72, 88 Isnardi Parente)—and thus already presupposes the many—it is evidently the many itself that originally comes forth from the one. We can thus develop in Speusippus a two-stage original act in which the many, in the first stage, comes forth from the one as unlimited in order, then, to be limited by it in the second stage. The unlimitedness of that which comes forth corresponds to what Speusippus accepts as the unlimitedness of the one itself (Proclus, *In Parm.* 1118, 1019 Cousin).[66] With regard, however, to the first stage of the original act, the coming-forth of the many from the one itself is not part of the tradition, but can nonetheless be developed with sufficient certainty in terms of the idea—attributed to Speusippus by Aristotle and Iamblichus independently of one another—of the coming-forth of reality out of the absolute and in terms of its function in the coherence of the derivation of the system of stages. The two-stage original act in Speusippus corresponds perfectly with the two-stage original act in Plotinus by which the many likewise comes forth "at first" as indefinite from the superiority of the one in order to limit itself by turning toward the one; thereby the coming-forth as such takes place in a discursively unknowable way.[67]

Particularly informative in connection with this is the version of the old Academic doctrine of principles—dependent upon Speusippus and Plato's *Parmenides*—that the middle Platonic philosopher, Eudorus from Alexandria, ascribes to the Pythagoreans:

> On the highest level [κατὰ τὸν ἀνωτάτω λόγον], the Pythagoreans posit the one as the origin of all; but, on the second level [κατὰ δὲ τὸν δεύτερον λόγον], they assume two constitutive principles of reality, namely, the one and the essence opposed to it. Everything that one knows as oppositional is then classified under the opposites; specifically, the valuable under the one and the invaluable under the opposite essence. Thus, this school does not understand these principles as absolutely first; for, if the former is a principle of

> one column of opposites and the latter is a principle of the other column of opposites, then they are not, like the absolute one, the common principles of all. . . . Therefore, they also taught that the absolute one is the origin of all in a completely different sense, because matter as well as every being comes forth from it. This [sc., the absolute one] is the transcendent god [ὑπεράνω θεός]. . . . I therefore say that the doctrine of the Pythagoreans leads to the one as the original principle [ἀρχή] of all; while, in another sense, they also posit two highest elements [στοιχεῖα] so that the absolute one emerges as the origin, but the [second] one and the indefinite dyad as the elements, whereby each of these both elementary principles is again a unity [ἀρχαὶ ἄμφω ἓν ὄντα πάλιν]. It is also evident that the highest one, the origin of all, is differentiated from the one of the two opposed elements, which they also designate as monads.[68]

Eudorus therefore leads the two-pole structure of reality back to the *two* principles of the one and the indefinite dyad, but thereby differentiates, like Speusippus and like Plato in the *Parmenides*, between the absolute one as the transcendent ἀρχή of *all things* and the ontic one or the monad as the immanent στοιχεῖον of being.[69] Together with the monad, the indefinite dyad, as the material principle, constitutes the bivalentstructure of being. Eudorus, accordingly, differentiates between a *monistic* ἀνωτάτω λόγος and a *dualistic* δεύτερος λόγος, and this seems to correspond exactly with the relation of the monistic reduction to the absolute and the dualistic derivation of being, which we find in Plato. Eudorus maintains the coherence of these two levels on the assumption that, according to him, the indefinite dyad "as well as every being" has come forth from the transcendent one. The remarkable argument by Eudorus thus reads: ἀρχαὶ ἄμφω ἓν ὄντα πάλιν. This argument is genuinely Platonic, since we know from Aristotle that the ἀόριστος δυάς itself was also a unity for Plato (*TP* 49). It is thus fair to assume that Plato had already accepted a coming-forth of the principle of the many from the one, but also that it could not be explained any further.

NOTES

1.The following essay was presented on April 29, 1994, at the University of Tübingen at a colloquium in honor of Prof. Dr. H. J. Krämer's sixty-fifth birthday; it also appears in the commemorative publication for H. J. Krämer: Th. A. Szlezák, ed., *Platonisches Philosophieren* (Hildesheim: Georg Olms, 2001). I would like to thank Thomas Szlezák and Georg Olms Publishers, Hildesheim, for their gracious permission to publish it here.The most important work by H. J. Krämer on the interpretation of Plato's unwritten doctrine of principles and its coherence with his written work are Krämer 1959; Krämer 1964; Krämer 1964(2); Krämer 1966; Krämer 1967;

Krämer 1968; Krämer 1969 (see chap. 2 of this volume); Krämer 1971; Krämer 1973; Krämer 1980; Krämer 1981; Krämer 1982; Krämer 1990; Krämer 1982(2); Krämer 1983; Krämer 1986; Krämer 1988; Krämer 1989; Krämer 1990(2); Krämer 1993; Krämer 1994; Krämer 1996; Krämer 1997; and Krämer 1997(2). H. J. Krämer gives a detailed bibliography regarding Plato's unwritten doctrine in Krämer 1990, 287–300.

2. Gaiser 1963/1968, 12–13.

3. The diverse possibilities of conceptualizing the relation of the principles to one another and also the many possible varieties of monism and dualism as well as the interpenetration of both have, in principle, been distinguishedby Ph. Merlan in Merlan 1965. A number of scholars examine diverse forms of monism and dualism in the history of Platonism such as: (1) Vogel 1970; (2) Theiler 1964; also Theiler 1965, esp. 205ff.; (3) Rist 1965; (4) Dillon 1977, esp. 12ff. (Speusippus), 119ff. (Ps.-Pythagorean), 126ff. (Eudorus), 342ff. (Alexander Polyhistor and Sextus Empiricus), 346ff. (Moderatus); also Dillon 1981, esp. 11, 17ff.

4. Findlay 1974, esp. 322ff.

5. Wilpert 1949, esp. 173ff.; Happ 1971, esp. 141ff.; also quite similar is Reale 1993, esp. 205ff.

6. De Vogel 1959, esp. 31; and de Vogel 1986; Weizsäcker 1971, 474–491, esp. 476; Weizsäcker 1981, 57f., 74f.

7. Gaiser 1963, esp. 12–13, 27, 200–201, 506 (200: "A final 'foundation' can only be given, if, behind the antinomies resolved in the doctrine of opposites, a comprehensive ground became evident that would entail both being and non-being within itself").

8. Hösle 1984, 478–490 (481: "In a certain sense, Platonic philosophy brings itself to the formula . . . that it has thought the unity of unity and plurality; what is important in this determination is the structure, which combines a positive and a negative category within the positive").

9. Krämer 1964, esp. 332–334.

10. Kullmann 1991, esp. 11ff. and 18ff.; cf. 21: "The doctrine of a second principle was first developed according to the composition of the 'state' and remained, in this strict form, entirely unconsidered in the dialogues because it could not be reconciled with the basic positions of Platonic philosophy."

11. In addition, a thorough interpretation of this claim is given in Reale 1993, 293ff., 315ff., 355ff., esp. 443–521, regarding the *Timaeus*. See also Migliori 1990 and Movia 1990.

12. Here, the information about my own relevant publications might be appropriate: Halfwassen 1992, esp. 98ff., 201ff., 282ff., 363ff.; Halfwassen 1992(2); Halfwassen 1993, esp. 342ff., 350ff., 360ff.; Halfwassen 1996; Halfwassen 1998, 29–42; Halfwassen 1999, esp. 175–196.

13. Fundamental to the understanding of the central passages in the *Republic* in light of the doctrine of principles are the works of Krämer: Krämer 1959, 135–145, 473–480, 533ff.; Krämer 1964, esp. 214f., 221; Krämer 1969, 96–103; Krämer 1997. The interpretations of the "analogy of the sun" by Reale and myself, which are based on Krämer's findings, should also be referred to: Reale 1993, 257–291; Halfwassen 1992, 220–264. Szlezák 1985 is also very important because of the precisely developed proof that the "help" for the proper logos establishes the consistently carried out

principle of composition in the Platonic dialogues by reverting to the τιμιώτερα—i.e., to a more *principled* foundation; further, through his thoroughgoing analysis of the dialogues' immanent reference functions, Szlezák produced an indirect proof that the dialogues need to be completed both in whole and in part by the unwritten doctrine of principles and aims toward it; cf. also Szlezák 1993, esp. 67ff., 85ff.

14. Plato, *Rep.* 506E, 509C.

15. Aristotle, *Met.* N.4, 1091b13–15; *EE* A.8, 1218a19–21. The same also comes in Aristoxenus, *Harm.* II 39–40 da Rios (according to Aristotle); Aristotle, *Met.* A.6, 988a14f., Λ.8, 1075a35f., Λ.8, 1084a34f., 1092a29ff.; *Physics* A.9, 192a15; Sextus Empiricus, *Adv. Math.* X.268–275; Hermodorus in Simplicius, *In Phys.* 248, 2ff.—Plato refers, in an encoded way, to the one as the essence of the good through the appeal to Apollo (509C1), whose name isinterpreted as the negation of the many (A-pollo, not-many); cf. Plotinus, *Enn.* V.5.6.27f.; Plutarch, *De E apud Delphos* 20, 393C, and *De Iside* 75, 381F–382A (in the context of the Platonic doctrine of principles: everything is derived from ἕν—Ἀπόλλων—κατ' ἔλλειψιν καὶ ὑπερβολήν, ἰσότητι).

16. Plato, *Rep.* 534B.

17. For the explanation of this very important position in *Rep.* 534B–C, see Krämer 1996. That Plato conceived a negative theology at this point is rightly confirmed by Proclus, *In Remp.* I.285, 5–28, and *In Parm.* VII.64, 16–27. Proclus' interpretation of the position as the *via negativa* of the pure one fundamentally agrees with Krämer's interpretation, but does not explicitly differentiate between the generalizing and elementary ascent to the one; furthermore, Proclus combines it with the first Hypothesis of the *Parmenides*, in which Plato, like Proclus, carries out the ἀφαίρεισις of the ἓν ἀγαθὸν ἀπὸ τῶν ἄλλων πάντων, the "abstraction" of the "one good among all others."

18. Plato, *Rep.* 509B; cf. *Parm.* 141E. For the absolute transcendence of the one and the good in particular cf. Halfwassen 1992, 19ff., 188ff., 221ff., 257ff., 277ff., 302ff., 392ff.

19. Plato, *Parm.* 142f. Cf. the informative parallel in Speusippus, fr. 72 Isnardi Parente (Iamblichus, *De comm. math. sc.* IV.15, 7–10): τὸ ἓν ὅπερ δὴ οὐδὲ ὄν πω δεῖ καλεῖν, διὰ τὸ ἁπλοῦν εἶναι καὶ διὰ τὸ ἀρχὴν μὲν ὑπάρχειν τῶν ὄντων, τὴν δὲ ἀρχὴν μηδέπω εἶναι τοιαύτην οἷα ἐκεῖνα ὧν ἐστιν ἀρχή ("the one, which should not even be called being because it is simple and constitutes the principle of existent things, and the principle does not have the properties of the things of which it is the principle"). For this, see Halfwassen 1992, 281ff., also 339ff., 356ff., 393ff.

20. Plato, *Rep.* 511B6: τὸ ἀνυπόθετον.

21. Ibid., 510B7: ἀνυπόθετος ἀρχή.

22. Ibid., 511B7: ἡ τοῦ παντὸς ἀρχή.

23. Ibid., 511B.

24. Ibid., 511B, 533C.

25. Ibid., 476A5–7: πάντων τῶν εἰδῶν πέρι ὁ αὐτὸς λόγος, αὐτὸ μὲν ἓν ἕκαστον εἶναι, τῇ δὲ τῶν πράξεων καὶ σωμάτων καὶ ἀλλήλων κοινωνίᾳ πανταχοῦ φανταζόμενα πολλὰ φαίνεσθαι ἕκαστον ("The same argument applies then to . . . all the forms; each is itself one, but, by showing up everywhere in a community with actions, bodies, and one another, each is an apparitional many" [trans. Bloom]). This

corresponds exactly to the argumentation for thenumber-character of the ideas in the reports by Sextus Empiricus, *Adv. Math.* X.258: ἐπείπερ ἑκάστη ἰδέα κατ᾽ ἰδίαν μὲν λαμβανομένη ἓν εἶναι λέγεται: κατὰ σύλληψιν δὲ ἑτέρας ἢ ἄλλων δύο ἢ τρεῖς ἢ τέσσαρες. ("because, taken on its own, every idea is said to be one, but in conjunction with others, it is two, three, or four.")

26. Plato, *Rep.* 524C, 525A, 524C11: τί οὖν ποτ᾽ ἐστὶ τὸ μέγα αὖ καὶ τὸ σμικρόν, "what are the big and the small?" Cf. also: ἅμα γὰρ ταὐτὸν ὡς ἕν τε ὁρῶμεν καὶ ὡς ἄπειρα τὸ πλῆθος ("[f]or we see the same thing at the same time as both one and as an unlimited multitude").—οὐκοῦν εἴπερ τὸ ἕν . . . καὶ σύμπας ἀριθμὸς ταὐτὸν πέπονθε τοῦτο ("If this is the case with the one . . . won't it be the same for all number?" [trans. Bloom]). Also, the principles of mathematics named by Plato in the simile of the divided line (510C)—the even and the odd, the figures, and the three kinds of angle—have been led back to the two universal principles in the unwritten doctrine concerning the equal and the unequal with respect to the πέρας and ἄπειρον as highest genera (cf. *TP* 37–38; also Gaiser 1986, esp. 100ff.). It is more typical of Plato to speak only of the one ἀνυπόθετον as the "origin of the whole," toward which it ascends, from the principles of mathematics outward; this can only mean that the indefinite dyad is not, for Plato, an ἀνυπόθετος ἀρχή.

27. Kullmann 1991, esp. 11ff.

28. Recall Krämer's fundamental clarification in Krämer 1964, 332f.: "If one thinks through more precisely the possibilities and problems of the academic doctrine of principles against the background of the 'later' solutions, then it immediately appears that the alternative is not simply monism or dualism, but, more determinately, monism with subsequent dualism or original dualism . . . or differently expressed: The monistic solution corresponds to a reflection [*Rückgriff*] behind the opposition of the two principles without sublating it."

29. The agreement between the second part of the *Parmenides* and the reports of the indirect tradition has been repeatedly emphasized from Stenzel to Reale and Migliori. For Aristotle's account see *Met.* A.8, 989b18, M.7, 1081a25, M.7, 1082a13ff., M.8, 1083b23f., N.4, 1091a25; Alexander, *In Met.* 56, 19f., 26ff. and 57, 4; Simplicius, *In Phys.* 454, 14 and 455, 6f.; Sextus Empiricus, *Adv. Math.* X.276–277. Cf. Speusippus in Iamblichus, *De comm. math. sc.* IV.16, 17f.; also Xenocrates, fr. 68 Heinze.

30. Plato, *Parm.* 141E–142A.

31. Plato, *Parm.* 141E.

32. Cf. Plato, *Rep.* 509B; *TP* 50, 52.

33. Plato, *Rep.* 534B–C.

34. Cf. my interpretation of Hypothesis I in Halfwassen 1992, 276ff., 302–405. I hold that the interpretation of Hypothesis I, as a negative theology, is the only historically possible interpretation for the following reasons: (1) The one's transcendence to being is repeatedly attested in the indirect tradition of Plato; the idea of the good identical with the one is confirmed in the *Republic* 509B. A principle *beyond being*, however, can only be grasped by *via negationis*, since every positive determination would already imply being. Plato requires the determination of the idea of the good ἀπὸ τῶν ἄλλων πάντων ἀφελών, "abstracting from all other things" (*Rep.* 534B9), i.e., through negative theology. (2) Plato criticizes the Eleatic one in

the *Sophist* (243Ef.), but not because it is absolutely simple and therefore without determination—as one would have to expect, if Hypothesis I were intendedin an anti-Eleatic manner—but precisely because it is being and the whole at the same time and, thus, *not* absolutely simple and free from every plurality; consequently, the Eleatic one has parts and this would be impossible for "the one" (*Sophist* 245A5f.). Platothereforecriticizes the Eleatic one because it is *not* a pure, absolutely simple one. He states in *Soph.* 245A8–9: ἀμερὲς δήπου δεῖ παντελῶς τό γε ἀληθῶς ἓν κατὰ τὸν ὀρθὸν λόγον εἰρῆσθαι: "what is truly one must, according to the right account, be said, indeed, to be without parts." This is a more exact reference to the *Parmenides*, 137Cf., where the one is posited in this way as absolutely partless and free from plurality. If Hypothesis I, for Plato, is the ὀρθὸς λόγος of the ἕν, it cannot be a *reductio ad absurdum* and, therefore, has to be understood as negative theology. (3) The "Neoplatonic" interpretation of Hypothesis I is not only demonstrably pre-Plotinian, as Dodds 1928 has shown, but it may already in principle be traceable back to Speusippus, which Dodds had assumed (140); that is to say, it can be shown that Speusippus in Proclus, *In Parm.* VII, 40, 1ff. (= *TP* 50), relates to the first two Hypotheses of the *Parmenides* (cf. Halfwassen 1993, esp. 365ff.). And with this, the correctness of the interpretation of Hypothesis I as a negative theology has been confirmed by a member of Plato's Academy. Incidentally, Proclus quotes the fragment of Speusippus in his commentary in order to show precisely this; in this context, he deals critically with the interpretation as a *reductio ad absurdum*. The "Neoplatonic" interpretation of the *Parmenides*, specifically, of Hypothesis I, in terms of the doctrine of principles, is now defended in Horn 1995.

35. Speusippus, *TP* 50; Aristotle, *TP* 28A; cf. *Met.* N.5, 1092a14f.; Porphyry, *TP* 52; Hermodorus, *TP* 31. For the transcendence of the one, there are additional references in Speusippus, fr. 48, 57, 62, 72 Isnardi Parente; Aristotle, Περὶ εὐχῆς, fr. 1 Ross; *EE* VIII.2, 1248a27–29; for the privative character of the principle of the many see, especially, Aristotle *Phys.*, I.9, 192aff.

36. Cf. Plato, *Parm.* 165E–166C.

37. Plato, *Parm.* 165E; cf. 159D.

38. Plato, *Parm.* 166C.

39. Aristotle, *Met.* N.1, 1087b9–12, 1088a15. Cf. also Szlezák 1987, 45–67.

40. Plato, *Phil.* 14Cf.

41. Plato, *Phil.* 23E4–6: πολλὰ ἑκάτερον ἐσχισμένον καὶ διεσπασμένον ἰδόντες, εἰς ἓν πάλιν ἑκάτερον συναγαγόντες, νοῆσαι πῇ ποτε ἦν αὐτῶν ἓν καὶ πολλὰ ἑκάτερον: "Seeing that each is split into many, [let us try] to gather them back into one and understand how each of them was both one and many."

42. Esp. Plato, *Phil.* 25A1–4: εἰς τὸ τοῦ ἀπείρου γένος ὡς εἰς ἓν δεῖ πάντα ταῦτα τιθέναι, κατὰ τὸν ἔμπροσθεν λόγον ὃν ἔφαμεν ὅσα διέσπασται καὶ διέσχισται συναγαγόντας χρῆναι κατὰ δύναμιν μίαν ἐπισημαίνεσθαί τινα φύσιν: "Everything that seems to us to become more or less . . .—we must put all of them into the genus of the infinite as into one, according to the account we gave a little while ago, so as to collect those things that are potentially scattered and split, and to mark them with some one nature"; 25C10–11: ὁπόσα ἐν τῷ πρόσθεν τῆς τὸ μᾶλλόν τε καὶ ἧττον δεχομένης ἐτίθεμεν εἰς ἕν φύσεως: "what we earlier posited in *one genus of nature* as what admits of more and less" (author's emphasis). Cf. Reale 1993, 417ff.

43. Cf. the convincing interpretation of Reale 1993, 429ff., esp. 440ff.

44. However, even this argument, namely, that the duality of the equally original, but combining principles necessarily presupposes an original principle as the ground of its coordination and that only the one itself can be the ground of the last and most comprehensive unification [*Einung*] was, for Proclus, the decisive refutation of every irreducible dualism. Cf. *Theol. Plat.* II.1, 12–14, and II.2, 15–16, and similarly *In Parm.* 619, 30–620, 3; 695, 39–697, 20; 706, 19–27; 709, 6–36; 724, 27, in the systematic working out of Zeno's argument against the many (Plato, *Parm.* 127E).

45. Cf. also Plato, *Phil.* 30D8: ὡς ἀεὶ τοῦ παντὸς νοῦς ἄρχει, "intellect always rules the whole."

46. Cf. Plato, *Rep.* 517C2: The idea of the good is πᾶσι πάντων . . . ὀρθῶν τε καὶ καλῶν αἰτία, "the cause in every case of all that is right and beautiful."

47. Cf. the role of the demiurgic νοῦς and its thoroughgoing relation to the absolute one in Reale 1993, 487ff. and 526ff.; also Halfwassen 2000, 39–61.

48. Sextus Empiricus, *Adv. Math.* X.261: καὶ ταύτην [τὴν μονάδα] κατ' αὐτότητα μὲν ἑαυτῆς νοουμένην μονάδα νοεῖσθαι, ἐπισυντεθεῖσαν δ' ἑαυτῇ καθ' ἑτερότητα ἀποτελεῖν τὴν καλουμένην ἀόριστον δυάδα: "and thought by its being itself, it [monad] is thought as monad, but added to itself according to otherness produces the so-called indefinite dyad."

49. Cf. Halfwassen 1992, 34f.n.221.

50. Hypothesis I, *Parm.* 139B–E; see also Halfwassen 1992, 336–352.

51. Hermodorus in Simplicius, *In Phys.* 248, 11ff.: αὐτῶν ἀμφοτέρων τῶν συζυγιῶν πάντα πλὴν τοῦ ἑνὸς στοιχείου τὸ μᾶλλον καὶ τὸ ἧττον δεδεγμένον. ὥστε ἄστατον καὶ ἄπειρον καὶ οὐκ ὂν τὸ τοιοῦτον λέγεσθαι κατὰ ἀπόφασιν τοῦ ὄντος. τῷ τοιούτῳ δὲ οὐ προσήκειν οὔτε ἀρχῆς οὔτε οὐσίας [ὄνομα emend. Theiler], ἀλλ' ἐν ἀκρισίᾳ τινὶ φέρεσθαι.

52. Aristotle, *Met.* N.1, 1087b9–12: καὶ γὰρ ὁ τὸ ἄνισον καὶ ἓν λέγων τὰ στοιχεῖα, τὸ δ' ἄνισον ἐκ μεγάλου καὶ μικροῦ δυάδα, ὡς ἓν ὄντα τὸ ἄνισον καὶ τὸ μέγα καὶ τὸ μικρὸν λέγει καὶ οὐ διορίζει ὅτι λόγῳ ἀριθμῷ δὲ οὔ: "for even the philosopher who says the unequal and the one are the elements, and the unequal is a dyad composed of the great and small, treats the unequal, or the great and the small, as being one, and does not draw the distinction that they are one in definition, but not in number" (trans. Ross). Porphyry also attests to the character of unity in the indefinite dyad in Simplicius, *In Phys.* 454, 8f.: ἐν τούτοις δὲ καὶ ἡ ἀόριστος δυάς ὁρᾶται ἔκ τε τῆς ἐπὶ τὸ μέγα καὶ τῆς ἐπὶ τὸ μικρὸν μονάδος συγκειμένη (author's emphasis): "In these the indefinite dyad is also seen, consisting of the *unit* tending towards the great and that tending towards the small" (trans. J. O. Urmson).

53. Aristotle, *Met.* N.1, 1087b27ff.: εἰ δ' ἐστίν, ὥσπερ βούλονται, τὰ ὄντα ἐξ ἐναντίων, τῷ δὲ ἑνὶ ἢ οὐθὲν ἐναντίον ἢ εἴπερ ἄρα μέλλει, τὸ πλῆθος: "if, as they claim, things consist of contraries, and to the one either there is nothing contrary, or if there is to be anything, it is plurality" (trans. Ross).

54. Proclus uses the expression, *Theol. Plat.* II 12, 66 Saffrey and Westerink: τὴν τῶν πολλῶν πρὸς τὸ ἓν οἷον ἀντίθεσιν: "a sort of opposition between the many and the one." See *In Parm.* 1095, 18f. Cousin: ἀναίνεται γὰρ ἡ τοῦ ἑνὸς ἔννοια τὸ πλῆθος: "for the concept of 'one' rejects multiplicity" (trans. Morrow and Dillon).

55. Aristotle, *Met.* Λ.10, 1075b17–20: καὶ τοῖς δύο ἀρχὰς ποιοῦσιν ἄλλην ἀνάγκη ἀρχὴν κυριωτέραν εἶναι, καὶ τοῖς τὰ εἴδη ὅτι ἄλλη ἀρχὴ κυριωτέρα. διὰ τί γὰρ μετέσχεν ἢ μετέχει; "and those who suppose two principles must suppose another,

a superior principle, and so must those who believe in the form; for why did things come to participate, or why do they participate?" (trans. Ross).

56. Cf. Aristotle, *Met.* A.6, 988a10–11: τὰ γὰρ εἴδη τοῦ τί ἐστιν αἴτια τοῖς ἄλλοις τοῖς δ' εἴδεσι τὸ ἕν; A.6, 988b4–6: τὸ τί ἦν εἶναι ἑκάστῳ τῶν ἄλλων τὰ εἴδη παρέχοντα—τοῖς δ' εἴδεσι τὸ ἕν: "the forms are causes of the essences of all other things, and the one is the cause of the essences of the forms" (trans. Ross).

57. This is also a negation of the principle-character of the one itself because that would imply a relation to the derivatives. Besides *TP* 50, cf. also Plotinus, *Enn.* VI.8.8.9ff.: [τὸ ἕν ἐστιν] ἀρχή: καίτοι ὅπερ τρόπον οὐκ ἀρχή . . . δεῖ δὲ ὅλως πρὸς οὐδὲν αὐτὸν λέγειν: ἔστι γὰρ ὅπερ ἐστὶ καὶ πρὸ αὐτῶν [sc., τῶν ἄλλων πάντων]: ἐπεὶ καὶ τὸ "ἔστιν" ἀφαιροῦμεν, ὥστε καὶ τὸ πρὸς τὰ ὄντα ὁπωσοῦν: "[the One is the principle] yet, all the same, in another way not the principle . . . but we must say that it is altogether unrelated to anything; for it is what it is before them; for we take away the 'is,' and so also any kind of relations to the real beings" (trans. Armstrong, with changes). *Enn.* VI 9, 3, 49ff.: ἐπεὶ καὶ τὸ αἴτιον λέγεν οὐ κατηγορεῖν ἐστι συμβεβηκός τι αὐτῷ, ἀλλ' ἡμῖν, ὅτι ἔχομέν τι παρ' αὐτοῦ ἐκείνου ὄντον ἐν αὐτῷ: "For to say that it is the cause is not to predicate something incidental of it but of us, because we have something from it while that one is in itself" (trans. Armstrong). In addition, cf. Halfwassen 1992, 106–130. As for Plotinus, so for Plato: the absolute is not in itself, but only with respect to being a principle, insofar as being stands in a one-sided relation of dependence to the absolute, which does not correspond to any relation on the side of the absolute itself; this also seems to confirm the report of Aristotle, *EE* A.8, 1218a15–30.

58. Speusippus, as reported by Proclus, *In Parm.* VII 40, 1–5 (fr. 62 Isnardi Parente = *TP* 50): "Le unum enim melius ente putantes et a quo le ens, et ab ea que secundum principium habitudine ipsum liberaverunt. Existimantes autem quod, si quis le unum ipsum seorsum et solum meditatum, sine aliis, secundem se ipsum ponat, nullum alterum elementum ipsi apponens, nihil utique fiet aliorum, interminabilem dualitatem entium principium induxerunt." "For they thought that the One is higher than being and is the source of being; and they delivered it even from the status of the principle. For they held that given the One, in itself, conceived as separated and alone, without the other things, with no additional element, nothing else would come into existence. And so they introduced the indefinite duality as the principle of beings" (trans. Tarán 1981, 350–351). See also Halfwassen 1992, 282ff.; Halfwassen 1993, 365ff.

59. Hegel 1971, vol. 19, 447; Hegel 1995, 415: "But out of the first all proceeds, owing to its revealing itself. . . . But the Absolute cannot be conceived as creative. . . . This transition [to the second] is thus not made by Plotinus philosophically or dialectically, but the necessity of it is expressed in representations and images." In addition, cf. chap. 5 of Halfwassen 1999.

60. Cf. also Halfwassen 1992, 98–130, with the proof, esp. 107ff. and 188ff.

61. Cf. Plato, *Parm.* 137D7–8 (ἄπειρον ἄρα τὸ ἕν, εἰ μήτε ἀρχὴν μήτε τελευτὴν ἔχει, "the one is infinite, if it has neither beginning nor end") with *Rep.* 509B910 (ἐπέκεινα τῆς οὐσίας πρεσβείᾳ καὶ δυνάμει ὑπερέχοντος, "residing beyond being in dignity and power"); see also Halfwassen 1992(2), 50ff., 65f., 70f.

62. Plato, *Rep.* 508B6–7: οὐκοῦν καὶ τὴν δύναμιν ἣν ἔχει [τὸ ὄμμα] ἐκ τούτου [τοῦ ἡλιοῦ] ταμιευομένην ὥσπερ ἐπίρρυτον κέκτηται: "Doesn't it get the power it

[the eyesight] has as a sort of overflow from the sun's treasury?" (trans. Bloom).

63. Cf. Aristotle, *Met.* N.4, 1091a35: προελθούσης τῆς τῶν ὄντων φύσεως ("when the nature of beings has progressed"); Iamblichus, *De comm. math. sc.* IV.16, 12: προϊούσης γὰρ πορρωτέρω ἀπὸ τῶν ἐν ἀρχῇ φύσεως: "for the nature [of the beautiful and the good] has progressed further from their principle"; IV.17, 5 and 12–16: καίπερ τοῦ ἑνὸς ὁμοίου ἐγγιγνομένου διὰ παντός . . . τὸ γὰρ ἁπλούστατον πανταχοῦ στοιχεῖον εἶναι. λοιπὸν οὖν τινα ἑτέραν μεγέθους αἰτίαν ὑποθεμένους, ὡς ἐν ἀριθμοῖς μονάδα κατὰ τὸ ἕν, οὕτως στιγμὴν ἐν γραμμαῖς τιθέναι: "although the one equally occurs in everything . . . for the simplest should be the element everywhere. Therefore, it remains to assume a different cause for [spatial] magnitude, so as in numbers the monad corresponds to the one, thus in lines the point should be posited."

64. In Aristotle, *Met.* Z.2, 1028b21–24 (Speusippus, fr. 48 Isnardi Parente), the one appears as the sole original principle beyond the hierarchically arranged levels of being and its (dualistically) special principles: Σπεύσιππος δὲ καὶ πλείους οὐσίας ἀπὸ τοῦ ἑνὸς ἀρξάμενος <οἴεται εἶναι>, καὶ ἀρχὰς ἑκάστης οὐσίας, ἄλλην μὲν ἀριθμῶν ἄλλην δὲ μεγεθῶν, ἔπειτα ψυχῆς· καὶ τοῦτον δὴ τὸν τρόπον ἐπεκτείνει τὰς οὐσίας (author's emphasis): "And Speusippus considers more kinds of substance, beginning *with the One*, and making principles for each kind of substance, one for numbers, another for spatial magnitudes, and then another for the soul; and in this way he multiplies the kinds of substance" (trans. Ross, with changes). The one itself is, therefore, also in Aristotle's report—just as in Iamblichus, *De comm. math. sc.* IV.17, 14f.—differentiated from the principle in the realm of numbers.

65. Cf. Halfwassen 1993, 361ff.

66. Cf. Halfwassen 1992(2).

67. Cf. Halfwassen 1992, 114–149, with the proof. Fundamental for the historical analysis of the Platonic "original act (*Urakt*)" is Krämer 1964, 312–337, which is completed, in particular, through the source analysis by Szlezák 1979, 52–119.

68. Eudorus reported in Simplicius, *In Phys.* 181, 10ff. (word-for-word quotation). On the dependence of Speusippus on Plato's *Parmenides*, cf. Halfwassen 1993, 350ff. and 359ff. (Further literature can also be found there.)

69. The distinction between ἀρχή and στοιχεῖον and the negation of the στοιχεῖον-character of the absolute one may be motivated by the immanence of the στοιχεῖον, which Aristotle stressed as constitutive in *Met.* Δ.3, 1014a26: στοιχεῖον λέγεται ἐξ οὗ σύγκειται πρώτου ἐνυπάρχοντος: "element means the primary component immanent in a thing" (trans. Ross). For the same reason, Plotinus also rejected the στοιχεῖον-character of the one itself: *Enn.* V.3.11.16f.: τὸ δὲ πρὸ τούτων ἡ ἀρχὴ τούτων, οὐχ ὡς ἐνυπάρχουσα: τὸ γὰρ ἀφ' οὗ οὐκ ἐνυπάρχει ἀλλ' ἐξ ὧν: "But that which is before these is their principle, not as immanent in them; for it is not that from which something comes which is immanent, but the parts of which it is constituted" (trans. Armstrong). Incidentally, Speusippus also rejects it similarly in his report of Plato's doctrine of principles (*TP* 50): "Le unum enim melius ente putantes et a quo le ens [ἀφ' οὗ τὸ ὄν], et ab ea que secundum principium [στοιχεῖον] ipsum liberaverunt." In contrast, he calls the indefinite dyad here *elementum* and *principium entium*.

SEVEN

PLATO'S FOUNDATION OF THE EUCLIDEAN CHARACTER OF GEOMETRY

Vittorio Hösle

In grateful memory of Imre Tóth (1921–2010), who opened up a world.

1. NON-EUCLIDEAN GEOMETRIES AND THE OLD ACADEMY

Following numerous failed attempts during the last century, Gauss, János Bolyai, and Lobachevski became convinced that Euclid's fifth postulate could not be proven; it was this conviction, in turn, that established the most important basis for the development of so-called non-Euclidean geometries.[1] Now, the curious structure of the first book of the *Elements* could truly be seen: propositions I, 1–28 are theorems of Bolyai's absolute geometry, and Euclid draws on the fifth αἴτημα only for I, 29 (which is a reversal of I, 27f., and cannot be derived from those propositions). The use of this axiom, which had been postponed as long as possible, as well as the fact that it is explicitly introduced as an axiom by Euclid, seemed to suggest that Euclid was already intuitively aware of its unprovability. Such an insight stands in contrast to the many attempts at proving the axiom—attempts that had already begun in antiquity (Ptolemy, Proclus) and continue down to Wolfgang Bolyai. Thus, Pierce could claim: "I maintain that Euclid was himself a non-Euclidean geometer. I do not mean, in the complete, Gaussian and Besselian sense, but more so than Saccheri and Lambert."[2]

In his book *Platon et la recherche mathématique de son époque*,[3] Charles Mugler suggests that problems regarding the fundamental principles of non-Euclidean geometry were discussed already in the Academy, and that the hypothesis opposed to the Euclidean axiom had already been investigated. Unfortunately, Mugler did not provide convincing evidence; hence his suggestion, which was not sufficiently justified, has not been taken into account.[4]

Only the groundbreaking work of the best expert on the history and philosophy of non-Euclidean geometries, Imre Tóth, was able to provide clarity concerning their early development. Because the present essay builds on these conclusions, I will start by introducing them,[5] and subsequently proceed to present my own theses.

2. ANTI-EUCLIDEAN PASSAGES IN THE ARISTOTELIAN CORPUS

Tóth discovered a number of passages in the work of Aristotle "which nowadays belong to the domain of non-Euclidean geometry" (Tóth 1977, 395). In these passages one reads, for example, of a triangle having an angular sum which is unequal to, greater, or smaller than two right angles (2R).[6]

The fact that the topic recurs many times already makes it unlikely that we are dealing with arbitrarily chosen examples of what is absolutely impossible (e.g., in *An. post.* 90a13, the triangle is predicated with ἰσότης/ἀνισότης ["equality"/"inequality"] [sc., to 2R], just as the moon, earth, and sun are predicated with ἔκλειψις, "eclipse"). That these examples would have been arbitrarily chosen is even more implausible, given the equivalence that is clearly drawn between the impossibility of the existence of parallels (which impossibility today is a basic axiom of elliptic geometry), and that of the sum of the angles in a triangle being greater than 2R (*An. priora* 66a13f.: οἷον τὰς παραλλήλους συμπίπειν [cf. also *An. post.* 77b23] καὶ εἰ μείζων ἐστὶν ἡ ἐντὸς τῆς ἐκτὸς καὶ ἐι τὸ τρίγωνον ἔχει πλείους ὀρθὰς δυεῖν: "for example, that parallels meet, supposing that the interior angle is greater than the exterior and on the assumption that a triangle contains more than two right angles"). Such arbitrariness, finally, can be dismissed beyond any doubt by *De caelo* 281b3f.: In this passage a distinction is made between, on the one hand, that which is ἀδύνατον/δύνατον ("impossible"/"possible") (and respectively ψεῦδος/ἀληθές, "false"/"true") ἐξ ὑποθέσεως, from a hypothesis, and on the other hand that which is "unconditionally impossible" (ἀδύνατον ἁπλῶς). An example of the first case is: λέγω δ' οἷον τὸ τρίγωνον ἀδύνατον δύο ὀρθὰς ἔχειν, εἰ τάδε, καὶ ἡ διάμετρος σύμμετρος, εἰ τάδε[7] ("It is impossible, for instance, on a certain hypothesis that the triangle should have its angles equal to two right angles, and on another the diagonal is commensurable" [trans. Stocks]). It is extremely difficult, from the point of view of textual criticism, to provide an accurate reconstruction of this passage.[8] However, in any formulation, the hypothetical and non-*a priori* character of propositions[9] concerning the sum of the angles and commensurability is emphasized. At the same time, there is mention of the possibility that, given certain conditions, the sum of the angles would be unequal to 2R; hence the diagonal line would assume values that are commensurable with the side of the square. Such a statement, however, could only be meaningful if the listeners were already familiar with this condition: the negation of Euclid's fifth αἴτημα necessitates these consequences. The knowledge concerning this non-Euclidean theorem presupposes a rather extended engagement with a geometry that negates the fifth postulate: "such statements could not be conjectured based on mere dialectical intuitions. Without proof (which is complicated) it is impossible to arrive at them" (Tóth 1967, 396).

Thus, the passages show that, shortly before Aristotle, Greek mathematicians apparently attempted to derive conclusions from anti-Euclidean hypotheses. Tóth reconstructs the goal of these attempts based on *Prior Analytics* II.16, i.e., the chapter on the *petitio principii* (τὸ δ' ἐν ἀρχῇ αἰτεῖσθαι: "begging the original [question]" [64b28]). One example of a circular argument presented in the passage reads (65a4f.): ὅπερ ποιοῦσιν οἱ τὰς παραλλήλους οἰόμενοι γράφειν: λανθάνουσι γὰρ αὐτοὶ ἑαυτοὺς τοιαῦτα λαμβάνοντες ἃ οὐχ οἷόν τε ἀποδεῖξαι μὴ οὐσῶν τῶν παραλλήλων ("This is what those persons do who suppose that they are constructing parallel lines; for they fail to see that they are assuming facts which it is impossible to demonstrate unless the parallels exist" [trans. Jenkinson]).

As Tóth has shown,[10] the expression τὰς παραλλήλους γράφειν ("constructing parallel lines") refers to the attempt to prove Euclid I, 29, without relying on the fifth αἴτημα, i.e., by deducing it from its inverse propositions I, 27f. Such an attempt (which is destined to fail)[11] apparently already rested on I, 29 (or on a proposition deduced from it); Aristotle refers critically to this notoriously false procedure.[12] "The extremely dense allusive style of the passage proves the high level of acquaintance with this problem among his audience" (Tóth 1977, 396). Aristotle's allusion suddenly brings to light the mathematical development: "attempts were made to provide a strict, i.e., absolutely geometrical, proof for it [sc., I, 32.2], and in so doing came across circular arguments." It is plausible that after these attempts had failed, the search for an indirect proof was undertaken: the task was to reveal inconsistencies in those systems which were based on an anti-Euclidean hypothesis. Such systems were constructed and partially developed for the purpose of finding their inconsistencies;[13] "the heterodox propositions provided by Aristotle have to be regarded as sedimented fragments of indirect attempts to solve the problem" (Tóth 1977, 397; cf. also 399 regarding *DC* 281b5f.: "It can be assumed that the original goal was the refutation of the general anti-Euclidean hypothesis by means of revealing the absurdity 'that an uneven number is even,' which was supposed to be the result of the hypothesis of commensurability. This contradiction, however, can only be reached by means of the Euclidean proposition, *Elem.* I, 32.2").

The (elliptic) hypothesis of the obtuse angle can indeed be refuted since on this assumption the parallels would intersect (which is prohibited by Euclid, *Elem.*, def. 23). This point is also elaborated by Aristotle (*An. priora* 66a13f.; *An. post.* 77b23: γεωμετρικὸν πως καὶ ἀγεωμέτρητον, "geometrical in a way, but also un-geometrical");[14] the (hyperbolic) hypothesis of the acute angle, however, cannot be refuted without drawing on the fifth αἴτημα,[15] which for that reason is explicitly used by Euclid: "The *communis opinio* that the problem of parallels was created due to a lack of evidence for the parallel postulate is to be dismissed as historically inaccurate based on what has been stated above; to the contrary, the necessity of overcoming the already existing problem of parallels *necessitated* the introduction of the parallel postulate" (Tóth 1977, 399).[16]

Aristotle is fully aware of the merely posited, unprovable character of the Euclidean axiom. In *EE* 1222b39f., he states: "Supposing there were no further cause for the triangle's having the above property, then the triangle would be a sort of principle or cause of all that comes later."[17] Here the ἀρχή, i.e., axiom, is the theorem about the sum of the angles, which in its three variations is equivalent to the parallel postulate in its three possible versions. All other theorems depend on this axiom; if it is altered, the theorems will also change: "as are the principles, so is what comes from the principles. This can be seen more clearly in matters of geometry. For there also, when certain principles are assumed, as are the principles, so are what follow the principles; for instance, if the triangle has its angles equal to two right angles, and the quadrilateral to four" (an application of the contraposition follows, MM 1187a37f.; cf. 1189b10f.) (trans. Stock);[18] "[t]he strict sense of 'principle' is not to be found among principles without movement, e.g., those of mathematics, though by analogy we may use the name there also. For there, too, if the principle should change, practically all that is proved from it would alter" (*EE* 1222b23f.; trans. Solomon).[19]

It is striking that these passages are from the *Ethics*; Tóth has shown that the Stagirite establishes a parallel between the geometric concept of an ἀρχή and the ethical motif, the choice based on preferences, the choice of a goal that appears as a τέλος at the beginning of an action from which individual actions can be deduced: "for as in theoretical sciences the assumptions are our starting-points, so in the productive the end is starting point and assumed . . . as in geometry we argue, if the angles of the triangle are equal to two right angles, then so and so must be the case" (*EE* 1227b29f.; trans.

Solomon; cf. *NE* 1140b16f.).[20] Through a detailed interpretation of *NE* 1140b13f., Tóth finally reaches the conclusion that, for Aristotle, the choice between Euclidean and non-Euclidean axioms (just as in *EE* 1222b39f., the proposition about the sum of the angles is what is mentioned) is analogous to an ethical choice and an act of freedom. In contrast to ethical actions, such an act of freedom cannot even be influenced by pleasure or pain: this is the only difference given the established structural analogy "in the domain of ethics and geometry" (Tóth 1977, 409).[21] This meta-mathematical conception is fascinating due to its extremely modern character.

3. PLATO AND THE ONTOLOGICAL FOUNDATION OF EUCLIDEAN GEOMETRY

3.1 The Unwritten Doctrine and Mathematical Research in the Academy

In what follows I will attempt to interpret two passages by Plato in light of Tóth's research and the groundbreaking works by Krämer 1959 and Gaiser 1968 concerning Plato's esoteric, or inner-Academic, doctrine. This interpretation is necessary because the systematic doctrine which was reserved for oral teaching in the Academy more and more turns out to be the key to understanding the dialogues as well.[22]

Considered *a priori*, it is very likely that the aforementioned geometric statements by Aristotle (who did not achieve anything original in mathematics, contrary to his discoveries in almost all of the other sciences) date back to his time in the Academy (Tóth 1977, 367–347). The Academy was the center of mathematical research at the time; the conditions for Euclid's *Elements* were established in the Academy:[23] one may think of Theaetetus' treatment of irrational values (book X)[24] and his systematic construction of regular bodies (book XIII), as well as Eudoxus'[25] foundation for a universal doctrine of proportions in book V. In terms of its precision in dealing with irrationality, Eudoxus' discoveries in this field exhibit a level which has only been reached again by R. Dedekind: in this context I would like to refer to Hasse and Scholz 1928 (HS), which compares Eudoxus' and Dedekind's achievements in detail and emphasizes, on the one hand, that "this Eudoxic system . . . is *isomorphic* with regard to the system of Dedekind's cuts" (HS 23), and on the other hand that the difference between the two systems is the greater formality and level of abstraction, as well as the use of implicit definitions,[26] by Eudoxus: "However, then the definition of the proportion that is included in Eudoxus' system of definitions is indeed an implicit definition, i.e., a definition which only prescribes in what contexts the word 'proposition' can be used without explaining this term itself" (HS 17).[27] They continue:

> [I]n contrast, we have already clearly elaborated that Eudoxus defines his proportions *implicitly*. Thus, while Dedekind completely determines the elements of his domain, namely the cuts, *by their content*, Eudoxus refrains from giving a *substantive* determination of the elements of his domain, i.e., the proportions. . . . Thus Eudoxus *immediately* achieves the construction of his type of system, i.e., the totality of all systems of Eudoxic proportions, without regard to their content (proportions of lines, planes, bodies . . .). Dedekind's process of construction, however, which initially only provides the determinate system of real numbers, arrives at this type of expanded system only *subsequently*, namely, by way of adding all isomorphic systems. (HS 24f.)

The traces of Eudoxus in Euclid's book V (and XII!) show at what level of abstraction the foundational problems of geometry were discussed in the Academy. This result also[28] supports the initial thesis that the passages cited by Aristotle are traces of extended research concerning the axioms of geometry that was carried on in Plato's school.[29] Furthermore, it is completely implausible to believe that Plato would have related to such investigations without any reaction to them;[30] thus one can legitimately assume that in the dialogues there are traces of the disconcerting discovery of the unprovability of the fifth αἴτημα. However, these traces might not be explicit discussions, but rather only veiled allusions to the problem.

3.2 The Allegory of the Line

At the center of Plato's *opus magnum* there are three well-known allegories, with the allegory of the line at the very center (*Republic* 509Df.).[31] Because of its prominent position, the latter allegory already stands out as the most important and as the very heart of the *Republic*. In this passage, Socrates asks Glaucon to imagine cutting a (vertical) line whose top part represents "the domain of what can be thought" (νοητοῦ γένους) (509D2), and whose lower part represents what is visible (ὁρατοῦ) (509D3). Then both lines are to be cut again (according to the proportion of the first division): within the domain of the visible the bottom section represents copies, while the section on top represents the sensual world. "The partition of what can be thought" (τὴν τοῦ νοητοῦ τομήν) (510B2), which is the main issue here, corresponds to the relationship between philosophy and mathematics. Philosophy and mathematics are distinguished in terms of their diverging cognitive capacities: νοῦς ("intelligence") guides philosophical reason, and διάνοια ("thought") guides mathematical understanding, which mediates between νοῦς and sensory δόξα (διάνοιαν δὲ καλεῖν μοι δοκεῖς τὴν τῶν γεωμετρικῶν τε καὶ τὴν τῶν τοιούτων ἕξιν ἀλλ' οὐ νοῦν, ὡς μεταξύ τι δόξης τε καὶ νοῦ τὴν διάνοιαν οὖσαν: "you seem to me to call the habit of geometers and their likes thought and not intelligence, indicating that thought is something between opinion and intelligence" [511D2f.; trans. Bloom]). The explicit γεωμετρικῶν, to which καὶ . . . τῶν τοιούτων is added only later (511D3), as well as the emphasis on the fact that this science needs to make use of images (510B3f., D5f.) even though it deals with the square in itself and diagonal line in itself (510D7f.), sufficiently show that, of all the mathematical sciences, geometry is the real focus of interest here. What is it that distinguishes geometry from dialectic? The former starts with presuppositions (which are derived from sensuous images: εἰκόσιν χρωμένη ψυχὴ ζητεῖν ἀναγκάζεται ἐξ ὑποθέσεων: "a soul . . . is compelled to investigate on the basis of images" [510B4f.; trans. Bloom]) that are not questioned any further (οὐδένα λόγον οὔτε αὑτοῖς οὔτε ἄλλοις ἔτι ἀξιοῦσι περὶ αὐτῶν διδόναι ὡς παντὶ φανερῶν: "[geometers] don't think it worthwhile to give any further account of them to themselves or others, as though they were clear to all" [510C6f.; trans. Bloom]; this idea is repeated in 533B–C, where Plato even states that when the ἀρχή has not been grasped one cannot claim that mathematics is an ἐπιστήμη),[32] as though these ὑποθέσεις would be clear to everyone: what is important is the ὡς. In contrast to ἅτε, ὡς characterizes a merely subjective opinion, not an objective relationship. In the *Meno* (86Ef.), by ὑπόθεσις Plato means the starting point of a geometrical deduction, which in this context is apparently an absolute, irreducible mathematical foundation or axiom (cf. *Def.* 415B: ὑπόθεσις ἀρχὴ ἀναπόδεικτος, "a hypothesis is an indemonstrable principle"). It is noteworthy that, for Plato, these presuppositions are not self-evident, as the mathematicians (what is probably meant is the majority of mathematicians) falsely assume (ἀξιοῦσι) (510C7). Rather, they require a justification that apparently cannot be provided by mathematics itself unless mathematicians make reference to intuition. Such a reference, however, is contrary to the claim of mathematicians, according to which they deal with the figures themselves. Because Plato is not a skeptic, and because it is precisely mathematics that amounts for him to a domain of proof and a model of knowledge (as Gaiser 1968 has shown for many individual problems), it is very perplexing and needs to be explained why mathematics is not ultimately justified in itself. What is Plato thinking about when he speaks of ὑποθέσεις that are not self-evident in themselves? It has been argued that Plato is referring to basic geometric concepts (due to 510C3f.).[33] However, it is hardly convincing that Plato regarded the definitions provided in the ὅροι of book I of the *Elements* (which for the most part originated in the Academy) as impossible to obtain for mathematicians themselves.[34] He hardly would have regarded philosophical assistance in these matters so constitutive that he would have mentioned it at the very ὄμφαλος of the *Republic*. The use of the word ὑπόθεσις also speaks against this idea. In the *Meno*, ὑπόθεσις refers to a theorem that functions as a point of departure (cf. supra), and Aristotle equates the term with an ἀρχή, i.e., geometric axiom (*EE* 1222b39f.; see above) within the context of an anti-Euclidean passage: ὥσπερ γὰρ ταῖς θεωρητικαῖς αἱ ὑποθέσεις ἀρχαί . . . : "for as in the theoretical sciences the assumptions are our starting-points" (*EE* 1227b29; trans. Solomon).[35]

3.3 A Possible Philosophical Foundation for Geometry

Hence, one needs to attempt to conceive of ὑπόθεσις as an axiom for which the concepts mentioned in 510E3f. play a role: first I will focus on the γωνιῶν τριττὰ εἴδη ("three forms of angles"), which are mentioned at the end of the passage. If one keeps in mind that Aristotle repeatedly presents the proposition concerning the sum of the angles as an axiom (it can function in that manner being equivalent to the parallel postulate; cf. MM 1187a37f., 1189b10f.; *EE* 1222b39f., 1227b29f.; in *An. priora* 66a14f. the equivalence between the hypothesis of the obtuse angle and that of intersecting parallels is asserted), then the passage from the allegory of the line suddenly acquires a clear meaning: the question concerning the sum of the angles (and thus the question concerning the essence) of a triangle, Plato seems to believe, cannot be solved by means of mathematics alone. The analytic method reaches its absolute limit here. The only way out would be to draw on intuition.[36] For Plato, however, this approach would require paying too heavy a price, namely, the loss of the scientific character of geometry.[37] But how can the angle sum theorem become a true proposition instead of a mere ὑπόθεσις if we are supposed to abandon intuition? Γεωμετρία, which is situated between νοῦς and δόξα (511D5), can itself still turn—not to the δόξα situated below—but to the superior νοῦς, i.e., Platonic dialectic, which will provide assistance in the attempt at its justification. Based on the testimonies concerning Plato's esoteric doctrine, we can conclude how Plato conceived of this constitutive assistance of philosophy for mathematics.

Plato did not attempt to "apply" his dualism of the principles of ἕν and ἀόριστος δυάς only to ethics, the philosophy of nature, and the philosophy of history, but—as especially Gaiser has shown—also to mathematics: all the ontological structures that are reflected in all of reality, should be discovered in it.[38] One example is that of tracing back the forms of angles to the two principles: the one right angle corresponds to what is equal in itself. The opposite of the arbitrarily increasing and decreasing acute and obtuse angles corresponds to the inner opposition of the second principle, the μέγα-μικρόν.

Allusions to this reduction, which is documented to be part of Plato's esoteric teachings (cf. Proclus, *In Eucl.* 131.21–132.17, 133.20–134.1 = *TP* 37), were collected by Ž. Marković (Marković 1965). Thus, already Aristotle mentions the ontological priority of the right angle in *Met.* 1084b7f. (καὶ ἔστι μὲν ὡς ἡ ὀρθὴ προτέρα τῆς ὀξείας, ὅτι ὥρισται καὶ τῷ λόγῳ: "in a sense the right angle is prior to the acute, because it is definite and in virtue of its formula" [trans. Ross]), while "on the other hand, the acute and obtuse angles in Aristotle's *Problems* are immediately connected with the indefinite dyad of high and low tones" (Marković 1965, 310; 918a18ff. is cited); in Hero of Alexandria's *Definitiones*, a parallel between the right angle and the one and the νῦν is established (26–28; cf. also 116–118, 148–150 Heiberg); in Theon of Smyrna's *Expositio rerum mathematicarum* (101.2f. Hiller), the right angle is referred to as ὡρισμένη καὶ ἐξ ἴσου καὶ ὁμοίου συνεστῶσα ("determinate and composed of equality and similarity"); the problem is also spelled out in Iamblichus (*In Nicom. Arithm.*, 43.27–44.2 Pistelli) and Proclus (*In Eucl.* loc. cit.; and also 172.8f.): τὸ μέτρον[39] ἀπολαβοῦσα τῶν γωνιῶν τὸ μήτε ἐπίτασιν μήτε ἄνεσιν ἐπιδεχόμενον, "[the right angle] holds the measure of angles, a measure permitting neither increase nor decrease" (trans. Morrow). One could add another passage, which is missing in Marković, from Nicholas of Cusa (*De beryllo*, chaps. 8–9), where Cusanus claims about the acute and obtuse angles that they can always become more acute or obtuse (cf. also *De ven. sap.*, chap. 7, n. 18, where he cites his own passage); concerning Hegel, see previous footnote.

These multiple passages sufficiently document that this idea must have played a prominent role in the esoteric philosophy within the Academy: otherwise it would hardly have been emphasized so often during late antiquity.

It is tempting to connect this fragment from Plato's lecture Περὶ τἀγαθοῦ with *Republic* 510E (cf. Gaiser 1968, 512 and Marković 1965, 310). The conclusion that results from such a connection is that this esoteric reduction makes a different claim than in the other mathematical examples. The issue here is not just the exemplification of categorical structures within mathematical concepts (which could be irrelevant for a mathematician), but primarily to prove through dialectic that Euclidean geometry is a true science based on valid principles.[40]

In other words, with the allegory of the line, Plato seems to allude to an achievement of his doctrine of principles within the context of a large-scale crisis in the foundation of mathematics. We can assume that, following the despair that resulted from grasping the unprovability, i.e., the hypothetical character, of the fifth αἴτημα and the angle sum theorem (which, given the passages from Aristotle, must have occurred at that time), there was probably an attempt to refer to intuition. Plato's achievement most likely consisted in dismissing this attempt as unscientific. Furthermore, in this situation of crisis Plato probably argued in favor of Euclidean geometry for ontological reasons: in this kind of geometry the right angle functions as the measure of the σχήματα ("figures") (510C4),[41] which is a function it must possess not for mathematical reasons, but rather because of the doctrine of principles.[42] Plato's commitment to Euclidean geometry is thus an ontological commitment. No matter how this commitment may be evaluated,[43] we probably owe the Euclidean character of the geometry that was developed up to the nineteenth century to Plato.

3.4 A Noteworthy Passage from the Cratylus.

Plato's knowledge of the mathematical possibility of geometric systems that are opposed to the Euclidean system is probably also documented in the *Cratylus*, which was written around the time of the *Republic*.[44] Cratylus' answer to Socrates' question as to whether the Heraclitean δημιουργὸς τῶν ὀνομάτων, or "craftsman of names," could have been mistaken in creating his names is that it is impossible, because otherwise everything would fail to fit together so well (οὐ γὰρ ἄν ποτε οὕτω σύμφωνα ἦν αὐτῷ ἅπαντα: "for otherwise everything would not have been harmonious") (436C4). Socrates replies: "My dear Cratylus, surely this defense is flawed. If the name-giver had made a mistake at the beginning and then forced the other names to conform to it [συμφωνεῖν], then it would be no surprise, as sometimes occurs in the case of geometrical proofs [διαγραμμάτων],[45] when, after a false premise, even small and not obvious [σμικροῦ καὶ ἀδήλου ψεύδους], all the consequences that follow, even if very numerous, prove consistent with each other [ὁμολογεῖν]."

That the text involves an allusion to the relative consistency of anti-Euclidean systems is supported not only by its terminology, but also by the fact that the *reductio ad absurdum*, which was so decisive for Greek mathematicians, i.e., the apagogic method, is excluded here, as is implied *ex silentio*. The deductions described above do not lead to evident absurdities that suggest incorrect premises. This would only be the case if the premise were axiomatic, i.e., if we were dealing with a consciously constructed (anti-Euclidean) system whose falsity could not be determined by means of mathematics or logic but only from the view of ontological principles. This can be deduced by means of analogy from the dialogue's subsequent discussion of language. The claim of language to be true as a Parmenidean or Heraclitean language can be determined by inner-linguistic means just as little as the truth claim of Euclidean and non-Euclidean geometry can be determined by means of mathematics: "If the words thus enter into confrontation and some claim to be close to truth while the others claim the same, how or based on what are we supposed to make a decision? We certainly cannot refer again to other words than those, because there are none. Obviously we have to search for something different than words, something that can reveal to us, without words, which group of words is the right one. It would do so by way of revealing to us the essence of being [τὴν ἀλήθειαν τῶν ὄντων]" (438D).

One possible argument against this interpretation consists in referring to σμικροῦ καὶ ἀδήλου [ψεύδους], small and unnoticeable mistake (436D2f.), which seems to rule out the possibility of a consciously anti-Euclidean construction. But the argument can be mitigated: it conforms to Plato's ironic and allusive style to retrospectively characterize the problem responsible for causing the second foundational crisis of Greek mathematics[46] as small and not obvious.[47]

3.5 *The Allusive Character of Our Passages*

The fact that neither of the passages being discussed is very explicit and only alludes to the problem is not surprising, and yet the problem itself needs to be assumed in order to understand their meaning, as I hope to have shown. As the research coming out of Tübingen concerning Plato's esoteric inner-Academic philosophy has proven beyond doubt, Plato did not publish his fundamental ontological conception, which, however, was probably already present by the time of the *Protagoras* (for the reasons, see the *Ep.* VII 340Bf.;[48] *Phaedr.* 275Cf.; and Krämer 1959, 393ff.). At important points in his dialogues, Plato only schematically outlines the structure of his line of argument and even explicitly states that something was being withheld (cf. Krämer 1959, 389ff.), e.g., in the allegory of the sun (506E) and in the introductory remarks to the allegory of the line (509C). These passages show that what follows cannot be fully understood based on what is explicitly said alone; in 510B Glaucon confesses that he did not sufficiently grasp what had been said (when in 511D6 Socrates affirms that Glaucon has fully understood what has been said, he refers to the summary account of the formal points, which begins at 511C3). Moreover, Plato had additional significant grounds for withholding the anti-Euclidean crisis (the truth claim of mathematics was not supposed to have been ridiculed by sophistic skeptics [cf. DK 80B 7; perhaps also DK 68B 155] who rejected Plato's ontological construction while happily picking up the anti-Euclidean hypothesis), as well as immediate precursors. The discovery of irrationality (see note 46) is supposed to have become public only through an act of indiscretion, which was penalized by the gods (cf. DK 18.4; and Pappus [Abû 'Othmân al-Damaskhî], *In Eucl. Elem.* I, 1–2 Junge-Thomson = *TP* 20]). Plato is part of this Pythagorean tradition; it is only the incidental remarks by Aristotle, and then the interpretation of these remarks by Tóth, that today allow us to gain insight into the mathematical discussions about foundations within the Academy. Those discussions resulted in highly sophisticated logical conceptions, especially concerning the rigorous methodology of geometrical proof, which were soon forgotten and whose level of abstraction was only reached again in the nineteenth century.

3.6 The Role of Leodamas of Thasos in the Formulation of the Axioms

Tóth had assumed that the anti-Euclidean statements from the Aristotelian corpus were derived from Eudoxus' circle. He suggested in particular that their originators were Menaechmus and Theudius (Tóth 1977, 396f., 410). However, if the relevant passages have been interpreted correctly, then for chronological reasons it is quite impossible that the unprovability of the parallel postulate would have been first discovered by Eudoxus. (Of course, it remains possible that individual propositions were proven by him, e.g., the one concerning the equivalence of the persistent incommensurability between the side and diagonal of a square and the Euclidean character of geometry; it is even likely that the original approach was pursued and deepened over a longer period of time.) Because the *Republic* was published around "374 or shortly after" (Wilamowitz-Moellendorff 1919, vol. 1, 308; Gigon 1974, 10, does not "want to situate it later than the time of the catastrophe of Leuctra 372 AD"), while Eudoxus was probably born around 400 (one can hardly assume that his mathematical discoveries were made during his first period in Athens; also, he only returned to Athens in 368), Menaechmus is referred to as his student (Proclus, *In Eucl.* 67.9 = *TP* 15), and Theudius belongs to the generation of Aristotle (Fritz 1936, 244ff., based on the report by Proclus, *In Eucl.* = *TP* 15), these mathematicians cannot be responsible for the conclusions drawn during the time of the *Republic*.[49] It is quite plausible, however, that Leodamas of Thasos, who is "at least about the same age as Plato" (his age is reconstructed by Fritz 1940, 371ff., although this reconstruction is not cogent, because the difference in age between teacher and student can sometimes be quite small, so that Leodamas could have been younger) may be the author of these anti-Euclidean investigations. Both Diogenes Laertius (*Lives* III, 24 [= *TP* 18b]: καὶ πρῶτος τὸν κατὰ τὴν ἀνάλυσιν τῆς ζητήσεως τρόπον εἰσηγήσατο [sc., Πλάτων] Λεωδάμαντι τῷ Θασίῳ, "[Plato] was the first to explain to Leodamas of Thasos the method of solving problems by analysis" [trans. Hicks]), as well as Proclus (*In Eucl.* 211.18–212.4 = *TP* 18a]; cf. also *TP* 17: ἐγενήθ(η) γὰρ καὶ ἡ ἀνάλυσις), write that Leodamas was influenced by Plato to use (as the first) the analytic method. "According to Diogenes Laertius' version, this obviously also means that Plato invented the analytic method" (Fritz 1940, 371; von Fritz's position will be presented in what follows). This, however, can be rejected, because Plato already mentions the analytic method at *Meno* 86Ef. (ὥσπερ οἱ γεωμέτραι πολλάκις σκοποῦνται: "as geometers frequently inquire"). Also, for Hippocrates of Chios and probably even for Oenopides (cf. Fritz 1937) the method is documented, or at least has to be assumed. "However, this does not rule out the possibility that Plato, here as well as in other contexts, referred to the particular importance and productivity of a certain method, and that he argued for extending the scope of its application. It might also be the case that he contributed to a thorough investigation of a method, which until then was more or less practically applied, an investigation that concerned its theoretical foundation, its extension and its limits" (Fritz 1937). This, however, entails that Leodamas, who was urged on by Plato, must have reached the level of axioms (because this is what it would mean to develop the analytic method up to its very limits). This allows us to make sense of the πρῶτος in Favorinus-Diogenes Laertius: Plato and Leodamas for the first time were able to carry the analytic method to its end, i.e., to the axioms. This ancient note convincingly proves, I think, Plato's interest in the foundations of geometry and supports the stated thesis: that the allegory of the line presents an ontological interpretation of the research that Leodamas carried out by following Plato's suggestion. This must have led to the insight concerning the unprovability of the fifth postulate and to the fragmentary development of anti-Euclidean systems, which we find in Aristotle.[50]

Gaiser (1968, 468) already saw a connection between the axiomatic investigations of Leodamas and the Platonic νόησις. Unfortunately, he did not spell this thought out: "a pivotal philosophical problem lies in the question as to how the presuppositions (ἀρχαί, ὑποθέσεις), which according to the analytic method appear as axioms and elements, or beyond these as universal formal principles, can be ontologically justified and known with immediate certainty. To put it differently: the question as to how the analytic/hypothetic method can be related to noetic intuition or anamnesis" (cf. also page 425).

3.7 *A Possible Reinterpretation of the Fourth Postulate*

To conclude, I would like to present an interpretation of Euclid's fourth postulate, which concerns the equality of all right angles and whose function is generally understood as being problematic; my interpretation results from what has been said up to this point. In the footnotes to his translation, Clemens Thaer writes: "If one does not assume this [a thesis by Zeuthen about the univocity of the extension of lines, which Zeuthen himself later dismissed] then it is problematic to include this proposition among the postulates" (Thaer 1962, 419). Heath (1956, vol. I, 200) provides a very modern and thus hardly plausible interpretation: "and hence his postulate must be taken as equivalent to the principle of *invariability of figures* or its equivalent, the *homogeneity of space*." (However, on page 201 the connection to the fifth postulate is rightly emphasized: "As to the *raison d'être* and the place of Post. 4 one thing is quite certain. It was essential from Euclid's point of view that it should come before Post. 5, since the condition in the latter that a certain pair of angles are together less than two right angles would be useless unless it were first made clear that right angles are angles of determinate and invariable magnitude.") In my opinion, the fourth postulate is nothing but a remnant of the Platonic ontological justification of the fifth postulate, because the right angle is only one angle, whereas there are infinitely many acute and obtuse angles, except in parallel lines in which an intersecting line creates inner angles whose sum is equal to 2R—and thus the triangle has an angular sum of 2R.[51]

Let us summarize: based on Tóth's research on the anti-Euclidean τόποι in Aristotle, which prove that Aristotle understood the axiomatic character of the fifth αἴτημα and regarded any decision about it, in the last instance, to be an act of free choice,[52] and after some *a priori* considerations regarding the origin of Aristotle's information from the Academy, I suggested the following interpretation of the allegory of the line and a passage from the *Cratylus* (this interpretation was supported by remarks about the esoteric Plato and his relationship to Leodamas' analytic method, which, finally, have allowed me to suggest a new explanation of Euclid's fourth αἴτημα): based on the investigations stimulated by Plato, it was probably Leodamas who understood that there was a gap in the earlier proof of *Elements* I, 29. What is more, he was convinced that it would be necessary to bridge that gap by means of an unprovable axiom. This led to a radical crisis in geometry in which the reference to intuition appears to have played an important role. We can assume that Plato's achievement in this difficult situation was to insist on a strict (and thus very modern) conception of geometry,[53] one that rejected intuition. Plato also helped in overcoming this crisis by way of an ontological construction:[54] Euclidean geometry as "the geometry of the right angle" is true for ontological reasons. In this light, it is reasonable to assume that Plato was responsible for the decline of anti-Euclidean theories[55] until their revival during the eighteenth and nineteenth centuries. For this reason, Euclidean geometry might be called, justifiably, Platonic geometry.[56]

NOTES

1. According to its classical foundation by David Hilbert (Hilbert 1899), Euclidean geometry consists of twenty axioms which are divided into five groups (by means of which the six basic concepts are implicitly defined); as such, the axioms cannot be proven. The eighteenth axiom ("axiom of parallels") is equivalent to the fifth αἴτημα of Euclid. It states that there can only be one parallel, which leads through a given point A, to a given line *a* in the plane determined by A and

a. This proposition is also equivalent to *Elements* I, 32.2: the sum of the angles in a triangle equals two right angles (2R). If one leaves out this axiom, one ends up with Bolyai's incomplete "absolute geometry." According to "absolute geometry" it can, e.g., not be determined if the sum of the angles in a triangle is less than or equal to 2R (the "appendix scientiam spatii absolute veram exhibens a veritate auf falsitate Axiomatis XI Euclidei [a priori hand unquam decidenda] independentem" of János Bolyai to a work of his father, the mathematician Wolfgang Bolyai, appeared in 1832, and already separately in 1831); if this axiom is replaced by another one that postulates the existence in a given point of at least two (and thus infinitely many) lines that do not intersect and run into opposing directions, "hyperbolic geometry" comes into existence. In the latter, the sum of the angles of a triangle is always less than 2R. In Riemann's elliptic geometry there are no parallels, and the sum of the angles in a triangle is greater than 2R. Elliptic geometry is inconsistent with the absolute geometry of Bolyai (AGB). Hence, for a consistent construction of this geometry, some of the nineteen axioms of the AGB need to be eliminated. Hilbert's Euclidean geometry is distinguished from Euclid's geometry in terms of its twentieth axiom, which is Cantor's continuity postulate (which even today is not accepted by intuitionism). Tóth rightly insists on this fact (cf., e.g., Tóth 1977, 414): geometric objects whose construction requires an *actually* infinite number of steps (e.g., an equilateral heptagon), are nonexistent for Euclid, but not for Hilbert.

2. Peirce 1976, 704. Imre Tóth has kindly pointed me to this work; I would like to thank him as well as Helmut Flashar and Alexander Kleinlogel for their many observations and critical comments on the manuscript.

3. Mugler 1948.

4. Cf. the review by Willem van der Wielen (Wielen et al. 1949): "Les notions d'une quatrième dimension et d'une géométrie non-euclidienne sont si étranges à la science grecque que le fait de les suggérer est déjà dangereux" (348). Because the present work aims to prove, or at least render probable, Mugler's thesis, various passages from his book will be cited.

5. The work cited in note 1 is the basis for this account insofar as it is the most accessible; at this point I want to refer to some other works by Tóth on this subject as well. Dealing with the historical aspects are: Tóth 1967; Tóth 1977; Tóth 1979; Tóth 2010, 27–52. Concerning philosophical aspects of this subject, see Tóth 1962 and Tóth 1972.

6. Unequal: *An. post.* 90a13, 93a35; *Soph. El.* 171a16; *Phys.* 200a18ff.; *DC* 281b5f.; *Met.* 1052a7; *NE* 1140b15f.; and MM 1187b3f. Greater: *An. priora* 66a14f.; *An. post.* 90a33; *Probl.* 956a18; *EE* 1222b35f. Smaller: *An. post.* 90a33.

7. The text cited is from Allan 1973.

8. Tóth aims to write a treatise on this subject matter; probably the second εἰ τάδε, which is missing in the best written copies, needs to be deleted (in the edition by Oddone Longo [Aristotle, *DC* 1961], the phrase is placed in square brackets. In Moraux's edition [Aristotle, *DC* 1965] the phrase is deleted from the text [in the *apparatus criticus* one reads: "εἰ τάδε post σύμμετρος add. recc."]), and should be changed to εἶτα δέ with a colon placed in front of it (Prof. Tóth graciously told me that this is what he found in the manuscripts he consulted: *Vindob. Phil. Gr.* 100 [Saec. IX], fol. 65r. 6; *Marcianus* 214 [XII], fol. 220r. b16; as well as *Marcianus* 200

[copyist: Joh. Rhosos 1457], fol. 46, v. 14), so that the translation would read: "I say that, for example, as the triangle [sc., ἐξ ὑποθέσεως] cannot have an angular sum of 2R; then the diagonal line is also commensurable" [cf. Tóth 1979, 80–81n.31].

9. An example of something ἁπλῶς ἀδύνατον, absolutely impossible, is 281b12: τὸ δ' ἅμα ἑστάναι καὶ καθῆσθαι: "at once standing and sitting."

10. Tóth 1967, 257–267.

11. It is well known that I, 27–29, are the only set of propositions in Euclid's book I in which the second proposition, even though it is the inverse of the first, does not follow from it (cf. the normal case: I,18–19; I, 24–25; I 47–48). Cf. Mugler 1948, 330: "que la reconte d'un théorème opposant une résistance acharnée a toutes les tentatives d'intervertir la prémisse et la conclusion devait apparaître à leurs yeux comme un scandale logique non moins déconcertant que, un siècle auparavant, la découverte par les Pythagoriciens de la première dérogation à la loi des nombres entiers."

12. Cf. Mugler 1948, 148: "La théorie des parallèles contenait donc, à cette époque, une pétition de principe qui n'échappait d'ailleurs pas à Aristote."

13. This is also Giralomo Saccheri's procedure in his well-known "anti-Euclidean" work Saccheri 1733 (Tóth introduced the term "anti-Euclidean" to characterize non-Euclidean propositions which were presented as false; this was done by all geometricians in antiquity up to and including Taurinus [1825–1826]. Only Gauss, Bolyai, and Lobachevski have true non-Euclidean geometries, because they "gave up the philosophy of dogmatic unicity and replaced it with a liberal philosophy of a plurality of geometric systems and the coexistence of opposing universes" [Tóth 1979, 400]).

14. Mugler is thinking in particular of a form of geometry like Riemann's, because its finite space fits Plato's conception of finitude (cf., e.g., Mugler 1948, 143), but it is more likely that the alternative Euclidean-hyperbolic geometry was in the foreground. This is also the case with later developments, especially up to the eighteenth century. Cf. the detailed discussion in Tóth 1967, 271ff.

15. When interpreting the concept αἴτημα, Tóth refers to *An. post.* 76b32f., where αἴτημα is defined as: τὸ ὑπεναντίον τοῦ μανθάνοντος τῇ δόξῃ. Tóth writes: "It cannot be fully excluded that in the case of the first application of the term to Euclid's parallel postulate the meaning provided in *An. post.* I.10, 76b31 played a role" (Tóth 1977, 398).

16. Cf. Mugler 1948, 149: "Tout semble indiquer que c'est Euclide lui-mēme qui le premier reconnut la nécessité de mettre fin aux pétitions de principe autour de la question des parallèles par un postulat et qui eut le génie de choisir de plusieurs possibilités la plus simple." Also cf. Mugler 1948, 330: The fifth postulate "est l'aboutissement de la longue suite de réflexions et de travaux provoqués par l'étonnement philosophique de Platon et de ses disciples sur l'exception unique qu'ils avaient constatée à la loi de la réversibilité des propositions."

17. εἰ γὰρ μηδὲν ἄλλο αἴτιον τοῦ τὸ τρίγωνον οὕτως ἔχειν, ἀρχή τις ἂν εἴη τοῦτο καὶ αἴτιον τῶν ὕστερον.

18. ὡς γὰρ ἂν ἔχωσιν αἱ ἀρχαί, οὕτως καὶ ἐκ τῶν ἀρχῶν ἔχει. ἐναργέστερον δ' ἔστι κατιδεῖν τοῦτο ἐν τοῖς κατὰ γεομετρίαν. καὶ γὰρ ἔχει ἐπειδή τινες λαμβάνονται ἀρχαί, ὡς ἂν αἱ ἀρχαί ἔχωσιν οὕτω καὶ τὰ μετὰ τὰς ἀρχάς, οἷον εἰ τὸ τρίγωνον δυοῖν ὀρθαῖς ἴσας ἔχει, τὸ δὲ τετράγωνον τέτταρσιν.

19. ἐν δὲ ταῖς ἀκινήτοις ἀρχαῖς, οἷον ἐν ταῖς μαθηματικαῖς, οὐκ ἔστι τὸ κύριον, καίτοι λέγεταί γε καθ' ὁμοιότητα. καὶ γὰρ ἐνταῦθ' κινουμένης τῆς ἀρχῆς πάντα μάλιστ' ἂν τὰ δεικνύμενα μεταβάλλοι.

20. ὥσπερ γὰρ ταῖς θεωρητικαῖς αἱ ὑποθέσεις ἀρχαί, οὕτω καὶ ταῖς ποιητικαῖς τὸ τέλος ἀρχὴ καὶ ὑπόθεσις . . . ὥσπερ ἐκεῖ, εἰ ἔστι τὸ τρίγωνον δύο ὀρθαί, ἀνάγκη τοδὶ εἶναι.

21. Of course this comparison does not disqualify Aristotle from saying that one side of the alternative (similar to choices of action) is "good," while the other is "bad." The interpretation in Tóth 1977, 412, of a passage from the (probably spurious) *Problemata* can, by the way, also be understood in a more harmless manner; the opposition to *Top.* 106a38ff. is not necessary, because the sort of happiness mentioned there is based on θαυμάζειν before incommensurability, and not necessarily on the non-axiomatic character of the proposition. Leaving this *Problemata* passage out, of course, does not alter Tóth's larger conception.

22. The works of both Krämer and Gaiser, which originated a noteworthy controversy, have not been generally acknowledged; I have attempted a detailed justification as to why I fundamentally agree with them in Hösle 1984, 375ff. At this point I only want to refer to Vlastos' rather critical review of Krämer's book *Arete bei Platon und Aristoteles* (Vlastos 1963, which also appears in Vlastos 1973, 379–398; cf. the appendix [ibid., 399–403]); Krämer discusses it metacritically in Krämer 1964. A further engagement with more recent critical works on the group of problems surrounding Plato's esoteric philosophy, e.g., with Tigerstedt and Guthrie, can be found in Krämer 1980. Some more recent works by Gaiser are Gaiser 1980 and Gaiser 1980(2).

23. As is generally known, Euclid's Platonism is proven by his use of the perfect passive imperative (ἔχθω, γεγράφθω, and even ᾐτήσθω, for his postulates) which indicates the eternity of geometrical constructions. Cf. Mugler 1958, 19–21.

24. Cf. Gaiser 1968, 131f. (the term "binomial" [ἐκ δύο ὀνομάτων] probably dates back to Plato) and ibid., 302 (on the Platonic interpretation of the classification of irrational magnitudes). Cf. also *TP* 67b.

25. Eudoxus' relationship with Plato does not need to be discussed at this point; it is well known that the remark in the *Vita Marciana* (fol. 278 A 60; cf. Gigon 1962, 49f.) suggests that he was the head of the Academy during Plato's second visit to Sicily.

26. Earlier it was assumed that Hilbert was the first to have replaced explicit definitions (similar to Euclid, *Elements* I) with implicit ones in Hilbert 1899. To name only two opposing arguments concerning the legitimacy of this procedure, cf., e.g., Frege's criticism in the three articles in Frege 1967; and Reichenbach's elaborate defense in Reichenbach 1958, §14; regardless, Hilbert's formalism seems to have been anticipated in Eudoxus.

27. Cf. supra: "We regard definition 4 as an *implicit* definition of homogeneity."

28. Cf. Mugler 1948, 141: "Un tel penseur aurait donc entrevu la possibilité d'une géométrie autre que celle que les Grecs ont développée effectivement, et il aurait découvert, comme moyen de concilier ses conceptions spatiales avec ses vues cosmogoniques, une géométrie Riemannienne (see note 14). L'idée d'un pareil philosophe à l'époque de Platon et déjà à celle de ses précurseurs immédiats n'est pas un vain anachronisme. Certes l'invention des géométries non euclidiennes suppose

un très grand pouvoir d'abstraction et elle ne fut faite qu'au 19e siècle après des travaux préparatoires au cours du 18e. Mais nous verrons à propos de la réforme d'Eudoxe . . . que le pouvoir d'abstraction mathématique des Grecs ne le cédait en rien à celui des mathématiciens contemporains et que le penseur de Cnide anticipait en partie les théories par lesquelles Cauchy, Dedekind et d'autres essayaient de refonder le calcul infinitésimal au 19e siècle."

29. Tóth regards Eudoxus and his circle as having been a source for Aristotle; he especially mentions Menaechmus and Theudius, who are referred to as Eudoxus' and Plato's students in Proclus' well-known catalogue of geometers (*In Eucl.* 64.18–68.8 = *TP* 15); cf. below. It is almost the *opinio communis* that the foundations of the *Elements* were laid down in the Academy, without making this commonly held thesis concrete and explicit; cf. Hoppe 1911, 164: "In two respects Plato is a forerunner of present efforts. . . . [S]econdly through systematic investigations into the conditions that are the basis of mathematics and in particular geometry. . . . [A] mong his contemporaries and successors no one managed to continue to develop the idea. This is especially true of Aristotle, who *collected* but did not develop." Cf. also Solmsen 1929, 117: "Now we are in the lucky position of being able to prove that the axioms have been discovered nowhere else but in the Platonic Academy and by the mathematicians working under the influence of Plato"; and Gaiser 1968, 304: "that Plato's philosophical thinking which was directed at the most universal principles of being productively influenced, and for the first time reflectively theorized, the process of the systematization of mathematical knowledge . . . to trace back the individual theorems without exception as completely as possible to simple and self-evident axioms" (of course, the axioms are precisely not self-evident for Plato!).

30. Cf. Mugler 1948, 145: "le terme de παράλληλοι est attesté pour la première fois chez Aristote, mais il est probable qu'il était en usage déjà dans l'academie. . . . L'intérêt de Platon pour cette question touchante los fondements de la géometrie devait être au contraire très grand. La théorie des parallèles a reçu sa forme définitive par Euclide. Mais avant que le grand Alexandrin finît par reconnaître l'avantage de la fonder sur un postulat indémontrable au lieu d'en faire un théorème démontrable au moyen d'un autre postulat admis consciemment ou inconsciemment . . . il se passait un siècle d'expériences, de vaines tentatives et de cercles vicieux autour des parallèles, et ces recherches remontent à l'école de Platon"; and ibid., 149: "Cet examen des citations d'Aristote relatives aux parallèles . . . nous montre que les géomètres de l'académie s'occupaient d'une façon intense et méthodique du problème du parallèlisme, et il est impossible que Platon, qui était partout ailleurs l'instigateur des recherches concernant les fondements de la géométrie et aboutissant aux définitions et aux postulats d'Euclide, soit resté étranger à ces méditations."

31. As Wyller 1970 has shown, for almost all of the late dialogues, the ὀμφαλός of each work is for the most part almost exactly in the middle of each work (e.g., αὐτὸ τἀκριβές in the *Statesman* [284D2]).

32. Mugler 1948, 29, refers to this passage when he writes: "Entrevoyait-il dans son esprit, en anticipant les idées audacieuses des Gauss, Riemann, H. Poincaré, la possibilité d'une géométrie absolue indépendante des hypothèses physiques et de la part de contingence entraînée par ces dernières?"

33. For example, to name just one instance: Zekl 1971, 202: "In the domain of hypothetical sciences . . . the path leads downward from the hypothesis deductively—one might think of mathematical axioms, but the illustration (510C) shows that instead he is concerned with basic mathematical concepts." In contrast, Stachowiak states, although cautiously, in Stachowiak 1971, 103: "However, even the most careful interpretation of the quoted Platonic texts will not be able to simply dismiss as completely unjustified and unlikely the assumption that Plato wanted to include the *propositions* as the basics of mathematical proofs in the circle of philosophically justifiable knowledge."

34. To understand Euclid, *Elements* I, defs. 10–12, one certainly does not need to have studied Platonic philosophy.

35. Knowledge of the unprovable ἀρχαί for Aristotle—just as for Plato—derives from νοῦς: οὐδὲ νοῦς (λέγω γὰρ νοῦν ἀρχὴν ἐπιστήμης) οὐδ᾽ ἐπιστήμη ἀναπόδεικτος: "neither intelligence (for by intelligence I mean a principle of scientific knowledge) nor indemonstrable scientific knowledge" (*An. post.* 88b36f.); λείπεται νοῦν εἶναι τῶν ἄρχων: "it remains that intelligence concerns principles" (*NE* 1141a8); of course the concept of νοῦς has a much broader meaning in Aristotle.

36. Cf. 510D5f. The Euclidean parallel postulate and the corresponding theorem concerning the sum of the angles seem more intuitively plausible than the opposed hyperbolic or elliptic theorems.

37. When discussing the fifth αἴτημα, Proclus states, *In Eucl.* 192.26–30: εἰ δὲ καὶ οἱ διαμφισβητοῦντες λόγοι πρὸς τὴν σύμπτωσιν πολὺ τὸ πληκτικὸν ἔχοιεν, πῶς οὐχὶ πολλῷ πλέον ἂν τὸ πιθανὸν τοῦτο καὶ τὸ ἄλογον ἐκβάλλοιμεν τῆς ἡμετέρας παραδοχῆς ("although the arguments against the intersection of these lines may contain much that surprises us, should we not all the more refuse to admit into our tradition this unreasoned appeal to probability?" [trans. Morrow]); in a truly Platonic manner, he proceeds here against the "evidence" of intuition for the parallel postulate and does not exclude the possibility of the hyperbolic axiom *a priori*. (Proclus later attempts to prove the fifth αἴτημα, although mistakenly. This attempt is admittedly strange because, in his brilliant interpretation of the allegory of the line [29.14–32.20], Proclus, in truly Platonic fashion, distinguishes mathematics from philosophy as a hypothetical science.) Shortly prior to this passage, Proclus (192.11f.) explicitly refers to Plato, *Phaedo* 92D ("Because the latter [sc., speech] came to me without any proof, only out of a certain probability and appropriateness [ἄνευ ἀποδείξεως μετὰ εἰκότος τινὸς καὶ εὐπρεπείας] . . . but I know that the speeches, which become effective by way of such an illusion, are empty swaggerers and, if one does not watch out for them carefully, they can easily betray one in geometry [ἐν γεωμετρίᾳ] and all the other arts"). One can, but does not need to, place this passage in the same context as the allegory of the line. Cf. similarly *Theaet.* 162Ef.

38. This kind of "speculative mathematics" can be found very often in the Neoplatonic commentators (e.g., Proclus), in Nicholas of Cusa, and traces of it even in Hegel; cf., for example, Hegel 1964, vol. 5, 310, where he states that the transition from the rectangle to the square corresponds to "an equation between what is identical with itself, the square, to what is in itself uneven, the rectangle" (on this Platonic idea, cf. Gaiser 1968, 53f.). Hegel draws a parallel between the right angle and "that which is identical with itself" (ibid.). Finally, Hegel explains (314)

incommensurability in a way that is very similar to Plato (cf. Gaiser 1968, 58). It is also certainly Platonic, the way in which Hegel stipulates the axiomatic character of the parallel postulate and its unprovability by mathematics (Hegel 1964, 306f.).

39. On the function of the right angle as measure, cf. Euclid, *Elements* I, defs. 10–12.

40. Cf. Gaiser 1968, 304: "according to the Platonic conception, in the last instance the universal principles of being themselves *constitute* the mathematical phenomena and their regularities as well" (my emphasis; unfortunately a more detailed elaboration is missing); and ibid., 305: "because it [sc., mathematics] is according to its essence dependent on ontological presuppositions, which cannot be grasped by mathematics."

41. This also elucidates the meaning of σχήματα: of course the geometrical figures change according to the validity of the angle sum theorem, and thus are presupposed as well. I situate the τό τε περιττὸν καὶ τὸ ἄρτιον in the context of the generation of numbers out of ἕν and ἀόριστος δυάς (cf. *TP* 32, §276f.; *TP* 60; *Parm.* 142Bf., esp. 144A; and Suhr 1969, 36ff., 52f.). In arithmetic, the Platonic doctrine of the principles was supposed to provide the proof of the existence of numbers (*Parm.* 144A: "do you believe that any number remains that does not exist necessarily?"); the claim to completeness in the last passage brings to mind the (of course much more complex) fifth axiom of Peano. One can also assume an ontological justification (which, however, does not correspond to anything in modern mathematics) in the context of Plato's teaching about indivisible lines (cf. Gaiser 1968, 158ff.).

42. It is quite possible that hyperbolic geometry was connected by Plato, because of its infinitely many parallels, to the ἀόριστος δυάς. As Mugler rightly emphasizes, Euclidean geometry is most closely related to the Greek spirit because of the similarity of figures existing in it. This fact, however, has most likely not been adequately considered. (Mugler 1948, 132f.: "Mais les propriétés géométriques dont il se sert principalement nous montrent que la géométrie euclidienne était la plus adéquate au génie constructeur des Grecs. Nous pouvons en effet constater que les propriétés auxquelles le Démiurge fait appel sont précisément celles qui caractérisent l'espace euclidien : il se propose de faire de la similitude un principe d'ordre, et nous savons que seul l'espace euclidien admet des figures semblables, au point que certains géomètres modernes [Mugler is thinking of John Wallis—VH] ont proposé le postulat de l'existence de figures semblabes [*sic*!] comme équivalent du 5e postulat d'Euclide.")

43. An adequate evaluation of this construction, which appears awkward to us, should bear in mind that Plato is at least more modern than Kant insofar as he not only renounces a justification of the axioms based on intuition, but also explicitly rejects such attempts. Cf. Robinson 1953, 156: "They [sc., the ὑποθέσεις] were 'plain to all' or παντὶ φανερά in the physical sense of being there to see in the geometer's sand. In geometry the appeal to spatial intuition and the claim that one's postulates are certainties go together. Plato's contemporaries accepted both. Plato and the twentieth century reject both."

44. The *Cratylus* is the only Platonic dialogue for which the question as to whether it was written before or after the *Republic* has remained controversial. Based on the reasons provided by Gaiser 1974, and despite some reservations, I would like to accept his position (ibid., 97) that it should be situated after the *Republic*.

45. The term διαγραμμάτων cannot be translated as "geometrical figures"; it means "geometrical proofs"; the term ψεῦδος does not yet mean, as it does in Aristotle, "error" or "sophism," but "false statement"; and ὁμολογεῖν, finally, means "to be consistent." See Tóth 2010; one of the main conclusions of this terminological research is that the logical triplet συλλογίζεσθαι–συλλογισμός–παραλογισμός has its geometrical counterpart in γράφειν–διάγραμμα–ψευδογραφεῖν.

46. The first was the Pythagorean discovery of the irrationals, which was only mastered by Eudoxus. Mugler already compares both of these crises (Mugler 1948, 330).

47. Cf., for example, *Charm.* 154D8 and 173D8, as well as the spurious *Theages* 128B4 (the imitator knew Plato's stylistic mannerisms). *Crat.* 436D was already cited by Tóth in a non-Euclidean context (Tóth 1977, 400). However, he did not provide a more detailed interpretation.

48. Contrary to Cherniss 1945, 13; Müller 1949; and Edelstein 1966, I agree with most scholars that the *Seventh Letter* is authentic (Pohlenz 1913, 113ff.; Wilamowitz-Moellendorff 1919; Stenzel 1921; Patzer 1954; Krämer 1959, 401; Gaiser 1968, 452; Fritz 1978, 175–213). Concerning the question of authenticity cf. Irmscher 1960, 7, 49, who, in his "Introduction," remains undecided.

49. The Eudoxian achievement presupposes a level of understanding concerning what constitutes a rigorous proof, which is at least as sophisticated as understanding the possibility of anti-Euclidean systems; also in the nineteenth century, Dedekind is later than Bolyai.

50. Leon's research on determination can be seen in the context of these investigations on the foundations (on Leon, cf. the article by Orinsky 1935, 222).

51. The ontological primacy of the right angle known from Plato's unwritten doctrine is also mentioned by Proclus in his discussion of the fourth postulate (*In Eucl.* 188.12–15: ἡ τῶν ὀρθῶν ἰσότης μονάδος δὲ ἔχουσα λόγον ἢ ὅρον πρὸς τὴν ἐπ' ἄπειρον αὔξησιν καὶ ἐλάττωσιν τῶν ἐφ' ἑκατέρα γωνιῶν ἴση ἐστὶ πρὸς πᾶσαν ὀρθήν: "the equality of right angles [is clear from our common notions], having the relation of a first term or bound with respect to the indefinite increase or decrease of the angles on either side of it, the right angle is equal to every right angle" [trans. Morrow]; see also 191.5–11). Marković 1965, 311, already demands "interpreting the fourth postulate of Euclid's first book, which requires the equality of all right angles, in light of this theory: in this light, the postulate appears as one of its vestiges." Marković, however, does not see its importance for the fifth αἴτημα.

52. Aristotle's more liberal stance with regard to non-Euclidean geometries is certainly also a product of embarrassment: because in general terms he rejects an ontological foundation for mathematics (cf. the transition from *Met.* K.7 to E.1; and see Gaiser 1968, 317ff.), he robs himself of the possibility of an ontological commitment to Euclidean geometry. Hence, he can only admit that concerning the problem, νῦν δ' οὔτε μὴ λέγειν οὔτε λέγειν ἀκριβῶς οἷόν τε πλῆν τοσοῦτον, "for now we can neither affirm nor deny anything with precision" (*EE* 1222b38f.; trans. Solomon). His parallelization of ethics and geometry probably also has Platonic origins—except that, for Plato, both were grounded ontologically. Cf. Proclus, *In Eucl.* 131.12–132.17; 133.20–134.1 (= *TP* 37), where the right angle is compared to ἀρετή.

53. Cf. *Epin.* 990D (criticizing the deficiency in the name γεω-μετρία), and also Plutarch, *Vit. Marc.* 14, 5–6, p. 305E (= *TP* 21b); and *Quaest. conviv.* VIII.2, 1 p. 718E–F (= *TP* 21a): Plato rejects the application of mechanical devices in geometry.

54. On the relationship between mathematics and dialectic cf. also *Euthyd.* 290C: mathematicians themselves cannot do anything (χρῆσθαι) with their conclusions and hand these over to ontologists.

55. And thus for a philosophy of mathematics that was revolutionized only during the twentieth century, one might think of Descartes' *genius malignus*, who—in much more general terms—must have already troubled the academic mathematicians prior to the solution suggested by Plato (cf. *Rep.* 533B8f.: ὡς ὀνειρώττουσι μὲν περὶ τὸ ὄν: "they are only dreaming of being").

56. Thus, this conclusion is very different from the solution given by Szabó 1965, who in this influential and fundamental work—according to the conclusions of this article—clearly underestimates the importance of Plato for the development of the Euclidean system of axioms (cf. esp. ibid., 454f.).

BIBLIOGRAPHY

ANCIENT SOURCES

Collections

DK *Fragmente der Vorsokratiker*. Ed. H. Diels and W. Kranz. Zürich: Weidmann, 1985.

TP *Testimonia Platonica: Quellentexte zur Schule und mündlichen Lehre Platons*, in Gaiser 1963, 441–557.

Commentaria in Aristotelem Graeca. Ed. H. Diels. 23 vols. Berlin: G. Reimer, 1882–1909.

Supplementum Aristotelicum. 2 vols. Berlin: G. Reimer, 1887.

Div. Arist. *Divisiones quae vulgo dicuntur Aristoteleae*. Ed. H. Mutschmann. Leipzig: Teubner, 1906.

Single-Author Texts

ALCIDAMAS

Soph. *Peri sophiston*. In Antiphon, *Orationes et fragmenta, adiunctis Gorgiae Antisthenis Alcidamantis declamationibus*, ed. F. Blass, 202–204. Leipzig: Teubner, 1908.

"On Those Who Write Written Speeches, or On Sophists," in *The Works and Fragments*, ed. J. V. Muir, 2–21. London: Bristol Classical Press, 2001.

ALCINOUS

Didask. *Alcinoou Didaskalikos tōn Platonis dramatōn*, in vol. 6 of *Platonis dialogi secundum Thrasylli tetralogias dispositi*. Ed. C. F. Hermann. Leipzig: Teubner, 1853, pp. 152–189; 2nd ed., 1884; 3rd ed., 1907.

Alcinous: The Handbook of Platonism. Trans. John Dillon. Oxford: Clarendon Press, 1993.

ALEXANDER OF APHRODISIAS

In Met. *In Aristotelis Metaphysica commentaria*. Ed. M. Hayduck. Vol. 1 of *Commentaria in Aristotelem Graeca*. Berlin: G. Reimer, 1891.

ARISTOTLE

Opera. Ed. Immanuel Bekker. Berlin: G. Reimer, 1831.

An. post. *Analytica posteriora* (*Posterior Analytics*)

An. priora *Analytica priora* (*Prior Analytics*)

Prior Analytics. Trans. A. J. Jenkinson. In *Complete Works*, ed. J. Barnes, 39–113. Oxford: Oxford University Press, 1984.

DA *De anima*

DC *De caelo* (*On the Heavens*)

De caelo. Ed. Oddone Longo. Florence: Sansoni, 1961.

De caelo. Ed. P. Moraux. Paris: Les Belles Letters, 1965.

De caelo. Ed. D. J. Allan. Oxford: Oxford University Press, 1973.

EE *Ethica Eudemia* (*Eudemian Ethics*)

Eudemian Ethics. Trans. J. Solomon. In *Complete Works*, ed. J. Barnes, 1922–1981. Oxford: Oxford University Press, 1984.

Frag. *Fragmenta selecta*. Ed. W. D. Ross. Oxford: Oxford University Press, 1955.

GC *De generatione et corruptione* (*On Generation and Corruption*)

De lin. insecab. *De lineis insecabilibus* (*On Indivisible Lines*)

MM *Magna Moralia*

Magna Moralia. Trans. G. St. Stock. In *Complete Works*, ed. J. Barnes, 1868–1921. Oxford: Oxford University Press, 1984.

Met. *Metaphysica* (*Metaphysics*)

Metaphysics. Trans. W. D. Ross. Oxford: Oxford University Press, 1924.

NE *Ethica Nicomachea* (*Nicomachean Ethics*)

Phys. *Physica* (*Physics*)

Probl. *Problemata* (*Problems*)

Soph. El. *De sophisticis elenchis* (*Sophistical Refutations*)

Top. *Topica* (*Topics*)

ARISTOXENUS

Harm. *Elementa harmonica*. Ed. R. da Rios. Rome: Typis publicae officinae polygraphicae, 1954.

ASCLEPIUS

In Met. *In Aristotelis Metaphysica libros A–Z commentaria*. Ed. M. Hayduck. Vol. 6, pt. 2, of *Commentaria in Aristotelem Graeca*. Berlin: G. Reimer, 1888.

DIOGENES LAERTIUS

Lives *Vitae philosophorum*. Ed. M. Marcovich. 2 vols. Leipzig: Teubner, 1999.

Lives of Eminent Philosophers. Trans. R. D. Hicks. 2 vols. Cambridge: Harvard University Press, 1972.

EUCLID

Elem. *Elementa*. Ed. J. L. Heiberg. Leipzig: Teubner, 1883–1888.

EUDEMUS

Frag. *Werke*. Ed. F. Wehrli. Vol. 7 of *Die Schule des Aristoteles*. Basel: Schwabe, 1955.

EUDOXUS

Frag. *Die Fragmente des Eudoxos von Knidos*. Ed. F. Lasserre. Berlin: Walter de Gruyter, 1966.

HERO OF ALEXANDRIA

Opera. Ed. J. L. Heiberg. Leipzig: Teubner, 1899–1914.

IAMBLICHUS

De comm. math. sc. *De communi mathematica scientia*. Ed. N. Festa. 1891; rept. Stuttgart: Teubner, 1975.

De vita Pythag. *De vita Pythagorica*. Ed. H. Pistelli. 1937; repr. Stuttgart: Teubner, 1975.

In Nicom. arithm. *In Nicomachi arithmeticam introductionem*. Ed. H. Pistelli. Leipzig: Teubner, 1894; repr. Stuttgart: Teubner, 1975.

Protrepticus *Protrepticus*. Ed. H. Pistelli. 1888; repr. Stuttgart: Teubner, 1996.

Theol. arithm. *Theologumena arithmeticae*. Ed. V. de Falco. 1922; repr. Stuttgart: Teubner, 1975.

PAPPUS

In Eucl. Elem. *The Commentary of Pappus on Book X of Euclid's* Elements. Trans. W. Thomson. Ed. W. Thomson and G. Junge. Cambridge: Harvard University Press, 1930.

PHILODEMUS

Acad. *Academica*. Ed. K. Gaiser. Stuttgart: Frommann-Holzboog, 1988.

Index Acad. *Academicorum philosophorum index Herculanensis*. Ed. S. Mekler. Berlin: Weidmann, 1902.

PHILOPONUS

In de gen. et corr. *In Aristotelis libros De generatione et corruption commentaria*. Ed. Hieronymus Vitelli. Berlin: Reimer, 1897.

PLATO

Opera. Ed. Henri Estienne. Geneva, 1578.

Werke. Trans. F. Schleiermacher, 2nd ed. 1817–1826; rept. Berlin: Akademie, 1985.

Opera. Ed. John Burnet. 5 vols. Oxford: Clarendon Press, 1900–1907.

Alc. I *Alcibiades I*

Charm. *Charmides*

Crat. *Cratylus*

Def. *Definitions*

Epin. *Epinomis*

Epinomis. Trans. W. R. M. Lamb. Cambridge: Harvard University Press, 1967.

Ep. *Epistles (Letters)*

Euthyd. *Euthydemus*

Euth. *Euthyphro*

Legg. *Laws*

Laws. Trans. R. G. Bury. Cambridge: Harvard University Press, 1926.

Meno *Meno*

Parm. *Parmenides*

Phaedo *Phaedo*

Phaedr. *Phaedrus*

Phil. *Philebus*

Polit. *Politicus (Statesman)*

Prot. *Protagoras*

Rep. *Republic*

Republic. Trans. A. Bloom. 2nd ed. New York: Basic Books, 1991.

Soph. *Sophist*

Symp. *Symposium*

Theaet. *Theaetetus*

Theag. *Theages*

Tim. *Timaeus*

PLOTINUS

Enneads. Trans. A. H. Armstrong. 7 vols. Cambridge: Harvard University Press, 1969–1988.

Plotini opera. Ed. P. Henry and H.-R. Schwyzer. 3 vols. Oxford: Clarendon Press, 1964–1984.

PLUTARCH

Mor. *Moralia*. Ed. F. C. Babbitt. 15 vols. Cambridge: Harvard University Press, 1927–1969.

PROCLUS

De prov. *Proclus: Trois études sur la providence, II. Providence, fatalité, liberté*. Ed. D. Issac. Paris Les Belles Lettres, 1979.

Elem. Th. *The Elements of Theology*. Ed. E. R. Dodds. 2nd ed. Oxford: Clarendon, 1963.

In Eucl. *Procli Diadochi in primum Euclidis elementorum librum commentarii*. Ed. G. Friedlein. Leipzig: Teubner, 1873.

A Commentary on the First Book of Euclid's Elements. Trans. G. R. Morrow. Princeton: Princeton University Press, 1992.

In Parm. *Procli philosophi Platonici opera inedita*. Ed. V. Cousin. 2nd ed. 1820–1827; rept. Hildesheim: Georg Olms 1961.

In Remp. *Procli Diadochi in Platonis rem publicam commentarii*. Ed. W. Kroll. 2 vols. Leipzig: Teubner, 1899–1901.

Proclus: Commentaire sur la république. Trans. A.-J. Festugière. 3 vols. Paris: Vrin, 1970.

Procli Successoris Platonici in Platonis Theologiam Libri Sex. Ed. A. Portus. 1618; rept. Frankfurt am Main: Minerva, 1960.

In Tim. *Procli Diadochi in Platonis Timaeum commentaria*. Ed. E. Diehl. Leipzig: Teubner, 1903–1906.

Procli In Platonis Parmenidem commentaria. Ed. Carlos Steel. Vols. I–III. Oxford: Clarendon, 2007–2009.

Theol. Plat. *Proclus: Théologie platonicienne*. Ed. H. D. Saffrey and L. G. Westerink. 6 vols. Paris: Les Belles Lettres, 1968–1997.

SEXTUS EMPIRICUS

Opera. Ed. H. Mutschmann and J. Mau. Leipzig: Teubner, 1954–62.

SIMPLICIUS

In Cat. *In Aristotelis Categorias commentaria*. Ed. C. Kalbfleisch. Berlin: G. Reimer, 1907.

In De caelo *In Aristotelis De caelo commentaria*. Ed. J. L. Heiberg. Vol. 7 of *Commentaria in Aristotelem Graeca*. Berlin: G. Reimer, 1893.

In Phys. In *Aristotelis Physicorum libros quattor priores commentaria*. Ed. Hermann Diels. Vol. 9 of *Commentaria in Aristotelem Graeca*. Berlin: G. Reimer, 1882.

SPEUSIPPUS

Frag. *Frammenti*. Ed. M. Isnardi Parente. Naples: Bibliopolis, 1980.

THEMISTIUS

In Phys. *Themistii in Aristotelis Physica paraphrasis*. Ed. Henricus Schenkl. Berlin: Reimer, 1900.

THEON OF SMYRNA

Exp. *Expositio rerum mathematicarum ad legendum Platonem utilium*. Ed. E. Hiller. Leipzig: Teubner, 1878.

THEOPHRASTUS

Met. *Metaphysica*. Ed. W. D. Ross and F. H. Fobes. Oxford: Clarendon Press, 1929.

XENOCRATES

Frag. *Fragmenta*. Ed. R. Heinze. Leipzig: Teubner, 1892.

SECONDARY SOURCES

Adam, J. 1902. *The Republic of Plato*. 2 vols. Cambridge: Cambridge University Press.

Adam, J. 1929. *The Republic of Plato*. 2 vols. Cambridge: Cambridge University Press.

Allen, R. E., ed. 1965. *Studies in Plato's Metaphysics*. New York: Humanities Press.

Annas, J. 1975. On the 'Intermediates.' *Archiv für Geschichte der Philosophie* 57: 146–166.

Annas, J. 1976. *Aristotle's Metaphysics: Books M and N*. Oxford: Clarendon Press.

Annas, J. 1981. *An Introduction to Plato's Republic*. Oxford: Oxford University Press.

Assmann, A., Assmann, J., and Hardmeier, C., eds. 1983. (3rd ed. 1998) *Schrift und Gedächtnis: Beiträge zur Archäologie der literarischen Kommunikation*. Munich: Wilhelm Fink.

Assmann, J. 1992. *Das kulturelle Gedächtnis: Schrift, Erinnerung und politische Identität in frühen Hochkulturen*. Munich: Beck.

Baltes, Mathias. 1999. *Dianoemata. Kleine Schriften zu Platon und zum Platonismus*. Stuttgart-Leipzig: Teubner.

Baumgartner, H. M. 1965. *Von der Möglichkeit, das Agathon als Prinzip zu denken, Versuch einer transzendentalen Interpretation zu Politeia 509RB*. In *Parusia: Studien zur Philosophie Platons und zur Problemgeschichte des Platonismus, Festgabe für Johannes Hirschberger*, ed. K. Flasch, 89–101. Frankfurt: Minerva.

Berger, H. H. 1961. *Ousia in de dialogen van Plato: Een terminologisch onderzoek*. Leiden: Brill.

Boeder, H. 1968. Zu Platons eigener Sache. *Philosophisches Jahrbuch* 76: 37–66.

Böhme, G. 1976. Platons Theorie der exakten Wissenschaften. *Antike und Abendland* 22: 40–53.

Bonagura, P. 1991. *Exterioridad e interioridad*. Pamplona: Universidad de Navarra.

Brandis, C. A. 1823. *Scholia in Aristotelem*. Berlin: G. Reimer.

Brisson, L. 1993. Présupposés et conséquences d'une interprétation ésotériste de Platon. *Méthexis* 6: 11–35.

Brisson, L. 2000. *Plato the Myth Maker*. Trans. G. Naddaf. Chicago: University of Chicago.

Brisson, L. 2002. L'approche traditionelle de Platon par H.F. Cherniss. In *New Images of Plato: Dialogues on the Idea of the Good*, ed. G. Reale and S. Scolnicov, 85–97. Sankt Augustin: Academia.

Bröcker, W. 1958. Gorgias contra Parmenides. *Hermes* 86: 425–440.

Bröcker, W. 1966. Platos Vorlesungen. *Forschungen und Fortschritte* 40: 89–92.

Bröcker, W. 1967. *Platos Gespräche*. Frankfurt: Klostermann.

Bulmer-Thomas, I. 1983. Plato's Theory of Numbers. *Classical Quarterly* 33: 375–384.

Bulmer-Thomas, I. 1984. Plato's Astronomy. *Classical Quarterly* 34: 107–112.

Burkert, W. 1962. *Weisheit und Wissenschaft: Studien zu Pythagoras, Philolaos und Platon*. Nuremberg: Hans Carl.

Burkert, W. 1982. Konstruktion und Seinsstruktur: Praxis und Platonismus in der griechischen Mathematik. *Abhandlungen der Braunschweigischen Wissenschaftichen Gesellschaft* 34: 125–141.

Burnyeat, M. 1987. Platonism and Mathematics: A Prelude to Discussion. In *Mathematics and Metaphysics in Aristotle / Mathematik und Metaphysik bei Aristoteles*, ed. A. Graeser, 213–240. Bern-Stuttgart: P. Haupt.

Cattanei, E. 1992–1993. *La teoria platonica-accademica degli enti matematici nella* Metafisica *di Aristotele*. Milan: Vita e Pensiero.

Cattanei, E. 1996. *Enti matematici e metafisica: Platone, l'Accademia e Aristotele a confronto*. Milano: Vita e Pensiero.

Chen, L. C. H. 1992. *Acquiring Knowledge of the Ideas: A Study of Plato's Methods in the* Phaedo, *the* Symposium *and the Central Books of the* Republic. Stuttgart: Franz Steiner.

Cherniss, H. 1944. *Aristotle's Criticism of Plato and the Academy*. Baltimore: Johns Hopkins University Press. 3rd ed. New York, Russell and Russell, 1962.

Cherniss, H. 1945. *The Riddle of the Early Academy*. Berkeley: University of California Press; rept. New York: Russell and Russell, 1962.

Cherniss, H. 1951. Plato as Mathematician. *Review of Metaphysics* 4: 395–425.

Cherniss, H. 1953. Review of G. Müller, *Studien zu den platonischen Nomoi*. *Gnomon* 25: 367–379.

Cherniss, H. 1977. *Selected Papers*. Ed. L. Tarán. Leiden: Brill.

Cornford, F. M. 1932. Mathematics and Dialectic in the *Republic* VI–VII. *Mind* 41: 173–190.

Cornford, F. M. 1939. *Plato and Parmenides*. London: Routledge & Kegan Paul.

Cornford, F. M., trans. 1941. *The* Republic *of Plato*. Oxford: Oxford University Press.

Cosenza, P. 1977. *L'incommensurabile nell'evoluzione filosofica di Platone*. Naples: Editions Il Tripode.

Crombie, J. M. 1963. *An Examination of Plato's Doctrines*. London and New York: Routledge & Kegan Paul.

Cross, R. C., and Woozley, A. D. 1964. *Plato's* Republic*: A Philosophical Commentary*. London: Macmillan.

Cusanus, N. 1982. *De Venatione Sapientiae. De Apice Theoriae*. Ed. Raymond Klibansky and Hans G. Senger. Vol. 12 of *Opera Omnia*. Hamburg: Felix Meiner.

Cusanus, N. 1988. *De Beryllo*. Ed. Hans G. Senger and Karl Bormann. Vol. 11, part 1 of *Opera Omnia*. Hamburg: Felix Meiner.

Dempe, H. 1967. Platon und die moderne Philosophie. *Gymnasium* 74: 510–528.

Detienne, M., ed. 1988. *Les savoirs de l'ecriture en Grèce ancienne*. Lille: Presses Universitaires de Lille.

Diès, A., ed. 1932. *Platon*, Rèpublique. Vols. 6–7 of Œuvre Complètes. Paris: Les Belles Lettres.

Dillon, J. 1977. *The Middle Platonists*. London: Duckworth.

Dillon, J. 1981. Eudoros und die Anfänge des Mittelplatonismus. In *Der Mittelplatonismus*, ed. C. Zintzen, 2–32. Darmstadt: Wissenschaftliche Buchgesellschaft.

Dillon, J. 2003. *The Heirs of Plato: A Study of the Old Academy (347–274 BC)*. Oxford: Clarendon Press.

Dodds, E. R. 1928. The Parmenides of Plato and the Origin of the Neoplatonic 'One.' *Classical Quarterly* 22: 129–142.

Duranti, G. C. 1994. *Towards a "Third" Plato*. Venice.

Düring, I. 1966. *Aristoteles: Darstellung und Interpretation seines Denkens*. Heidelberg: Carl Winter.

Ebert, T. 1974. *Meinung und Wissen in der Philosophie Platons: Untersuchungen zum Charmides, Menon und Staat*. Berlin: Walter de Gruyter.

Edelstein, L. 1966. *Plato's* Seventh Letter. Leiden: Brill.

Erler, M. 1983. Zur Platon, Politeia 534D. *Hermes* 111: 221–226.

Erler, M. 1987. *Der Sinn der Aporien in den Dialogen Platons*. Berlin-New York: Walter de Gruyter.

Ferber, R. 1984. *Platos Idee des Guten*. Sankt Augustin: Richarz.

Ferguson, A. 1921. Plato's Simile of Light: Part I: The Similes of the Sun and the Line. *Classical Quarterly* 15: 131–52.

Ferguson, A. 1922. Plato's Simile of Light: Part II: The Allegory of the Cave (Continued). *Classical Quarterly* 16: 15–28.

Ferguson, A. 1934. Plato's Simile of Light Again. *Classical Quarterly* 15: 131–152.

Festugière, A. J. 1935. *Contemplation et vie contemplative selon Platon.* Paris: Vrin.

Field, G. C. 1952. *Die Philosophie Platons*. Trans. M. Soreth. Stuttgart: Kohlhammer.

Field, G. C. 1957. *Plato and His Contemporaries*. London: Methuen.

Field, G. C. 1969. *The Philosophy of Plato.* 2nd ed. Oxford: Oxford University Press.

Findlay, J. N. 1974. *Plato: The Written and Unwritten Doctrines*. London: Routledge & Kegan Paul.

Frank, E. 1923. *Plato und die sogenannten Pythagoreer*. Darmstadt: Wissenschaftliche Buchgesellschaft.

Fränkel, H. 1960. Zenon von Elea im Kampf gegen die Idee der Vielheit. In *Wege und Formen frühgriechischen Denkens*, 198–236. Munich: Beck.

Frege, G. 1967. *Kleine Schriften.* Vol. 1. Ed. I. Angelelli. Darmstadt: Wissenschaftliche Buchgesellschaft.

Frege, G. 1968. *Kleine Schriften.* Vol. 2. Ed. I. Angelelli. Hildesheim: Georg Olms.

Fritz, K. von. 1931. "Theudios." In vol. VIA, pt. 1, *Realencyclopädie der classischen Altertumswissenschaft*, ed. A. Pauly, G. Wissowa, et al. 244–246. Stuttgart: J. B. Metzler.

Fritz, K. von. 1932. (2nd ed. 1969) *Platon Theaetet und die antike Mathematik.* Darmstadt: Wissenschaftliche Buchgesellschaft.

Fritz, K. von. 1937. "Oinopides." In vol. XVII, *Real-Enzyklopädie der classischen Altertumswissenschaft*, ed. A. Pauly, G. Wissowa, et al., 262–266. Stuttgart: J. B. Metzler.

Fritz, K. von. 1940. "Leodamas von Thasos." In Supplement VII, *Real-Enzyklopädie der classischen Altertumswissenschaft*, A. Pauly, G. Wissowa, et al., 371–373. Stuttgart: J. B. Metzler.

Fritz, K. von. 1955. Die ΑΡΧΑΙ in der griechischen Mathematik. *Archiv für Begriffsgeschichte* 1: 13–103.

Fritz, K. von. 1961. Der Beginn universalwissenschaftlicher Bestrebungen und der Primat der Griechen. I, II. *Studium Generale* 14: 546–583, 601–636.

Fritz, K. von. 1966. Die philosophische Stelle im siebten platonischen Brief und die Frage der 'esoterischen' Philosophie Platon. *Phronesis* 11: 117–153.

Fritz, K. von. 1967. Zur Frage der 'esoterischen' Philosophie Platons. *Archiv für Geschichte der Philosophie* 49: 255–268.

Fritz, K. von. 1978. *Schriften zur griechischen.* 2 vols. Stuttgart: Frommann-Holzboog.

Furley, D. J. 1967. *Two Studies in the Greek Atomists*. Princeton: Princeton University Press.

Gadamer, H. G. 1931. (2nd ed. 1968) *Platos dialektische Ethik.* Leipzig: Felix Meiner.

Gadamer, H. G. 1964. *Dialektik und Sophistik im siebenten platonischen Brief: Sitzungsberichte der Heidelberger Akademie der Wissenschaften, phil.-hist. Kl.*, 2 Heidelberg.

Gadamer, H. G. 1968. Platons ungeschriebene Dialektik. In *Idee und Zahl: Studien zur platonischen Philosophie*, ed. H. G. Gadamer and W. Schadewaldt, 106–150. Heidelberg: Akademie der Wissenschaften.

Gadamer, H. G. 1978. *Die Idee des Guten zwischen Plato und Aristoteles*. Heidelberg: Carl Winter.

Gaiser, K. 1959. *Protreptik und Paränese bei Platon: Untersuchungen zur Form des platonischen Dialogs*. Stuttgart: Kohlhammer.

Gaiser, K. 1963. *Platons ungeschriebene Lehre: Studien zur systematischen und geschichtlichen Begrundung der Wissenschaften in der Platonischen Schule*. Stuttgart: Klett.

Gaiser, K. 1964. Platons Menon und die Akademie. *Archiv für Geschichte der Philosophie* 46: 241–292.

Gaiser, K. 1968. *Platons ungeschriebene Lehre: Studien zur systematischen und geschichtlichen Begrundung der Wissenschaften in der Platonischen Schule*. 2nd ed. Stuttgart: Klett.

Gaiser, K. 1968(2). Quellenkritische Probleme der indirekten Platonüberlieferung. In *Idee und Zahl. Studien zur platonischen Philosophie*, ed. H. G. Gadamer and W. Schadewaldt, 31–84. Heidelberg: Carl Winter.

Gaiser, K, ed. 1969. *Das Platonbild: Zehn Beiträge zum Platonverständnis*. Hildesheim: Georg Olms.

Gaiser, K. 1972. Exoterisch / esoterisch. In vol. 2 of *Historisches Wörtherbuch der Philosophie*, ed. J. Ritter, 866–867. Basel-Stuttgart: Schwabe.

Gaiser, K. 1974. *Name und Sache in Platons 'Cratylus.'* Heidelberg: Carl Winter.

Gaiser, K. 1980. *Das Philosophenmosaik in Neapel: Eine Darstellung der platonischen Akademie*. Heidelberg: Carl Winter.

Gaiser, K. 1980(2). Plato's Enigmatic "Lecture on the Good." *Phronesis* 25: 5–37.

Gaiser, K. 1983. La biografia di Platone in Filodemo: Nuovi dati dal Pherc. 1021. *Cronache Ercolanesi* 13: 53–62.

Gaiser, K. 1984. *Platone come scrittore filosofico: Saggi sull'ermeneutica dei dialoghi platonici*. Naples: Bibliopolis.

Gaiser, K. 1986. Platons Zusammenschau der mathematischen Wissenschaften. *Antike und Abendland* 32: 89–124

Gaiser, K. 1987. Platonische Dialektik—damals und heute. *Gymnasium Beiheft* 9: 77–107.

Gaiser, K. 1988. Platons esoterische Lehre. In *Gnosis und Mystik in der Geschichte der Philosophie*, ed. P. Koslowski, 13–40. Zürich-München: Artemis und Winkler Verlag.

Gaiser, K. 1998. *Platons ungeschriebene Lehre: Studien zur systematischen und geschichtlichen Begrundung der Wissenschaften in der Platonischen Schule*. 3rd ed. Stuttgart: Klett.

Gaiser, K. 1998(2). *Testimonia Platonica: Le antiche testimonianze sulle dottrine non scritte di Platone*. Milan: Vita e Pensiero.

Gaiser, K. 2004. *Gesammelte Schriften*. Ed. Th. A. Szlezák and K. Stanzel. Sankt Augustin: Academia.

Gauss, H. 1958. *Philosophische Handkommentar zu den Dialogen Platons*. Bern: Francke.

Geach, P. 1956. The Third Man Again. *Philosophical Review* 65: 72–82.

Gentile, M. 1930. *La dottrina platonica delle idee numeri e Aristotele*. Pisa: Pacini-Mariotti.

Gentili, B., and Paioni, G., eds. 1985. *Oralità: Cultura, letteratura, discorso*. Rome: Edizione dell'Ateneo.

Gigon, O. 1936. Gorgias 'Über das Nichtsein.' *Hermes* 71: 186–213.

Gigon, O., ed. 1962. *Vita Aristotelis Marciana*. Berlin: Walter de Gruyter.

Gigon, O. 1974. Introduction to *Platon: Der Staat*. Trans. R. Rufener. Ed. Th. A. Szlezák. Zurich and Munich: Artemis and Winkler.

Gomperz, H. 1930. Platons philosophische System. In *Proceedings of the Seventh International Congress of Philosophy*, 426–431. London: Milford.

Gomperz, H. 1953. *Philosophical Studies*. Boston: Christopher Publishing House.

Goody, J. 1986. *The Logic of Writing and the Organisation of Society*. Cambridge: Cambridge University Press.

Görgemanns, H. 1960. Beiträge zur Interpretation von Platons Nomoi. *Zetemata* 25: 119–122.

Gosling, J. C. B. 1973. *Plato*. London: Routledge & Kegan Paul.

Gould, J. 1955. *The Development of Plato's Ethics*. Cambridge: Cambridge University Press.

Graeser, A. 1983. Die Philosophie der Antike 2: Sophistik und Sokratik, Plato and Aristoteles. In vol. 2 of *Geschichte der Philosophie*, ed. V. W. Röd, 151–157. Munich: Beck.

Graeser, A., ed. 1987. *Mathematics and Metaphysics in Aristotle*. Bern-Stuttgart: P. Haupt.

Griswold, C. 1986. *Self-Knowledge in Plato's* Phaedrus. New Haven: Yale University Press.

Guthrie, W. K. C. 1975. *A History of Greek Philosophy*. 6 vols. (1962–1981), vol. 4. Cambridge: Cambridge University Press.

Halfwassen, J. 1992. *Der Aufstieg zum Einen: Untersuchungen zu Platon und Plotin, Beiträge zur Altertumskunde* 9. Stuttgart: Teubner.

Halfwassen, J. 1992(2). Speusipp und die Unendlichkeit des Einen: Ein neues Speusipp-Testimonium bei Proklos und seine Bedeutung. *Archiv für Geschichte der Philosophie* 74: 43–73.

Halfwassen, J. 1993. Speusipp und die metaphysische Deutung von Platons 'Parmenides.' In *Hen kai plēthos: Einheit und Vielheit: Festschrift für Bormann*, ed. L. Hagemann and R. Glei, 339–373. Würzburg: Oros.

Halfwassen, J. 1994. Monismus und Dualismus in Platons Prinzipienlehre. In *Platonisches Philosophieren: Zehn Vorträge zu Ehren von Hans Joachim Krämer*, ed. H. J. Krämer, Th. A. Szlezák, and K.-H. Stanzel, 67–85. Hildesheim: Georg Olms.

Halfwassen, J. 1996. Das Eine als Einheit und Dreiheit: Zur Prinzipientheorie Jamblichs. *Rheinisches Museum* 139: 52–83.

Halfwassen, J. 1998. Philosophie als Transzendieren: Der Aufstieg zum höchsten Prinzip bei Platon und Plotin. *Bochümer Philosophisches Jahrbuch für Antike und Mittelalter* 3: 29–42.

Halfwassen, J. 1999. *Hegel und der spätantiken Neuplatonismus: Untersuchungen zur Metaphysik des Einen und des Nous in Hegels spekulativer und geschichtlicher Deutung*. Bonn: Bouvier.

Halfwassen, J. 2000. Der Demiurg: Seine Stellung in der Philosophie Platons und seine Deutung im antiken Platonismus. In *Le Timée de Platon: Contributions à l' historie de sa* réception, ed. A. B. Neschke, 39–61. Löwen: Peeters.

Halfwassen, J. 2002. Monism and Dualism in Plato's Doctrine of Principles. *Graduate Faculty Philosophy Journal* 23: 125–144.

Halfwassen, J. 2010. Ist die Tübinger Schule der Platonismus unserer Tage? In *Hermeneutik und Geschichte der Philosophie. Festschrift für Hans Krämer zum 80. Geburtstag*, 33–53. Ed. Dagmar Mirbach. Hildesheim: Georg Olms.

Happ, H. 1971. *Hyle: Studien zum aristotelischen Materiebegriff*. Berlin: Walter de Gruyter

Harder, R. 1960. *Kleine Schriften*. 3 vols. Munich: Beck.

Hare, R. M. 1965. Plato and the Mathematicians. In *New Essays on Plato and Aristotle*, ed. R. Bambrough. London: Routledge & Kegan Paul.

Hartmann, N. 1909. *Platos Logik des Seins*. (2nd ed., 1965) Berlin: Walter de Gruyter.

Hartmann, N. 1957. Das Problem des Apriorismus in den platonischen Philosophie. In vol. 2 of *Kleinere Schriften*. Berlin: Walter de Gruyter.

Hasse, H., and Scholz, H. 1928. *Die grundlagenkrisis der griechischen mathematik*. Charlottenburg: Metzner.

Havelock, E. 1976. *Origins of Western Literacy*. Toronto: The Ontario Institute for Studies in Education.

Havelock, E. 1982. *Preface to Plato*. Cambridge: Harvard University Press.

Havelock, E. 1988. *The Muse Learns to Write: Reflections on Orality and Literacy from Antiquity to the Present*. New Haven: Yale University Press.

Heath, T., ed. 1956. *The Thirteen Books of Euclid's Elements*. 3 vols. New York: Dover.

Hegel, G. W. F. 1964. *Sämtliche Werke*, ed. H. Glockner. Stuttgart-Bad Cannstatt: Frommann.

Hegel, G. W. F. 1971. *Werke in zwanzig Bänden*. Ed. E. Moldenhauer and K. M. Michel. Frankfurt: Suhrkamp.

Hegel, G. W. F. 1995. *Lectures on the History of Philosophy*. 3 vols. Trans. E. S. Haldane and F. H. Simson. Lincoln: University of Nebraska Press.

Heidegger, M. 1929. Vom Wesen des Grundes. In *Wegmarken*. Frankfurt: Klostermann.

Heidegger, M. 1953. *Einführung in die Metaphysik*. Tübingen: Max Niemeyer.

Hilbert, D. 1899. *Grundlagen der Geometrie*. Stuttgart: Teubner; rept. P. Bernays, ed. New York: Springer, 1968.

Hinüber, O. 1996. A *Handbook of Pali Literature*. Berlin: Walter De Gruyter.

Hirschberger, J. 1940. Omne ens est bonum. *Philosophisches Jahrbuch* 53: 292–305.

Hoppe, E. 1911. *Mathematik und Astronomie im klassischen Altertum*. Heidelberg: Carl Winter.

Horn, C. 1995. Der Platonische Parmenides und die Möglichkeit seiner prinzipientheoretischen Interpretation. *Antike und Abendland* 41: 95–114.

Hösle, V. 1982. Platons Grundlegung der Euklidizität der Geometrie. *Philologus* 126: 184–197.

Hösle, V. 1984. *Wahrheit und Geschichte*. Stuttgart-Bad Cannstatt: Frommann-Holzboog.

Hösle, V. 1984(2). Zu Platons Philosophie der Zahlen. *Theologie und Philosophie* 59: 321–355.

Hösle, V. 1994. *I fondamenti dell'aritmetica e della geometria in Platone*. Milano: Vita e Pensiero.

Hösle, V. 1996. Die Philosophie und ihre Medien. In *Platonisches philosophieren: Zehn Vorträge zu Ehren von Hans Joachim Krämer*, ed. H. J. Krämer, K. Albert, Th. A. Szlezák, and K.-H. Stanzel. Hildesheim: Georg Olms.

Hyland, D. 2004. *Questioning Platonism: Continental Interpretations of Plato*. Albany: State University of New York Press.

Irmscher, J., ed. 1960. *Platon: Briefe*. Berlin: Akademie.

Jäger, G. 1967. "Nus" in Platons Dialogen. *Hypomnemata* 17: 13–45.

Joseph, H. W. B. 1948. *Knowledge and the Good in Plato's* Republic. Oxford: Oxford University Press.

Jowett, B., and Campbell, J. 1894. *Plato's* Republic. 3 vols. Oxford: Oxford University Press.

Kahn, C. 2005. The Philosophical Importance of the Dialogue Form in Plato. *Graduate Faculty Philosophy Journal* 26: 13–28.

Kamerbeek, J. C., Vardenius, W. J., Viljoen, H. G., and Wielen, W. van der 1949. De Novis Libris Iudica. *Mnemosyne* 2, 1: 340–349.

Kant, I. 1977. Von einem neuerdings erhobenen vornehmen Ton in der Philosophie. In vol. 6 of *Werkausgabe*, 377–397. Frankfurt: Suhrkamp.

Klein, J. 1968. *Greek Mathematical Thought and the Origin of Algebra.* Trans. E. Brann. Cambridge and London: MIT Press.

Klibansky, R., ed. 1940–1962. *Corpus Platonicum Medii Aevi, Plato Latinus.* 4 vols. London: Warburg Institute.

Klibansky R., and Labowsky, C., eds. 1953. *Parmenides usque ad finem primae hypothesis nec non Procli Commentarium in Parmenidem pars ultima adhuc inedita inter prete Guillelmo de Moerbeka.* London: Warburg Institute.

Kobusch, T., and Mojsisch, B., eds. 1996. *Platon: Seine Dialoge in der Sicht der neueren Forschung.* Darmstadt: Wissenschaftliche Buchgesellschaft.

Koller, H. 1959. Harmonie und Tetraktys. *Museum Helveticum* 16: 238–248.

Koller, H. 1960. Zum Aufsatz über Harmonie und Tetrakys. *Museum Helveticum* 17: 115–116.

Krafft, F. 1965. Der Mathematikos und der Physikos: Bemerkungen zu der angeblichen Platonischen Aufgabe, die Phänomene zu retten. In *Alte Probleme—Neue Ansätze.* Wiesbaden: Franz Steiner.

Krafft, F. 1971. *Geschichte der Naturwissenschaft.* Freiburg: Rombach.

Krämer, H. J. 1959. *Arete bei Platon und Aristoteles: Zum Wesen und zur Geschichte der platonischen Ontologie.* Heidelberg: Carl Winter.

Krämer, H. J. 1964. *Der Ursprung der Geistmetaphysik: Untersuchungen zur Geschichte des Platonismus zwischen Platon und Plotin.* Amsterdam: B. R. Grüner.

Krämer, H. J. 1964(2). Retraktationen zum Problem des esoterischen Platon. *Museum Helveticum* 21: 137–167.

Krämer, H. J. 1964(3). Die platonische Akademie und das Problem einer systematischen Interpretation der Philosophie Platons. *Kant-Studien* 55: 69–101.

Krämer, H. J. 1966. Aristoxenos über Platons Περὶ τἀγαθοῦ. *Hermes* 94: 111–112.

Krämer, H. J. 1966(2). Über den Zusammenhang von Prinzipienlehre und Dialektik bei Platon: Zur Definition des Dialektikers 534 B–C. *Philologus* 110: 35–70.

Krämer, H. J. 1966(3). Über den Zusammenhang von Prinzipienlehre und Dialektik bei Platon: Zur Definition des Dialektikers 534 B–C. *Philologus* 110: 35–70. Rpt. in: Wippern, J., ed. 1972: 394–448.

Krämer, H. J. 1967. Das Problem der Philosophenherrschaft bei Platon. *Philosophisches Jahrbuch* 74: 254–270.

Krämer, H. J. 1967(2). *Der Ursprung der Geistmetaphysik: Untersuchungen zur Geschichte des Platonismus zwischen Platon und Plotin.* Amsterdam: B. R. Grüner.

Krämer, H. J. 1968. Die grundsätzlichen Fragen der indirekten Platonüberlieferung. In *Idee und Zahl: Studien zur platonischen Philosophie*, ed. H. G. Gadamer and W. Schadewaldt, 106–150. Heidelberg: Akademie der Wissenschaften.

Krämer, H. J. 1969. ΕΠΕΚΕΙΝΑ ΤΗΣ ΟΥΣΙΑΣ: Zu Platon, Politeia 509B. *Archiv für Geschichte der Philosophie* 51: 1–30.

Krämer, H. J. 1971. *Platonismus und hellenistische Philosophie*. Berlin: Walter de Gruyter.

Krämer, H. J. 1973. Aristoteles und die akademische Eidoslehre: Zur Geschichte des Universalienproblems im Platonismus. *Archiv für Geschichte der Philosophie* 55: 119–190.

Krämer, H. J. 1980. Neues zum Streit um Platons Prinzipientheorie. *Philosophische Rundschau* 27: 1–38.

Krämer, H. J. 1981. Zum neuen Platon-Bild. *Deutsche Vierteljahrsschrift für Literaturwissenschaft und Geistesgeschichte* 55: 1–18.

Krämer, H. J. 1982. Kritische Bemerkungen zu den jüngsten Äußerungen von W. Wieland and G. Patzig über Platons Ungeschriebene Lehre. *Rivista di Filosofia* neo-scolastica 74: 579–592.

Krämer, H. J. 1982(2). *Platone e i fondamenti della metafisica: Saggio sulla teoria dei principi e sulle dottrine non scritte di Platone*. Milan: Pubblicazioni della Università Cathòlica del Sacro Cuore.

Krämer, H. J. 1983. Die Ältere Akademie. In Ältere Akademie—Aristoteles—Peripatos, vol. 3 of Überwegs Grundriss der Geschichte der Philosophie: Philosophie der Antike, ed. H. Flashar, 3–174. Basel/Stuttgart: Schwabe.

Krämer, H. J. 1986. *La nuova immagine di Platone*. Naples: Bibliopolis.

Krämer, H. J. 1988. Fichte, Schlegel und der Infinitismus in der Platondeutung. *Deutsche Vierteljahrsschrift für Literaturwissenschaft und Geistgeschichte* 62: 583–621.

Krämer, H. J. 1989. *Dialettica e definizione del Bene in Platone: Interpretazione e commentario storico-filosofico di Repubblica VI, 534B3–D2*. Trans. Enrico Peroli. Milan: Vita e Pensiero.

Krämer, H. J. 1989. Neue Literatur zum neuen Platonbild. *Allgemeine Zeitschrift für Philosophie* 14: 59–81.

Krämer, H. J. 1990. *Plato and the Foundations of Metaphysics*. Trans. J. R. Catan. Albany: State University of New York Press.

Krämer, H. J. 1990(2). Zur aktuellen Diskussion um den Philosophiebegriff Platons. *Perspektiven der Philosophie* 16: 1–20.

Krämer, H. J. 1993. Altes und neues Platonbild. *Methexis* 6: 95–114.

Krämer, H. J. 1994. Das neue Platonbild. *Zeitschrift für philosophische Forschung* 48: 1–20.

Krämer, H. J. 1996. Platons ungeschriebene Lehre. In *Platon: Seine Dialoge in der Sicht neuer Forschungen*, ed. T. Kobusch and B. Mojsisch, 249–275. Darmstadt: Wissenschaftliche Buchgesellschaft.

Krämer, H. J. 1996. The New View of Plato. Trans. J. Uhlaner. *Graduate Faculty Philosophy Journal* 19: 25–41.

Krämer, H. J. 1997. Die Idee des Guten: Sonnen- und Liniengleichnis (Buch VI, 504a-511e). In *Platon: Politeia*, ed. O. Höffe, 179–203. Berlin: Akademie.

Krämer, H. J. 1997(2). Zu neuen Büchern über Platon. *Allgemeine Zeitschrift für Philosophie* 22: 49–68.

Krämer, H. J. 1999. Fichte, Schlegel, and the Infinite Interpretation of Plato. Trans. C. Colvin. *Graduate Faculty Philosophy Journal* 21: 69–111.

Kucharski, P. 1971. *La spéculation platonicienne*. Paris: Publications de la Sorbonne.

Kuhn, H. 1968. Platon und die Grenze philosophischer Meitteilung. In *Idee und Zahl: Studien zur platonische Philosophie*, ed. H.-G. Gadamer and W. Schadewaldt, 151–173. Heidelberg: Carl Winter.

Kullmann, W. 1958. Zenon und die Lehre des Parmenides. *Hermes* 86: 157–172.

Kullmann, W. 1991. Platons Schriftkritik. *Hermes* 119: 2–21.

Kullmann, W., and Reichel, M. 1990. *Der Ubergang von der Mündlichkeit zur Literatur bei den Griechen*. Tübingen: Gunter Narr.

Kytzler, B. 1959. Die Weltseele und der musikalische Raum. *Hermes* 87: 393–414.

Lacey, A. R. 1956. The Mathematical Passage in the *Epinomis*. *Phronesis* 1: 81–104.

Lang, P. 1965. *De Speusippi Academici scriptis: accedunt fragmenta*. Hildesheim: Georg Olms.

Lee, H. D. P. 1936. *Zeno of Elea: A Text, with Translation and Notes*. Cambridge: Cambridge University Press; rept. Amsterdam: Hakkert, 1967.

Lord, A. B. 1960. *The Singer of Thales*. Cambridge: Harvard University Press.

Loewenclau, I. von. 1965. Die Wortgruppe πλάνη in den platonischen Schriften. In *Synusia: Festgabe für Wolfgang Schadewaldt*, ed. H. Flashar and K. Gaiser, 111–122. Pfullingen: Neske.

Luther, W. 1965. Wahrheit, Licht, Sehen und Erkennen im Sonnengleichnis von Platons Politeia. *Studium Generale* 18: 479–496.

Manasse, E. M. 1976. *Bücher über Platon III*. Tübingen: Mohr Siebeck.

Mann, W.-R. 2006. Plato in Tübingen. *Oxford Studies in Ancient Philosophy* 31: 349–400.

Marc-Wogau, K. 1941. Der Staat und der Begriff des Guten in Platons Politeia. *Theoria* 7: 20–45.

Marković, Z. 1965. Platons Theorie über das Eine und die unbestimmte Zweiheit und ihre Spuren in der griechischen Mathematik. In *Zur Geschichte der griechischen Mathematik*, ed. O. Becker, 308–318. Darmstadt: Wissenschaftliche Buchgesellschaft.

Marten, R. 1967. Selbstprädikation bei Platon. *Kant-Studien* 58: 209–226.

McLuhan, M. 1964. *Understanding Media: The Extensions of Man*. New York: McGraw-Hill; rept. Cambridge: MIT Press, 1994.

Merlan, P. 1953. *From Platonism to Neoplatonism*. 3rd ed. 1968. The Hague: Martinus Nijhoff.

Merlan, P. 1965. Monismus und Dualismus bei einigen Platonikern. In *Parousia: Festschrift für J. Hirschgerger*, ed. K. Flasch, 143–153. Frankfurt: Minerva.

Merlan, P. 1967. Τὸ ἀπορῆσαι ἀρχαϊκῶς (Arist., *Met*. XIV.2, 1089a1). *Philologus* 111: 119–121.

Merlan, P. 1969. Bemerkungen zum neuen Platobild. *Archiv für Geschichte der Philosophie* 51: 111–126.

Migliori, M. 1990. *Dialettica e verità: Commentario filosofico al 'Parmenide' di Platone*. Milan: Vita e Pensiero.

Miller, M. 1995. 'Unwritten Teachings' in the 'Parmenides.' *Review of Metaphysics* 48, 3: 591–633.

Miller, M. 1999. Dialectical Education and 'Unwritten Teachings' in Plato's *Statesman*. In *Plato and Platonism*, ed. J. M. Van Ophuijsen, 218–241. Washington, D.C.: The Catholic University of America Press.

Mittelstraß, J. 1985. Die geometrischen Wurzeln der platonischen Ideenlehre. *Gymnasium* 92: 399–418.

Mohr, R. D. 1981. The Number Theory in Plato's *Republic* VII and *Philebus*. *Isis* 72: 620–627.

Morrison, J. S. 1977. Two Unresolved Difficulties in the Line and Cave. *Phronesis* 22: 212–234.

Mourelatos, A. P. D. 1980. Plato's 'Real Astronomy,' *Republic* 527D–531D. In *Science and Sciences in Plato*, ed. J. P. Anton, 33–72. New York: EIDOS.

Mourelatos, A. P. D. 1981. Astronomy and Kinematics in Plato's Project of Rationalist Explanation. *Studies in History and Philosophy of Science* 12: 1–32.

Movia, G. 1990. *Apparenze, essere e verità: Commentario storico-filosofico al 'Sofista' di Platone*. Milan: Vita e Pensiero.

Mugler, C. 1948. *Platon et la recherche mathématique de son époque*. Strasbourg: Heitz.

Mugler, C. 1958. *Dictionnaire historique de la terminologie géométrique des grecs*. Paris: Librairie C. Klincksieck.

Müller, G. 1949. Die Philosophie im pseudoplatonischen 7. Brief. *Archiv für Philosophie* 3: 251–276.

Murphy, N. R. 1951. *The Interpretation of Plato's* Republic. Oxford: Oxford University Press.

Muth, R. 1966. Zur Bedeutung von Mündlichkeit und Schriftlichkeit der Wortkunst. *Wiener Studien* 79: 246–260.

Nails, D. 2002. *The People of Plato: A Prosopography of Plato and Other Socratics*. Indianapolis: Hackett.

Napolitano Valditara, L. M. 1988. *Le idee, i numeri, l'ordine: La dottrina della mathesis universalis dall'Accademia antica al Neoplatonismo*. Naples: Bibliopolis.

Natorp, P. 1921. *Platons Ideenlehre: eine Einführung in der Idealismus*. 2nd ed. (first ed. 1903) Leipzig: Felix Meiner.

Nettleship, R. L. 1929. *Lectures on the* Republic *of Plato*. London: Macmillan.

Nietzsche, F. 1913. Einführung in das Studium der platonischen Dialoge. In vol. 19 of *Werke*, ed. O. Crusius and W. Nestle, 367–443. Leipzig: Kröner.

Nietzsche, F. 1975. *Kritische Gesamtausgabe Briefwechsel*, ed. G. Colli and M. Montinari. 24 vols. Berlin: Walter de Gruyter.

Nikulin, D. 2000. A New Interpretation of Plato's Cosmology: *Timaeus* 36 b–d. *Méthexis* 13: 113–118.

Nikulin, D. 2002. *Matter, Imagination and Geometry: Ontology, Natural Philosophy and Mathematics in Plotinus, Proclus and Descartes*. Aldershot: Ashgate.

Nikulin, D. 2012. Indivisible Lines and Plato's Mathematical Ontology. In *Platons Hermeneutik und Prinzipiendenken im Licht der Dialoge und der antiken Tradition. Festschrift für Thomas Alexander Szlezák zum 70. Geburtstag*, 291–326. Ed. Ulricke Bruchmüller. Hildesheim: Spudasmata.

Novotný, F. 1957. De Platonis Miraculo Geometrico. *Listy Filologické* 80: 14–20.

Novotný, F. 1960. *Platonis Epinomis commentariis illustrata*. Prague: Academia Sceientarum Bohemoslovenicae.

Oehler, K. 1962. *Die Lehre vom noetischen und dianoetischen Denken bei Platon und Aristoteles*. Munich: Felix Meiner.

Oehler, K. 1965. Der entmythologisierte Platon: Zur Lagbe der Platonforschung. *Zeitschrift für philosophische Forschung* 10: 393–420.

Oehler, K. 1966. Der geschichtliche Ort der Entstehung der formalen Logik. *Studium Generale* 19: 453–461.

Ong, W. 1982. *Orality and Literacy: The Technologizing of the Word*. London: Methuen.

Orinsky, K. 1935. "Leon, der Mathematiker." In Supplement VI, *Real-Enzyklopädie der classischen Altertumswissenschaft*, ed. A. Pauly, G. Wissowa, et al., 222. Stuttgart: J. B. Metzler.

Ostwald, M. 1965. Review of Gadamer's *Dialektik und Sophistik im siebenten platonischen Brief*. *Gnomon* 37: 822–823.

Owen, G. E. L. 1961. Τιθέναι τὰ φαινόμενα. In *Aristote et les problèmes de méthode*. Louvain/Paris: Publications Universitaires de Louvain.

Owen, G. E. L. 1986. *Logic, Science, and Dialectic*. Ed. Martha Nussbaum. Ithaca: Cornell University Press.

Parry, M. 1971. *The Making of the Homeric Verse: The Collected Papers of Milman Parry*. Oxford: Clarendon.

Patzer, H. 1954. Mitteilbarkeit der Erkenntnis und Philosophie. *Archiv für Philosophie* 5: 19–36.

Pauly, A., Wissowa, G., Kroll, W., Witte, K., Mittelhaus, K., and Ziegler, K., eds. 1894–1980. *Realencyclopädie der klassischen Altertumswissenschaft*. Stuttgart: Metzler.

Peirce, C. S. 1976. *The New Elements of Mathematics*. Ed. C. Eisele. 3 vols. The Hague and Paris: Mouton.

Pépin, J. 1968. Redécouverte de Platon. *Preuves* 206: 76–84.

Pohlenz, M. 1913. *Aus Platons Werdezeit*. Berlin: Weidmann.

Postman, N. 1985. *Amusing Ourselves to Death: Public Discourse in the Age of Show Business*. New York: Penguin.

Raible, W., ed. 1987–. *ScriptOralia*. 135 vols. Tübingen: Gunter Narr.

Reale, G. 1984. *Per una nuova interpretazione di Platone*. Milan: Vita e Pensiero.

Reale, G. 1992. *Per una nuova interpretazione di Platone*. 2nd ed. Milan: Vita e Pensiero.

Reale, G. 1993. *Zu einer neuen Interpertation Platons: Eine Auslegung der Metaphysik der großen Dialoge im Lichte der 'ungeschiebenen Lehre.'* Paderborn: Schöningh. (Italian: *Per una nuove interpretazione di Platone*. Milan: Vita e Pensiero, 1994.)

Reale, G. 1996. Alles, was tief ist, liebt die Maske: Aristophanes' Rede im Symposion als sinnbildliche Verhüllung der ungeschriebenen Lehren Platons. In *Platonisches philosophieren: Zehn Vorträge zu Ehren von Hans Joachim Krämer*, ed. H. J. Krämer, K. Albert, Th. A. Szlezák, and K.-H. Stanzel, 87–108. Hildesheim: Georg Olms.

Reichenbach, H. 1958. *The Philosophy of Space and Time*. Trans. M. Reichenbach. New York: Dover.

Richard, M.-D. 1986. *L'enseignement orale de Platon: Une nouvelle interprétation du platonisme*. (2nd ed. 2005). Paris: Cerf.

Rist, J. M. 1965. Monism: Plotinus and Some Predecessors. Harvard Studies in *Classical Philology* 69: 329–344.

Robin, L. 1908. *La théorie platonicienne des idées et des nombres d'après Aristote*. Paris: Alcan.

Robin, L. 1935. *Platon*. Paris: Alcan.

Robinson, R. 1953. *Plato's Earlier Dialectic*. 2nd ed. Oxford: Oxford University Press.

Ross, W. D. 1963. *Plato's Theory of Ideas*. 4th ed. (first ed. 1951). Oxford: Oxford University Press.

Runciman, W. G. 1962. *Plato's Later Epistemology*. Cambridge: Cambridge University Press.

Saccheri, G. 1733. *Euclides ab omni naevo vindicatus*. Mediolani.

Santas, G. 1983. The Form of the Good in Plato's *Republic*. In vol. 2 of *Essays in Ancient Greek Philosophy*, ed. J. P. Anton and A. Preus, 232–263. Albany: State University of New York Press.

Sayre, K. 1969. *Plato's Analytic Method*. Chicago: University of Chicago Press.

Sayre, K. 1983. *Plato's Late Ontology: A Riddle Resolved*. Princeton: Princeton University Press.

Schleiermacher, F. 1804. Einleitung zu *Platons Werke, Ersten Theiles erster Band*. (3rd ed., 1855) Berlin; rept. in *Das Platonbild*, ed. K. Gaiser, 1-31. Hildesheim: Georg Olms, 1969.

Schleiermacher, F. 1838–. *Gesamtausgabe der Werke Schleiermachers*. Berlin.

Schleiermacher, F. 1974. *Hermeneutik*. Ed. H. Kimmerle. 2nd ed. Heidelberg: Carl Winter.

Schleiermacher, F. 1984–. *Kritische Gesamtausgabe*. Berlin: New York: Walter de Gruyter.

Schleiermacher, F. 1999. *Hermeneutik und Kritik*. Ed. M. Frank. 7th ed. Frankfurt am Main: Suhrkamp.

Schleiermacher, F. 2001. *Dialektik*. Ed. M. Frank. 2 vols. Frankfurt am Main: Suhrkamp.

Schmalzriedt, E. 1969. *Platon: Der Schriftsteller und die Wahrheit*. Munich: Piper.

Schmitz-Moormann, K. 1959. *Die Ideenlehre Platons im Lichte des Sonnengleichnisses des sechsten Buches des Staates*. PhD Diss. Munich.

Schneider, K. 1966. *Die schweigenden Götter*. Hildesheim: Georg Olms.

Schulz, W., ed. 1960. *Festschrift für H.-G. Gadamer*. Tübingen: Mohr Siebeck.

Shorey, P. 1895. The Idea of the Good in Plato's *Republic*. *Studies in Classical Philology* 1: 188–239.

Shorey, P., trans. 1946. *Plato's* Republic. 2 vols. Cambridge: Harvard University Press.

Sinaiko, H. L. 1965. *Love, Knowledge, and Discourse in Plato: Dialogue and Dialectic in Phaedrus, Republic, Parmenides*. Chicago: University of Chicago Press.

Solmsen, F. 1929. *Die Entwicklung der aristotelischen Logik und Rhetorik*. Berlin: Weidmann.

Solmsen, F. 1931. Platos Einfluß auf die Bildung der mathematischen Methode. *Quellen und Studien zur Geschichte der Mathematik B 1*, 93–107.

Solmsen, F. 1940. Plato and the Unity of Science. *Philosophical Review* 49: 567–571.

Solmsen, F. 1960. *Aristotle's System of the Physical World: A Comparison with His Predecessors*. Ithaca: Cornell University Press.

Solmsen, F. 1977. Plato and Science. In *Interpretations of Plato: A Swarthmore Symposium*, ed. H. F. North, 86–105. Mnemosyne Suppl. 50. Leiden: Brill.

Stachowiak, H. 1971. *Rationalismus im Ursprung: Die Genesis des axiomatischen Denkens*. New York: Springer.

Stahl, H.-P. 1960. Ansätze zur Satzlogik bei Platon. *Hermes* 88: 409–451.

Stenzel, J. 1921. Über den Aufbau der Erkenntnis im 7: platonischen Brief. In *Jahresberichte des Philologischen Vereins Berlin: Sokrates* 47: 63–84.

Stenzel, J. 1924. *Zahl und Gestalt bei Platon und Aristoteles*. Leipzig: Teubner. 3rd ed. Darmstadt: Wissenschaftliche Buchgesellschaft, 1959.

Stenzel, J. 1931. *Metaphysik der Altertums*. Munich/Berlin: Oldenbourg.

Stewart, J. A. 1909. *Plato's Doctrine of Ideas*. Oxford: Clarendon.

Strauss, L. 1988. *Persecution and the Art of Writing*. Chicago: Chicago University Press.

Suhr, M. 1969. *Platons Kritik and den Eleaten*. Hamburg: Stiftung Europa-Kolleg.

Swift Riginos, A. 1976. *Platonica: The Anecdotes concerning the Life and Writings of Plato*. Leiden: Brill.

Szabó, Á. 1965. Anfänge des Euklidischen Axiomensystems. In *Zur Geschichte der griechischen Mathematik*, ed. O. Becker, 355–461. Darmstadt: Wissenschaftliche Buchgesellschaft.

Szabó, Á. 1970. Ein Lob auf die altpythagoreische Geometrie (*Epinomis* 990D1–6). *Hermes* 98: 405–421.

Szabó, Á. 1978. *The Beginnings of Greek Mathematics*. Dordrecht/Boston/London: D. Reidel.

Szilasi, W. 1946. *Macht und Ohnmacht des Geistes*. Freiburg: Alber.

Szlezák, Th. A. 1979. *Platon und Aristoteles in der Nuslehre Plotins*. Basel/Stuttgart: Schwabe.

Szlezák, Th. A. 1985. *Platon und die Schriftlichkeit der Philosophie: Interpretation Zu Den Fruehen Und Mittleren Dialogen*. Berlin: New York: Walter de Gruyter.

Szlezák, Th. A. 1987. Die Lückenhaftigkeit der akademischen Prinzipientheorie nach Aristoteles' Darstellung in Metaphysik M und N. In *Mathematik und Metaphysik bei Aristoteles: Akten des 10: Symposium Aristotelicum*, ed. A. Graeser, 45–67. Bern/Stuttgart: Haupt.

Szlezák, Th. A. 1992. *Platone e la scrittura della filosofia: Analisi di struttura dei dialoghi della giovinezza e della maturitŕ alla luce di un nuovo paradigma ermeneutico*. Trans. G. Reale. Milan: Vita e Pensiero.

Szlezák, Th. A. 1993. *Platon lesen*. Stuttgart-Bad Cannstatt: Frommann-Holzboog.

Szlezák, Th. A. 1997. Das Höhlengleichnis. In *Platon: Politeia*, ed. O. Höffe, 205–228. Berlin: Akademie.

Szlezák, Th. A. 1999. *Reading Plato*. Trans. Graham Zanker. London-New York: Routledge.

Szlezák, Th. A. 2003. Die Idee des Guten als *arche* in Platons *Politeia*. In *New Images of Plato: Dialogues on the Idea of the Good*, ed. G. Reale and S. Scolnicov, 49–68. Sankt Augustin: Academia.

Szlezák, Th. A. 2004. *Das Bild des Dialektikers in Platons spaten Dialogen. Platon und die Schriftlichkeit der Philosophie, Teil II*. Berlin: Walter de Gruyter.

Tarán, L. 1975. *Academica: Plato, Philip of Opus and the Pseudo-Platonic Epinomis*. Philadelphia: Memoirs of the American Philosophical Society.

Tarán, L. 1981. *Speusippus of Athens: A Critical Study with a Collection of the Related Texts and Commentary*. Leiden: Brill.

Taylor, C. C. W. 1967. Plato and the Mathematicians: An Examination of Professor Hare's Views. *Philosophical Quarterly* 17: 193–203.

Thaer, C., ed. 1962. *Euklid: Elemente*. Darmstadt: Wissenschaftliche Buchgesellschaft.

Theiler, W. 1964. Einheit und unbegrenzte Zweiheit von Platon bis Plotin. In *Isonomia: Studien zur Gleichheitsvorstellung im griechischen Denken*, ed. J. Mau and E. G. Schmidt, 89–109. Berlin: Akademie.

Theiler, W. 1965. Philo von Alexandria und der Beginn des kaiserzeitlichen Platonismus. In *Parousia: Festschrift für J. Hirschgerger*, ed. K. Flasch, 199–218. Frankfurt: Minerva.

Theiler, W. 1970. *Untersuchung zur antiken Literatur*. Berlin: Akademie.

Thiel, D. 1990. Über die Genese Philisophischer Texte: Studien zu Jacques Derrida. Freiburg/Munich: Alber.

Tóth, I. 1962. La géometrie non euclidienne dans le développement de la pensée. In Études d'histoire *et de philosophie des sciences*, 53–70. Bucharest: Éditions de l'Académie de la République Populaire Roumaine.

Tóth, I. 1967. Das Parallelenproblem im Corpus Aristotelicum. *Archive for History of Exact Sciences* 3: 249–422.

Tóth, I. 1972. Die nicht-euklidische Geometrie in der Phänomenologie des Geistes: Wissenschaftstheoretische Betrachtungen zur Entwicklungsgeschichte der Mathematik. In *Philosophie als Beziehhungswissenschaft: Festschrift für Julius Schaaf*, ed. W. F. Nebel and D. Leisegang. Frankfurt am Main: Horst Heiderhoff.

Tóth, I. 1977. Geometria more ethico. *In PRISMATA: Festschrift für Willy Hartner*, ed. Y. Maeyama and W. G. Saltzer, 395–415. Wiesbaden: Franz Steiner.

Tóth, I. 1977(2). La révolution non euclidienne. *La Recherche* 8: 143–151.

Tóth, I. 1979. Spekulationen über die Möglichkeit eines nicht euklidischen Raumes vor Einstein. In vol. 100 of *Lecture Notes in Physics*, 46–83. New York: Springer.

Tóth, I. 2010. *Fragmente und Spuren nichteuklidischer Geometrie bei Aristoteles*. Berlin: Walter de Gruyter.

Trendelenburg, F. A. 1826. *Platonis de ideis et numeris doctrina ex Aristotele illustrata*. Berlin.

Untersteiner, M., ed. 1966. *Platone, Repubblica, Libro X*. Naples: Bibliopolis.

Vasilieva, T. V. 1985. *Afinskaya shkola filosofii: filosofskii yazyk Platona i Aristotelya*. Moscow: Nauka.

Vlastos, G. 1963. On Plato's Oral Doctrine. *Gnomon* 41: 641–655.

Vlastos, G. 1973. *Platonic Studies*. Princeton: Princeton University Press.

Vlastos, G. 1980. The Role of Observation in Plato's Conception of Astronomy. In *Science and Sciences in Plato*, ed. J. P. Anton, 1–31. New York: EIDOS.

Vogel, C. J. de. 1959. La théorie de l'ἄπειρον chez Platon et dans la tradition platonicienne. *Revue Philosophique de la France et de l'Etranger* 84: 21–39.

Vogel, C. J. de. 1970. The Monism of Plotinus. In *Philosophia: Studies in Greek Philosophy*. Assen: van Gorcum.

Vogel, C. J. de. 1986. *Rethinking Plato and Platonism*. Leiden: Brill.

Weizsäcker, F. von. 1971. *Die Einheit der Natur*. Munich: Hanser.

Weizsäcker, F. von. 1981. *Ein Blick auf Platon: Ideenlehre, Logik und Physik*. Stuttgart: Reclam.

White, N. P. 1976. *Plato on Knowledge and Reality*. Indianapolis: Hackett.

Wieland, W. 1982. *Platon und die Formen des Wissens*. Göttingen: Vandenhoek & Ruprecht.

Wielen, W. van der, Kamerbeek, J. C., Vardenius, W. J., and Viljoen, H. G. 1949. De Novis Libris Iudica. *Mnemosyne* 2, 1: 340–349.

Wilamowitz-Moellendorff, U. von. 1919. *Platon.* 2 vols. Berlin: Weidmannsche Buchhandlung.

Wilpert, P. 1949. *Zwei aristotelische Frühschriften über die Ideenlehre*. Regensburg: Habbel.

Wippern, J. 1965. Eros und Unsterblichkeit in der Diotima-Rede des Symposions. In *Synusia: Festgabe für Wolfgang Schadewaldt*, ed. H. Flashar and K. Gaiser, 123–160. Pfullingen: Neske.

Wippern, J., ed. 1972. *Das Problem der ungeschriebenen Lehre Platons: Beiträge zum Verständnis der Platonischen Prinzipienphilosophie*. Darmstadt: Wissenschaftliche Buchgesellschaft.

Wolff, H. M. 1957. *Plato: der Kampf ums Sein*. Bern: Francke.

Wyller, E. A. 1970. *Der späte Platon*. Hamburg: Felix Meiner.

Zekl, H. G. 1971. *Der Parmenides: Untersuchungen über innere Einheit, Zielsetzung und begriffliches Verfahren eines platonischen Dialogs*. Marburg: Elwert.

Zeller, E. 1844–. *Philosophie der Greichen in ihrer geschichtlichen Entwicklung*. Tübingen: Fues.

INDEX LOCORUM

INDEX